INDEX TO PERIODICAL LITERATURE
ON THE APOSTLE PAUL

NEW TESTAMENT TOOLS
AND STUDIES

EDITED BY

BRUCE M. METZGER, Ph.D., D.D.

Professor of New Testament Language and Literature
Princeton Theological Seminary

VOLUME I

LEIDEN
E. J. BRILL
1960

INDEX TO PERIODICAL
LITERATURE
ON THE APOSTLE PAUL

COMPILED UNDER THE DIRECTION OF

BRUCE M. METZGER

LEIDEN
E. J. BRILL
1960

PRINTED IN THE NETHERLANDS

TABLE OF CONTENTS

INTRODUCTION

This index of periodical literature on the Apostle Paul had its inception during the Spring term of 1957. While conducting a Seminar on the Apostle Paul it became apparent that the ordinary bibliographic aids were either too cumbersome to use or quite inadequate to disclose the existence of many valuable studies on Paul. Therefore, partly as an exercise in bibliographic research itself and partly with a view to compiling a tool for the work of the Seminar, each member became responsible for canvassing one or more periodicals with an eye for articles on Paul. Such a rich harvest was secured that during the following academic year a similar program was pursued as an adjunct to another graduate course.

It is fitting that the names of the students who participated in the making of this index should be recorded here; they are Messrs. Robert C. D. Brow, Frank G. Carver, Demetrios J. Constantelos, David L. Eiler, Lyle B. Gangsei, Raymond Harms, Koji Kayama, Earl W. Kennedy, Andrew Kuyvenhoven, Donald B. Landis, John B. Mathews, Osmundo A. Miranda, William R. Nelson, Vernon H. Neufeld, Marcus B. Prince, III, Graydon F. Snyder, George S. Stephanides, Mark W. Thomsen, Henry E. Turlington, and Donald C. Ziemke. These twenty men surveyed a total of about sixty periodicals. The present writer is responsible for canvassing more than fifty other periodicals, and for supplementing the work of some of those who had not completed their original assignment. The index includes articles written in fourteen languages, namely Dutch, English, French, German, Greek, Italian, Latin, Lithuanian, Norwegian, Polish, Russian, Serbian, Spanish, and Swedish. Every periodical mentioned in the list below (pp. XIII ff.) has been indexed completely, from the first year of its publication to the end of 1957 (or, if it ceased being issued prior to 1957, to the last year of its publication). [1] All articles on Paul, except a few of a purely homiletic nature, have been cited. Cross references will serve to call attention to articles that fall into more than one category of the

---

[1] Thirty of the periodicals span fifty years or more of publication, and several cover more than a century.

classification. In the section on Lexicography (III. C. 1) the articles are arranged alphabetically in accord with the Greek words which are treated in the articles. In the several sections which deal with the exegesis of individual passages, the articles are arranged in accord with the Scriptural sequence of the passages. For the rest, the articles stand in chronological order.

It is the pleasant duty of the compiler to acknowledge the courtesies shown him by the librarians of Princeton Theological Seminary (where the major part of the work was done), Princeton University, The Institute for Advanced Study, Harvard Divinity School, and Union Theological Seminary, as well as the Bayerische Staatsbibliothek of Munich, the British Museum, and the Pontifical Biblical Institute of Rome. Gratitude must also be expressed to several friends who kindly supplied information as to articles on Paul contained in several volumes of certain periodicals which were not available in complete sets at the libraries which the compiler visited. They are Professor Teófilo Ayuso of Zaragoza, Dr. A. F. J. Klijn of Utrecht, and Mr. Ralph S. Hamburger, a former student at Princeton Theological Seminary and later at Basel. Mr. John B. Mathews, Teaching Fellow in New Testament at Princeton Theological Seminary, prepared the index of the names of the authors.

In musing upon both the drudgery of assembling bibliographies and their potential usefulness in lightening the labors of others, one recalls the truism that a part of erudition is knowing where to find information. According to the jingling couplet of Alexander Pope,

> ". . . Index-learning turns no student pale,
> Yet holds the Eel of science by the Tail."
> *Dunciad*, Bk. I, 11. 233 f.

In a less jocular mood, and with an overtone of complaint (which the present writer, who has published several other bibliographies, [1] does not share), are the words of the Director of the New York Historical Society, R. W. G. Vail, who writes as follows: "Bibliographers are the jackdaws of scholarship, for they build into their nests the colorful feathers of other birds of more brilliant plumage.

---

[1] Namely, an *Index of Articles on the New Testament and the Early Church Published in Festschriften* (being vol. V of the Monograph Series issued by the Society of Biblical Literature, 224 North Fifteenth Street, Philadelphia 2, Pa., 1951), a *Supplement* to this index (Philadelphia, 1955), and an *Annotated Bibliography of the Textual Criticism of the New Testament, 1914-1939* (published by Ejnar Munksgaard, Copenhagen, 1955).

But, having completed their nests, they fly away and leave other
scholarly birds, who have no taste for bibliographical nest-building,
to occupy them and bring forth their broods of historical treatises
in the comfortable quarters supplied by the nest builders." [1]

BRUCE M. METZGER

Princeton Theological Seminary
Princeton, New Jersey
February 9, 1959

---

[1] R. W. G. Vail, *The Voice of the Old Frontier* (Philadelphia, 1949), p. vii.

LIST OF PERIODICALS

ABR   Australian Biblical Review (Melbourne, 1951 ff.)
AJP   American Journal of Philology (Baltimore, 1880 ff.)
AJT   American Journal of Theology (Chicago, 1897-1920)
ATR   Anglican Theological Review (New York; Evanston, Ill., 1918 ff.)
B   Biblica (Rome, 1920 ff.)
BA   Biblical Archaeologist (New Haven, 1938 ff.)
BBC   Bulletin of the Bezan Club (Leiden, [1926]-1937)
Bes   Bessarione, pubblicazione periodica di studi orientali (Rome, 1896-1923)
BibZ   Biblische Zeitschrift (Freiburg, 1903-1939; Paderborn, 1957)
BJRL   Bulletin of the John Rylands Library (Manchester, 1903 ff.)
BLE   Bulletin de littérature ecclésiastique (Paris, 1899 ff.)
BR   Biblical Review (New York, 1916-1930)
BS   Bibliotheca Sacra (New York; Andover; Oberlin; St. Louis; Dallas, 1844 ff.)
BP   Biblical Theology (Belfast, 1950 ff.)
BW   Biblical World (Chicago, 1893-1920)
CBQ   Catholic Biblical Quarterly (Washington, 1939 ff.)
CJRT   Canadian Journal of Religious Thought (Toronto, 1924-1932)
CJT   Canadian Journal of Theology (Toronto, 1955 ff.)
CQ   Crozer Quarterly (Chester, Pa., 1924-1952)
CTM   Concordia Theological Monthly (St. Louis, Mo., 1930 ff.)
DS   Dominican Studies (Oxford, 1948-1954)
EB   Estudios bíblicos (Madrid, 1929-1936); segunda época (Madrid, 1941 ff.)
EE   Estudios eclesiásticos (Madrid, 1926 ff.)
EQ   Evangelical Quarterly (London, 1929 ff.)
Er   Eranos, acta philologica suecana (Gotoburgi, 1900 ff.)
ET   Expository Times (Edinburgh, 1889 ff.)
Exp   The Expositor (London, 1880-1925)
FZPT   Freiburger Zeitschrift für Philosophie und Theologie (Freiburg [Schweiz], 1954 ff.)
GTT   Wat zegt de Schrift?; from 1909, Nieuwe reeks = Gereformeerd theologisch tijdschrift (Heusden, 1900 ff.)
Herm   Hermathena; a Series of Papers on Literature, Science, and Philosophy by Members of Trinity College, Dublin (Dublin, 1873 ff.)
HJ   Hibbert Journal (London, 1902 ff.)
HTR   Harvard Theological Review (Cambridge, Mass., 1908 ff.)
Interp   Interpretation; a Journal of Bible and Theology (Richmond, Va., 1947 ff.)
ITQ   Irish Theological Quarterly (Dublin; Maynouth, 1906 ff.)
JBL   Journal of Biblical Literature (New Haven; Boston; Philadelphia, 1881 ff.)
JBR   Journal of Bible and Religion (Wolcott, N. Y.; Brattleboro, Vt., 1933 ff.)
JCSP   Journal of Classical and Sacred Philology (Cambridge, England, 1854-1859)

JEH   Journal of Ecclesiastical History (London, 1950 ff.)
JJS   Journal of Jewish Studies (London, 1948 ff.)
JNES   Journal of Near Eastern Studies (Chicago, 1942 ff.)
JQR   Jewish Quarterly Review (London, 1889-1908; New Series, Philadelphia, 1910 ff.)
JR   Journal of Religion (Chicago, 1921 ff.)
JSS   Journal of Semitic Studies (Manchester, 1956 f.)
JTS   Journal of Theological Studies (Oxford, 1899 ff.)
KD   Kerygma und Dogma, Zeitschrift für theologische Forschung und kirchliche Lehre (Göttingen, 1955 ff.)
KhV   Христіанскій Востокъ. (St. Petersburg, 1912-1922)
LCQ   Lutheran Church Quarterly (Gettysburg, Pa., 1928-1949)
LCR   Lutheran Church Review (Philadelphia, 1882-1927)
LQ   The Quarterly Review of the Evangelical Lutheran Church; from 1878, The Lutheran Quarterly (Gettysburg, Pa., 1871-1927; revived in 1949 ff.)
Luth   Luthertum (= NKZ, Erlangen, 1934-1939)
Mn   Mnemosyne, bibliotheca classica batava (Leiden, 1852 ff.)
MTZ   Münchener theologische Zeitschrift (München, 1950 ff.)
NedTT   Nederlands theologisch tijdschrift (Wageningen, 1946 ff.)
NKZ   Neue kirchliche Zeitschrift; from 1934, Luthertum (Erlangen, 1890-1939)
Num   Numen; International Review for the History of Religions (Leiden, 1954 ff.)
NT   Novum Testamentum; an International Quarterly for New Testament and Related Studies based on International Cooperation (Leiden, 1956 f.)
NTS   Nieuwe theologische studiën (Groningen; Wageningen, 1918-1942)
NTSt   New Testament Studies; an International Journal Published Quarterly under the Auspices of Studiorum Novi Testamenti Societas (Cambridge, England, 1954 ff.)
NTT   Norsk teologisk tidsskrift (Christiana; Oslo, 1900 ff.)
Nunt   Nuntius sodalicii neotestamentici Upsaliensis (Lund, 1949-1952)
O   Orpheus; rivista di umanità classica e cristiana (Catania, 1954 ff.)
OC   Oriens christianus (Rome, 1901-1940; Wiesbaden, 1953 ff.)
OCP   Orientalia christiana periodica (Rome, 1935 ff.)
OS   L'orient syrien (Paris, 1956 f.)
Π   Παῦλος, ὁ ᾽Απόστολος τῆς ῾Ελλάδος (Cyparissia, 1956 f.)
PB   Przegląd biblijny (Kraków, 1937-1939)
PTR   Princeton Theological Review (Philadelphia; Princeton, 1903-1929)
RB   Revue biblique (Paris, 1892 ff.)
RBén   Revue Bénédictine (Maredsous, 1884 ff.)
RE   [Baptist] Review and Expositor (Louisville, Ky., 1904 ff.)
RET   Revista española de teología (Madrid, 1940 ff.)
RHLR   Revue d'histoire et de littérature religieuses (Paris, 1896 ff.)
RHPR   Revue d'histoire et de philosophie religieuses (Strasbourg, 1921 ff.)
RivB   Rivista biblica (Rome, 1953 ff.)
RL   Religion in Life (New York, 1932 ff.)
RMAL   Revue du moyen âge latin (Lyon; Strasbourg, 1945-1952)
ROC   Revue de l'orient chrétien (Paris, 1896-1946)
RR   Richerche religiose (also, Religio; also, Ricerche di storia religiosa) (Rome, 1925 ff.)
RSPT   Revue des sciences philosophiques et théologiques (Paris, 1907 ff.)

RSR   Recherches de science religieuse (= Science religieuse, travaux et recherches, 1943-1944), (Paris, 1910 ff.)

RTAM Recherches de théologie ancienne et médiévale (Louvain, 1929 ff.)

Σ   Σωτήρ. Religijos mokslo laikraštis (Kaunas, 1924-1935)

Scr   Scripture; The Quarterly of the Catholic Biblical Association (London, 1948 ff.)

SJT   Scottish Journal of Theology (Edinburgh, 1948 ff.)

SO   Symbolae osloenses (Osloae, 1922 ff.)

SOr   Studia orientalia, edidit societas orientalis fennica (Helsinki, 1925-1941)

SR   Science religieuse, travaux et recherches (cf. RSR) (Paris, 1943 f.)

ST   Studia theologica (Lund, 1948 ff.)

STK   Svensk teologisk kvartalskrift (Lund, 1925 ff.)

STZ   Theologische Zeitschrift aus der Schweiz; from 1900 = Schweizerische theologische Zeitschrift (Zürich, 1884-1920)

Θ   Θεολογία (Athens, 1923 ff.)

TB   Theologische Blätter (Leipzig, 1922—Mai, 1942)

Th   Theology; A Journal of Historic Christianity (London, 1920 ff.)

ThSt   Theological Studies (New York; Woodstock, Md., 1940 ff.)

TLZ   Theologische Literaturzeitung (Leipzig, 1876 ff.)

TQ   Theologische Quartalschrift (Tübingen; Ravensburg, 1819 ff.)

TR   Theologische Rundschau (Tübingen, 1897 ff.)

TS   Theologische Studiën (Utrecht, 1883 ff.)

TSK   Theologische Studien und Kritiken (Hamburg; Gotha, 1828-1938)

TT   Theologisch tijdschrift (Amsterdam; Leiden, 1867-1919)

TTod Theology Today (Princeton, N. J., 1944 ff.)

TZ   Theologische Zeitschrift (Basel, 1945 ff.)

USR   Union Seminary Magazine; since 1913, Union Seminary Review (Hampden-Sidney, Va.; Richmond, Va., 1890-1946)

VC   Vigiliae Christianae (Amsterdam, 1947 ff.)

VD   Verbum Domini (Rome, 1920 ff.)

VP   Vivre et Penser; recherches d'exégèse et d'histoire (= RB) (Paris, 1941-1944)

WTJ   Westminster Theological Journal (Philadelphia, 1938 ff.)

ŽA   Živa Antika (Skoplje, 1951 ff.)

ZKT   Zeitschrift für katholische Theologie (Innsbruck, 1876 ff.)

ZNW Zeitschrift für die neutestamentliche Wissenschaft und die Kunde des Urchristentums (Giessen; Berlin, 1900 ff.)

ZRGG Zeitschrift für Religions- und Geistesgeschichte (Köln, 1948 ff.)

ZST   Zeitschrift für systematische Theologie (Gütersloh, 1923-1955)

ZWT Zeitschrift für wissenschaftliche Theologie, ed. Adolf Hilgenfeld (Jena; Leipzig, 1858-1914)

ZWTh Zeitschrift für wissenschaftliche Theologie, ed. G. B. Winer (Sultzbach, 1826-1827)

SECTION I

BIBLIOGRAPHICAL ARTICLES ON PAUL

1. C. H. van Rhijn, "De jongste literatuur over de Schriften des Nieuwen Verbonds, IV: De Brieven van Paulus," *TS*, 2 (1884), 294-353.
2. E. Grafe, "Paulinische Theologie," *TR*, 1 (1897-1898), 23-30.
3. Paul W. Schmiedel, "Paulinische Briefe, I," *TR*, 1 (1897-1898), 142-150.
4. E. Grafe, "Paulinische Theologie," *TR*, 2 (1899), 306-316.
5. Carl Clemen, "Apostelgeschichte und apostolisches Zeitalter," *TR*, 3 (1900), 50-56.
6. Carl Clemen, "Apostelgeschichte und apostolisches Zeitalter," *TR*, 4 (1901), 66-79.
7. Adolf Jülicher, "Paulinische Theologie," *TR*, 4 (1901), 187-198.
8. Paul W. Schmiedel, "Paulinische Briefe, I," *TR*, 4 (1901), 498-522.
9. Carl Clemen, "Apostelgeschichte und apostolisches Zeitalter," *TR*, 6 (1903), 79-90.
10. Carl Clemen, "Apostelgeschichte und apostolisches Zeitalter," *TR*, 7 (1904), 278-286.
11. Paul W. Schmiedel, "Paulinische Briefe, I," *TR*, 7 (1904), 21-28, 62-75.
12. Eberhard Vischer, "Paulus," *TR*, 8 (1905), 470-481, 512-532.
13. R. Knopf, "Paulinische Briefe, II," *TR*, 9 (1906), 62-65.
14. W. Bousset, "Neueste Forschungen zur Apostelgeschichte," *TR*, 11 (1908), 185-205.
15. Eberhard Vischer, "Jesus und Paulus," *TR*, 11 (1908), 301-313.
16. Walter Bauer, "Das apostolische und nachapostolische Zeitalter," *TR*, 12 (1909), 459-469.
17. Eberhard Vischer, "Paulus," *TR*, 13 (1910), 439-453, 462-481.
18. Walter Bauer, "Apostelgeschichte und apostolisches Zeitalter," *TR*, 14 (1911), 269-295.
19. Rudolf Knopf, "Paulinische Briefe, II," *TR* 16 (1913), 22-32; 20 (1917), 239-247.

20. Eberhard Vischer, "Paulus, I und II," *TR*, 16 (1913), 247-262, 294-307.
21. Walter Bauer, "Apostelgeschichte und apostolisches Zeitalter," *TR*, 17 (1914), 209-223; 20 (1917), 115-138.
22. Rudolf Knopf, "Paul and Hellenism," *AJT*, 18 (1914), 497-520.
23. Eberhard Vischer, "Paulus," *TR*, 18 (1915), 151-159; 19 (1916), 294-323; 20 (1917), 368—376.
24. Eberhard Vischer, "Paulus im Lichte der neuesten Forschung," *STZ*, 34 (1917), 1-9, 49-68.
25. Frederick C. Grant, "A New Testament Bibliography, 1914-1917," *ATR*, 1 (1918-1919), 58-91.
26. Hans Windisch, "Literature on the NT in Germany, Austria, Switzerland, Holland, and the Scandinavian Countries, 1914-1920," *HTR*, 15 (1922), 115-216.
27. A. van Veldhuizen, "Paulus," *NTS*, 7 (1924), 144-151.
28. Frederick C. Grant, "A New Testament Bibliography for 1918-1922 Inclusive," *ATR*, 7 (1924-1925), 40-54.
29. Hans Windisch, "Literature on the NT in Germany, Holland, and the Scandinavian Countries, 1921-1924," *HTR*, 19 (1926), 1-114.
30. A. van Veldhuizen, "Paulus," *NTS*, 10 (1927), 301-304; 11 (1928), 268-272.
31. Rudolf Bultmann, "Zur Geschichte der Paulusforschung," *TR*, N.F. 1 (1929), 26-59.
32. L. Murillo, "Notulae bibliographicae in Pauli scripta," *VD*, 2 (1932), 181-186.
33. A. van Veldhuizen, "Paulus," *NTS*, 16 (1933), 281-283.
34. Rudolf Bultmann, "Neueste Paulusforschung," *TR*, N.F. 6 (1934), 229-246; 8 (1936), 1-22.
35. Sydney Cave, "After Fifty Years; VIII, The Significance of the Apostle Paul," *ET*, 50 (1938-1939), 452-456.
36. Werner G. Kümmel, "Das Urchristentum," *TR*, N.F. 14 (1942), 81-95, 155-173; 17 (1948-1949), 3-50, 103-142; 18 (1950), 1-53; 22 (1954), 138-170, 191-211.
37. John M. T. Barton, "Catholic Bibliography of St. Paul's Life and Writings," *Scr*, 1 (1946), 61-65; 6 (1953), 56-58.
38. A. M. Hunter, "St. Paul in the Twentieth Century," *ET*, 61 (1949-1950), 356-360.
39. St. Lyonnet, "Bulletin d'exégèse paulinienne," *B*, 32 (1951), 104-113, 281-297, 432-439, 569-586; 33 (1952), 240-257.

40. C. K. Barrett, "New Testament Commentaries; III, Epistles and Revelation," *ET*, 65 (1953-1954), 177-180.
41. C. J. Bjerkelund, "Albert Schweitzer's Paulus-forskning — en karakteristik," *NTT*, 58 (1957), 65-89.

See also numbers 1755, 1898, 2031, 2102, 2194, 2196, 2310, and 2555.

SECTION II

HISTORICAL STUDIES ON THE LIFE OF PAUL

A. The Chronology of Events in Paul's Life

42. [M. V.] Aberle, "Zur Chronologie der Gefangenschaft Pauli," *TQ*, 65 (1883), 553-572.
43. W. M. Ramsay, "A Fixed Date in the Life of St. Paul," *Exp*, 5th series, 3 (1895), 336-345.
44. J. Weiss, "Paulinische Probleme: Die Chronologie der Paulinischen Briefe," *TSK*, 68 (1895), 252-296.
45. K. Kühn, "Letzte Reise und Todesjahr des Apostels Paulus," *NKZ*, 7 (1896), 271-277.
46. W. M. Ramsay, "Pauline Chronology," *Exp*, 5th series, 5 (1897), 201-211.
47. B. W. Bacon, "A Criticism of the New Chronology of Paul," *Exp*, 5th series, 7 (1898), 123-136; 10 (1899), 351-367, 412-430.
48. J. Belser, "Zur Chronologie des Paulus," *TQ*, 80 (1898), 353-379.
49. George H. Gilbert, "The New Chronology of Paul's Life," *BS*, 55 (1898), 244-258.
50. E. Schürer, "Zur Chronologie des Lebens Pauli," *ZWT*, 41 (1898), 21-41.
51. Vernon Bartlet, "Some Points in Pauline History and Chronology," *Exp*, 5th series, 10 (1899), 263-280.
52. W. P. Workman, "A New Date-Indication in Acts," *ET*, 11 (1899-1900), 316-319. [Paul's voyage was probably in A.D. 58].
53. G. A. Simcox, "A Point in Pauline Chronology," *JTS*, 2 (1901), 586-590.
54. G. Hoennicke, "Die Chronologie des Lebens des Apostels Paulus," *NKZ*, 12 (1902), 569-620.
55. Joseph Aberle, "Chronologie des Apostels Paulus von seiner Bekehrung bis zur Abfassung des Galaterbriefes," *BibZ*, 1 (1903), 256-279, 372-377.
56. G. Hoennicke, "Der Todestag des Apostels Paulus," *NKZ*, 14 (1903), 905-932.
57. T. Zahn, "Zur Lebensgeschichte des Apostels Paulus," *NKZ* 15 (1904), 23-41, 189-201.

58. Joseph Aberle, "Chronologie des Apostels Paulus vom Apostelkonzile bis zum Märtyrertode des Apostels in Rom," *BibZ*, 3 (1905), 371-400.

59. G. Wohlenberg, "Eine Claudius-Inschrift von Delphi in ihrer Bedeutung für die paulinische Chronologie," *NKZ*, 23 (1912), 380-396.

60. F. W. Grosheide, "De chronologie van het leven van Paulus," *GTT*, 19 (1918-1919), 349-361.

61. Maurice Jones, "A New Chronology of the Life of St. Paul," *Exp*, 8th series, 17 (1919), 363-383, 424-446; 18 (1919), 99-120.

62. Oswald Gerhardt, "In welchem Jahre wurde der Apostel Paulus in Jerusalem gefangen gesetzt?" *NKZ*, 33 (1922), 89-114.

63. L. G. Da Fonseca, "A Moyse ad Paulum (aetas Abrahami et chronologia S. Pauli, iuxta Kugler)," *VD*, 3 (1923), 350-352.

64. John Knox, "The Pauline Chronology," *JBL*, 58 (1939), 15-30.

65. Paul S. Minear, "The Jerusalem Fund and Pauline Chronology," *ATR*, 25 (1943), 389-396.

66. Gilmore H. Guyot, "The Chronology of Saint Paul," *CBQ*, 6 (1944), 28-36.

67. George Ogg, "A New Chronology of Saint Paul's Life," *ET*, 64 (1952-1953), 120-123.
See also numbers 94, 134, 201, 321, and 327.

B. Paul's Conversion

68. C. Holsten, "Die Christus-Vision des Paulus und die Genesis des Paulinischen Evangeliums," *ZWT*, 4 (1861), 223-284.

69. R. D. C. Robbins, "Remarks Upon Some Passages in the Acts of the Apostles," *BS*, 14 (1857), 258-279 [Paul's Conversion Experience, Acts 9 : 7; 22 : 9; 26 : 14].

70. W. Beyschlag, "Die Bekehrung des Apostels Paulus," *TSK*, 37 (1864), 197-264.

71. A. Hilgenfeld, "Die Bekehrung und apostolische Berufung des Paulus," *ZWT*, 7 (1864), 155-191.

72. J. K. Koch, "De bekeering van Paulus volgens Straatman," *TT*, 9 (1875), 45-54.

73. F. Zimmer, "Die drei Berichte der Apostelgeschichte über die Bekehrung des Paulus," *ZWT*, 25 (1882), 465-482.

74. John Massie, "Conversion of St. Paul," *Exp*, 3rd series, 10 (1889), 241-262.

75. Ernest DeW. Burton, "Saul's Experience on the Way to Damascus," *BW*, 1 (1893), 9-23.

76. A. B. Scherer, "The Conversion of Saul as Evidence for Christianity," *LQ*, 25 (1895), 331-357.

77. Russell Cecil, "The Psychological Aspects of the Conversion of the Apostle Paul," *USR*, 9 (1897), 168-176.

78. C. J. Klumker, "Die Bekehrung des Paulus," *ZWT*, 41 (1898), 335-363.

79. C. W. Votaw, "The Conversion and Early Ministry of Paul," *BW*, 33 (1909), 272-278.

80. Howell M. Haydn, "Paul's Transformation in Character," *BS*, 69 (1912), 522-526.

81. Alfred Loisy, "La conversion de saint Paul et la naissance du christianisme," *RHLR*, N.S. 5 (1914), 289-331.

82. R. A. Falconer, "The Aramaic Source of Acts 1 : 15 and Paul's Conversion," *Exp*, 8th series, 19 (1920), 271-285.

83. B. R. Lacy, Jr., "An Introduction to Paul's Spoken Messages — His Conversion," *USR*, 34 (1922-1923), 50-54.

84. E. G. Selwyn, "Studies in Texts: Acts 9 : 5," *Th*, 6 (1923), 100-102.

85. A. M. Pope, "The Objective Focus of Paul's Religious Experience," *CJRT*, 2 (1925), 290-298.

86. G. J. Inglis, "The Problem of St. Paul's Conversion," *ET*, 40 (1928-1929), 227-231.

87. E. Hirsch, "Die drei Berichte der Apostelgeschichte über die Bekehrung des Paulus," *ZNW*, 28 (1929), 305-312.

88. E. von Dobschütz, "Die Berichte über die Bekehrung des Paulus," *ZNW*, 29 (1930), 144-147.

89. Fred C. Anderson, "The Call of Saul of Tarsus," *ET*, 42 (1930-1931), 90-92.

90. Mary S. Thomas, "The Nature of Paul's Conversion," *CQ*, 8 (1931), 468-492.

91. H. Windisch, "Die Christusepiphanie vor Damaskus (Acts 9, 22 u. 26) und ihre religionsgeschichtlichen Parallelen," *ZNW*, 31 (1932), 1-23.

92. J. Louw, "De beteekenis van het licht voor de bekeering van Paulus," *NTS*, 18 (1935), 190-192.

93. Robert H. Miller, "Jesus Finds Paul — Paul Finds his Job," *RE*, 33 (1936), 183-187.

94. Otto Procksch, "Pauli Todesjahr 62 n. chr.," *NKZ*, 47 (1936), 225-234.

95. G. J. Inglis, "St. Paul's Conversion in his Epistles," *Th*, 34 (1937), 214-228.

96. A. Ben Oliver, "Did Paul's Companions Hear the Voice?" *RE*, 37 (1940), 63-66.

97. Mary E. Andrews, "The Conversion of Paul," *JBR*, 9 (1941), 147-154.

98. Joseph L. Lilly, "The Conversion of Saint Paul (The Validity of his Testimony to the Resurrection of Jesus Christ)," *CBQ*, 6 (1944), 180-204.

99. A. Wikenhauser, "Die Wirkung der Christophanie vor Damaskus auf Paulus und seine Begleiter nach den Berichten der Apostelgeschichte," *B*, 33 (1952), 313-323.

100. David M. Stanley, "Paul's Conversion in Acts: Why the Three Accounts?" *CBQ*, 15 (1953), 315-338.

101. H. G. Wood, "The Conversion of St. Paul: its Nature, Antecedents and Consequences," *NTSt*, 1 (1955), 276-282.

102. Walenty Prokulski, "The Conversion of St. Paul," *CBQ*, 19 (1957), 453-473.
    See also numbers 397, 1612, 2375, 2477, and 2516.

C. Paul's Missionary Journeys

103. F. Märcker, "Ist Paulus zweimal oder dreimal in Korinth gewesen?" *TSK*, 45 (1872), 153-162.

104. J. H. Scholten, "De onderstelde derde reis van Paulus naar Corinthe," *TT*, 12 (1878), 559-589.

105. W. M. Ramsay, "St. Paul's First Journey in Asia Minor," *Exp*, 4th series, 5 (1892), 29-39; 6 (1892), 161-175, 281-297, 373-385.

106. J. Belser, "Pauli Reisen nach Korinth," *TQ*, 76 (1894), 15-47.

107. W. M. Ramsay, "St. Paul in Athens," *Exp*, 5th series, 2 (1895), 209-22, 261-277.

108. W. Sanday, "St. Paul the Traveller," *Exp*, 5th series, 3 (1895), 81-94.

109. R. Scott, "Paul's 'Missionary Journeys,' " *ET*, 7 (1895-1896), 425-426.

110. W. S. Currell, "A Model Missionary — the Apostle Paul," *USR*, 9 (1897), 1-13.

111. John Reid, "The Missionary Method of the Apostles," *ET* 11 (1899-1900), 55-60, 156-159, 266-269, 360-364, 411-414, 448-451, 508-512, 544-547.

112. N. J. D. White, "The Visits of St. Paul to Corinth," *Herm*, 12 (1903), 79-89.

113. Thomas C. Johnson, "Paul's Obligations to Missionary Effort and the Way in Which He Met Them," *USR*, 15 (1903-1904), 163-174.

114. O. Holtzmann, "Die Jerusalemreisen des Paulus und die Kollekte," *ZNW*, 6 (1905), 102-104.

115. John W. Bailey, "Paul's Second Missionary Journey," *BW*, 33 (1909), 414-423.

116. W. P. Behan, "Paul's Third Missionary Journey," *BW*, 34 (1909), 120-130.

117. T. G. Soares, "Paul's Missionary Method," *BW*, 34 (1909), 326-336.

118. James Kelso, "Paul's Roman Citizenship as reflected in his Missionary Experiences and his Letters," *BS*, 79 (1922), 173-183.

119. James Kelso, "Key Cities in Paul's Missionary Program," *BS*, 79 (1922), 481-486.

120. T. Vargha, "Paulus missionarii popularis exemplar," *VD*, 9 (1929), 24-27, 39-42, 87-90.

121. G. Palomero Díaz, "Los viajes apostólicos de S. Pablo," *EB*, 6 (1934), 195-213.

122. W. A. McDonald, "Archaeology and St. Paul's Journeys in Greek Lands," *BA*, 3 (1940), 18-24.

123. W. H. Murray Walton, "The Over-ruling Purpose of God as shown in Paul's Missionary Travels," *ET*, 55 (1943-1944), 33-36.

124. W. H. Murray Walton, "St. Paul's Movements between the Writing of 1 and 2 Corinthians," *ET*, 56 (1944-1945), 136-138.

125. Donald T. Rowlingson, "The Geographical Orientation of St. Paul's Missionary Interests," *JBL*, 69 (1950), 341-344.

126. Henry Turlington, "Paul's Missionary Practice," *RE*, 51 (1954), 168-186.

127. Thomas H. Campbell, "Paul's 'Missionary Journeys' as Reflected in his Letters," *JBL*, 74 (1955), 80-92.
See also number 2110.

D. Paul at Athens (the Areopagus Speech)

128. H. B. Hackett, "The Discourse of Paul at Athens. A Commentary on Acts 17 : 16-34," *BS*, 6 (1849), 338-356.

129. F. W. Laufs, "Über die areopagische Rede des Apostels Paulus: Apostelg. 17, 22-32," *TSK*, 23 (1850), 583-595.

130. M. Michelsen, "Über einige sinnverwandte Aussprüche des Neuen Testaments: Apg. 17, 31," *TSK*, 46 (1873), 120-124.

131. Émile Beurlier, "Saint Paul et l'Aréopage," *RHLR*, 1 (1896), 344-366.

132. Eberhard Nestle, "Acts 17 : 29," *ET*, 9 (1897-1898), 381 [οὐκ ὀφείλομεν νομίζειν].

133. J. M. English, "Elements of Persuasion in Paul's Address on Mars' Hill, at Athens," *AJT*, 2 (1898), 97-109.

134. J. Belser, "Paulus in Athen im Sommer 50," *TQ*, 81 (1899), 63-88.

135. Ernst Curtius, "St. Paul in Athens," *Exp*, 7th series, 4 (1907), 436-455.

136. W. N. Stearns, "The Apostle Paul in Athens," *BW*, 37 (1911), 411-419.

137. Basil Mathews, "Where did Paul speak at Athens?" *ET*, 26 (1914-1915), 281-283.

138. J. Q. Adams, "Paul at Athens," *ET*, 32 (1920-1921), 376-377.

139. A. Sizoo, "Het spotten der Atheners met de opstanding der dooden," *GTT*, 24 (1923-1924), 289-297.

140. L. Feuerbringer, "Paulus in Athen," *CTM*, 1 (1930), 735-742, 804-810, 881-887.

141. J. H. Maclean, "St. Paul at Athens," *ET*, 44 (1932-1933), 550-553.

142. J. McKee Adams, "Paul at Athens," *RE*, 32 (1935), 50-56.

143. W. A. McDonald, "Archaeology and St. Paul's Journeys in Greek Lands; Part II, Athens," *BA*, 4 (1941), 1-10.

144. P. P. Parente, "Saint Paul's Address before the Areopagus," *CBQ*, 11 (1949), 144-150.

145. Walther Eltester, "Zur Areopagrede," *TLZ*, 79 (1954), 367-368.
See also number 2465.

E. Paul's Ephesian Imprisonment (*pro et contra*)

146. B. W. Robinson, "An Ephesian Imprisonment of Paul," *JBL*, 29 (1910), 181-189.

147. E. Ch. Babut et Alfred Loisy, "Le proconsul Gallion et saint Paul," *RHLR*, N. S. 2 (1911), 139-144.

148. Ernst Dubowy, "Paulus und Gallio," *BibZ*, 10 (1912), 143-153.

149. E. W. Burch, "Was St. Paul in Prison at Ephesus?" *BS*, 71 (1914), 490-493.

150. B. W. Bacon, "Again the Ephesian Imprisonment of Paul," *Exp*, 8th series, 9 (1915), 235-242.

151. E. W. Winstanley, "Pauline Letters from an Ephesian Prison," *Exp*, 8th series, 9 (1915), 481-498.

152. H. Coppieters, "Saint Paul fut-il captif à Éphèse pendant son troisième voyage apostolique?" *RB*, N.S. 16 (1919), 404-418.

153. C. R. Bowen, "Are Paul's Prison Letters from Ephesus?" *AJT*, 24 (1920), 112-135, 277-287.

154. C. R. Bowen, " 'I fought with Beasts at Ephesus,' " *JBL*, 42 (1923), 59-68.

155. W. Tom, "Heeft Paulus te Efeze gevangen gezeten?" *GTT*, 24 (1923-1924), 451-460, 500-513.

156. W. Michaelis, "The Trial of St. Paul at Ephesus," *JTS*, 29 (1927-1928), 368-375.

157. Alberto Pincherle, "Paolo a Efeso," *RR*, 3 (1927), 422-439.

158. G. S. Duncan, "St. Paul's Ministry at Ephesus: A Reconstruction," *Th*, 22 (1931), 16-23.

159. G. L. Hurst, "A Footnote to Paul's Ephesian Ministry," *ET*, 43 (1931-1932), 235-236.

160. W. Grossow, "Fuitne Paulus Ephesi 'vinctus Christi Iesu'?" *VD*, 11 (1931), 294-297, 343-348.

161. G. S. Duncan, "Some Outstanding New Testament Problems; VI, The Epistles of the Imprisonment in Recent Discussion," *ET*, 46 (1934-1935), 293-298.

162. B. Brinkmann, "Num S. Paulus Ephesi fuerit captivus," *VD*, 19 (1939), 321-332.

163. B. Brinkmann, "Epistolae captivitatis S. Pauli num Ephesi scripta sint," *VD*, 21 (1941), 9-21.

164. D. T. Rowlingson, "Paul's Ephesian Imprisonment: An Evaluation of the Evidence," *ATR*, 32 (1950), 1-7.

165. G. S. Duncan, "Important Hypotheses Reconsidered; VI, Were Paul's Imprisonment Epistles written from Ephesus?" *ET*, 67 (1955-1956), 163-166.

See also numbers 431, 501, and 2225.

F. Paul's Caesarean Imprisonment

166. W. H. P. Faunce, "Paul Before Agrippa," *BW*, 7 (1896), 86-93.
167. W. M. Lewis, "St. Paul's Defense before King Agrippa in Relation to the Epistle to the Hebrews," *BW*, 13 (1899), 244-248.
168. C. B. Williams, "The Caesarean Imprisonment of Paul," *BW*, 34 (1909), 271-280.
169. U. Holzmeister, "Der hl. Paulus vor dem Richterstuhle des Festus (Ag. 25, 1-12)," *ZKT*, 23 (1912), 489-509, 742-783.
170. G. H. Whitaker, "The Words of Agrippa to St. Paul," *JTS*, 15 (1914), 82-83 [Acts 26 : 28].
171. J. E. Harry, "ἐν ὀλίγῳ με πείθεις," *ATR*, 28 (1946), 135-136 [Acts 26 : 28].

G. Paul's Voyage to Rome

172. H. B. Hackett, "The Voyage and Shipwreck of Paul as Related by Luke; A Commentary on Acts 27 : 1-44; 28 : 16," *BS*, 7 (1850), 743-771.
173. Edward Hull, "St. Paul's Voyage," *ET*, 7 (1895-1896), 476-477.
174. W. M. Ramsay, "S. Paul's Shipwreck," *Exp*, 5th series, 6 (1897), 154-157.
175. J. von Goerne, "Der Schiffbruch des Apostels Paulus, vom seemänischen Standpunkt," *NZK*, 9 (1898), 352-373.
176. E. J. Goodspeed, "Paul's Voyage to Rome," *BW*, 34 (1909), 337-345.
177. W. Montgomery, "St. Paul's Voyage and Shipwreck," *Exp*, 8th series, 9 (1915), 356-361.
178. W. Cowan, "Acts 27 : 39," *ET*, 28 (1916-1917), 330-331.
179. G. A. Sim, "Acts 27 : 39," *ET*, 28 (1916-1917), 187-188.
180. W. Cowan, "Acts 27 : 39," *ET*, 27 (1915-1916), 472-473.
181. W. P. Gillieson, "Acts 28 : 3," *ET*, 42 (1930-1931), 192.
     See also number 52.

H. Paul's Roman Imprisonment(s) and Death

182. Anonymous, "Die letzten Reisen und Schicksale der Apostel Petrus und Paulus, nach Clemens von Rom und Dionys von Korinth," *TQ*, 12 (1830), 621-648.

183. D. Schenkel, "Die zweite Gefangenschaft des Apostels Paulus," *TSK*, 14 (1841), 53-87.

184. John Macpherson, "Was there a Second Imprisonment of Paul in Rome?" *AJT*, 4 (1900), 23-48.

185. Th. Mommsen, "Die Rechtsverhältnisse des Apostels Paulus," *ZNW*, 2 (1901), 81-96.

186. Vernon Bartlet, "Paul in Rome," *BW*, 34 (1909), 346-354.

187. K. Lake, "The End of Paul's Trial in Rome," *TT*, 47 (1913), 356-365.

188. F. Pfister, "Die zweimalige römische Gefangenschaft und die spanische Reise des Apostels Paulus und der Schluss der Apostelgeschichte," *ZNW*, 14 (1913), 216-221.

189. Ernesto Buonaiuti, "St. Paul's Imprisonment at Rome and the Text of Acts," *ET*, 26 (1914-1915), 520-521.

190. W. W. Rockwell, "The Latest Discussion on Peter and Paul at Rome," *AJT*, 22 (1918), 113-124.

191. N. W. DeWitt, "Paul and Peter in Rome," *CJRT*, 1 (1924), 164-168.

192. A. M. Perry, "Acts and the Roman Trial of Paul," *HTR*, 17 (1924), 195-196.

193. Wilhelm Michaelis, "Die Gefangenschaftsbriefe des Paulus und antike Gefangenenbriefe," *NKZ*, 36 (1925), 586-606.

194. W. Bartlett, "Paul and Peter at Rome," *ET*, 40 (1928-1929), 92-93.

195. O. Cullmann, "Les causes de la mort de Pierre et de Paul d'après le témoignage de Clément Romain," *RHPR*, 10 (1930), 294-300.

196. L. P. Pherigo, "Paul's Life after the Close of Acts," *JBL*, 70 (1951), 277-285.

197. F. R. M. Hitchcock, "On What Charge was St. Paul Beheaded?" *Herm*, No. 77 (1951), 25-36.

198. J. A. D. Bentfort, "Enige beknopte beschouwingen met betrekking tot de processen van de Here Jezus Christus en van de Apostel Paulus," *GTT*, 55 (1955), 33-68.
See also numbers 45, 56, 58, 94, and 369.

I. PAUL AND THE PRIMITIVE CHURCH

199. A. Hilgenfeld, "Paulus und die Urapostel, der Galaterbrief und die Apostelgeschichte, und die neuesten Bearbeitungen," *ZWT*, 3 (1860), 101-168, 205-239.

200. T. H. Darlow, "St. Paul's Last Visit to Jerusalem," *Exp*, 5th series, 2 (1895), 152-158.
201. W. M. Ramsay, "St. Paul and the Jewish Christians in A.D. 46," *Exp*, 5th series, 3 (1896), 174-190.
202. W. M. Ramsay, "Paul's Attitude towards Peter and James," *Exp*, 5th series, 4 (1896), 43-56.
203. W. Sanday, "Paul's Attitude towards Peter and James," *Exp*, 5th series, 4 (1896), 56-64.
204. W. Sanday, "The Early Visits of St. Paul to Jerusalem," *Exp*, 5th series, 3 (1896), 253-263.
205. E. P. Gould, "St. Paul and the Twelve," *JBL*, 18 (1899), 184-189.
206. R. A. Falconer, "The Early Visits of St. Paul to Jerusalem," *ET*, 11 (1899-1900), 487-490.
207. S. J. Case, "Paul's Historical Relation to the First Disciples," *AJT*, 9 (1907), 269-286.
208. J. Kreyenbühl, "Der Apostel Paulus und die Urgemeinde," *ZNW*, 8 (1907), 81-109, 163-189.
209. Preserved Smith, "A New Light on the Relations of Peter and Paul," *HJ*, 11 (1913), 733-750.
210. Dr. Ritter, "Paulus und der 'Geist' der Urgemeinde," *NKZ*, 25 (1914), 449-471.
211. H. J. Toxopeus, "Nieuw licht op de betrekkingen tusschen Petrus en Paulus," *TT*, 49 (1915), 285-316.
212. H. Koch, "Petrus und Paulus im zweiten Osterfeierstreit?" *ZNW*, 19 (1919-1920), 174-179.
213. J. H. Philp, "Paul and the Jerusalem Church," *CJRT*, 2 (1925) 354-359.
214. C. H. Turner, "St. Peter and St. Paul in the New Testament and in the Early Church," *Th*, 13 (1926), 190-204.
215. W. Bartlett, "St. Paul and the Twelve," *ET*, 39 (1927-1928), 39-44.
216. A. S. Peake, "Paul and the Jewish Christians," *BJRL*, 13 (1929), 31-61.
217. S. M. Gilmour, "Paul and the Primitive Church," *JR*, 25 (1945), 119-128.
218. L. P. Pherigo, "Paul and the Corinthian Church," *JBL*, 68 (1949), 341-351.
219. J. Munck, "Paul, the Apostles, and the Twelve," *ST*, 3 (1949 [1950]), 96-110.

220. A. W. Argyle, "St. Paul and the Mission of the Seventy," *JTS*, N.S., 1 (1950), 63.
221. J. N. Sanders, "Peter and Paul in the Acts," *NTSt*, 2 (1955), 133-143.
222. J. Dupont, "La mission de Paul à Jérusalem (Acts 12 : 25)," *NT*, 1 (1956), 275-303.
223. Jacques Dupont, "Pierre et Paul à Antioche et à Jérusalem," *RSR*, 45 (1957), 42-60, 225-239.
224. Jacques Dupont, "Pierre et Paul dans les Actes," *RB*, 64 (1957), 35-47.
   See also numbers 235, 371, 389, 485, 2480, 2574, 2577, and 2878.

J. Paul's Companions

225. J. B. Lightfoot, "The Mission of Titus to the Corinthians," *JCSP*, 2 (1855), 194-205.
226. F. Spitta, "Über die persönlichen Notizen im zweiten Briefe an Timotheus," *TSK*, 51 (1878), 582-607.
227. A. H. Blom, "Paulus en Barnabas," *TT*, 16 (1882), 186-199.
228. G. G. Findlay, "Paul and Titus at Jerusalem," *Exp*, 3rd series, (1887), 435-442.
229. E. Medley, "The Character of Timothy as reflected in the Letters addressed to him by the Apostle Paul," *Exp*, 5th series, 2 (1895), 223-234.
230. Christian Roth, "Onesimus," *STZ*, 14 (1897), 1-13.
231. E. P. Boys-Smith, "Titus and Luke," *ET*, 18 (1906-1907), 380-381.
232. Alexander Souter, "A Suggested Relationship between Titus and Luke," *ET*, 18 (1906-1907), 285.
233. Alexander Souter, "The Relationship between Titus and Luke," *ET*, 18 (1906-1907), 335-336.
234. J. P. Alexander, "The Character of Timothy," *ET*, 25 (1913-1914), 277-285.
235. Xavier Roiron, "Saint Paul témoin de la primauté de saint Pierre," *RSR*, 4 (1913), 489-531.
236. A. J. Robertson, "Barnabas the Friend of the Friendless,' *Exp*, 8th series, 17 (1919), 1-19.
237. Ernesto Buonaiuti, "Paolo ed Apollos," *RR*, 1 (1925), 14-34.
238. T. J. Pennell, "Acts 13 : 13," *ET*, 44 (1932-1933), 476.

239. W. S. Reilly, "Saint Mark, the Disciple of Saint Peter and Saint Paul," *CBQ*, 1 (1939), 223-231.
240. A. Kappeler, "S. Barnabas in vita S. Pauli," *VD*, 22 (1942), 129-135.
241. Otto Bauernfeind, "Zur Frage nach der Entscheidung zwischen Paulus und Lukas," *ZST*, 23 (1954), 59-88.
See also numbers 190, 191, 194, 195, 199, 224, 398, 1615 ff., and 2408.

K. Paul's Infirmity

242. M. Krenkel, "Das körperliche Leiden des Paulus," *ZWT*, 16 (1873), 238-244.
243. Joh. Döller, "Der 'stimulus carnis' beim Apostel Paulus," *ZKT*, 26 (1902), 208-211.
244. A. Steffens, "Der 'stimulus carnis' des hl. Apostels Paulus," *ZKT*, 26 (1902), 606-607.
245. W. M. Alexander, "St. Paul's Infirmity," *ET*, 15 (1903-1904), 469-473, 545-548.
246. E. M. Merrins, "St. Paul's Thorn in the Flesh," *BS*, 64 (1907), 661-692.
247. Hugh Pope, "What was Paul's Infirmity?" *ITQ*, 10 (1915), 418-435.
248. Margaret L. Knopp, "Paul the Deaf," *BW*, 47 (1916), 311-317.
249. Eleanor A. Johnson, "St. Paul's Infirmity," *ET*, 39 (1927-1928), 428-429.
250. C. H. Nash, "Paul's 'Thorn in the Flesh' in its Bearing on his Character and Mission," *RE*, 28 (1931), 33-51.
251. V. A. Holmes-Gore, "The Thorn in the Flesh," *Th*, 32 (1936), 111-112.
252. A. C. Kruer, "Paul's Handicap," *RE*, 37 (1940), 173-180.
253. E. A. Mangan, "Was Saint Paul an Invalid?" *CBQ*, 5 (1943), 68-72.
254. Dorothy Donley, "The Epilepsy of Saint Paul," *CBQ*, 6 (1944), 358-360.
255. J. L. Lilly, "The Epilepsy of Saint Paul," *CBQ*, 7 (1945), 108-109.
256. J. E. Schulte, "De apostel Paulus en zijn 'ziekte(n),'" *NTT*, 11 (1956), 110-118.
257. T. Y. Mullins, "Paul's Thorn in the Flesh," *JBL*, 76 (1957), 299-303.

L. THE PERSONALITY AND APPEARANCE OF PAUL

258. W. H. Bradley, "Have We Authentic Portraits of St. Paul?" *BW*, 9 (1897), 179-184.
259. L. J. Koch, "Paulus som karakter," *NTT*, 12 (1911), 313-361.
260. H. Offermann, "The Personality of the Apostle Paul," *LCR*, 37 (1918), 318-327.
261. Alfred Loisy, "La carrière de l'apôtre Paul," *RHLR*, N.S. 6 (1920), 449-471.
262. H. Offermann, "The Personality of St. Paul," *LCR*, 39 (1920), 1-18.
263. L. Fonck, "Imagines 'authenticae' Ss. Petri et Pauli (?)," *VD*, 3 (1923), 320.
264. A. S. Peake, "Paul the Apostle: His Personality and Achievement," *BJRL*, 12 (1928), 363-388.
265. DuBose Murphy, "The Lighter Side of Paul's Personality," *ATR*, 11 (1928-1929), 242-250.
266. D. R. Fotheringham, "The Appearence of St. Paul," *ET*, 48 (1936-1937), 188.
267. W. S. Reilly, "Characteristics of Saint Paul," *CBQ*, 3 (1941), 214-219.
268. Werner Hannan, "The Real Heart of Saint Paul," *CBQ*, 6 (1944), 334-341.
269. R. W. Cousar, "The Moods of Paul," *USR*, 57 (1945-1946), 320-328.
270. B. H. Ioannides, "'ο στοργικὸς καὶ εὐαίσθητος χαρακτὴρ τοῦ 'Αποστόλου Παύλου," Π, 2 (1957), 298-300.
271. J. Schwartz, "A propos du statut personnel de l'apôtre Paul," *RHPR*, 37 (1957), 91-96.
    See also number 2374.

M. PAUL'S TOMB

272. Anonymous, "I varii seppellimenti degli apostoli Pietro e Paolo sull' Appia," *Bes*, 2 (1897), 317-330.
273. Hans Lietzmann, "Grabstätte d. Petrus und Paulus," *TLZ*, 40 (1915), 285-286.
274. George La Piana, "The Tombs of Peter and Paul *ad Catacumbas*," *HTR*, 14 (1921), 53-86.
275. Paul Styger, "Die erste Ruhestätte der Apostelfürsten Petrus und Paulus an der Via Appia in Rom," *ZKT*, 45 (1921), 549-572.

276. Hans Lietzmann, "The Tomb of the Apostles *ad Catacumbas*," *HTR*, 16 (1923), 147-162.
277. F. J. Foakes Jackson, "Evidence for the Martyrdom of Peter and Paul in Rome," *JBL*, 46 (1927), 74-79.
278. E. Griffe, "La légende du transfert des corps de saint Pierre et de saint Paul ad catacumbas," *BLE*, 52 (1951), 193-209.
279. H. Chadwick, "St. Peter and St. Paul in Rome: The Problem of the Memoria Apostolorum ad Catacumbas," *JTS*, N.S. 8 (1957), 30-52.

N. THE INFLUENCE OF PAUL

280. J. H. A. Michelsen, "Feestgave ter gelegenheid van de viering van het 1800-jarig martelaarschap van Petrus en Paulus," *TT*, 2 (1868), 58-62.
281. W. Seufert, "Das Abhängigkeitsverhältnis des 1 Pet. vom Römerbrief," *ZWT*, 17 (1874), 360-387.
282. Albr. Thoma, "Justins literarisches Verhältnis zu Paulus und zum Johannes-Evangelium," *ZWT*, 18 (1875), 383-412, 490-565.
283. J. H. A. Michelsen, "Paulinisme en Petrinisme in 't na-apostolisch tijdvak," *TT*, 9 (1875), 155-169; "II. Paulus en Simon Magus," 10 (1876), 70-82; "III. Paulinisme en Chiliasme," 11 (1877), 215-223.
284. A. H. Blom, "De Apokalypse en de brieven van Paulus aan de Korinthiërs," *TT*, 12 (1878), 84-95.
285. A. Hilgenfeld, "Der Paulinismus des Hebräerbriefs," *ZWT* 22 (1879), 415-436.
286. J. M. S. Baljon, "Is Marcion volgens Clemens Alexandrinus een bestrijder van 'Paulus canonicus'?" *TS*, 5 (1887), 163-166.
287. H. U. Meyboom, "Het Paulinisme van Lukas (naar aan-leiding van W. H. van de Sande Bakhuyzen, *Het dogmatisch karakter, dat aan het Evangelie van Lukas wordt toegekend*)," *TT*, 23 (1889), 366-406.
288. R. Steck, "Hat Lukas die Paulinischen Briefe gekannt?" *STZ*, 7 (1890), 153-185.
289. H. U. Meyboom, "Marcion en Paulus in de Clementijnen," *TT*, 25 (1891), 1-46.
290. M. Zimmer, "Das schriftstellerische Verhältnis des Jacobus-briefes zur paulinischen Literatur," *ZWT*, 36, 2 (1893), 481-502.

291. J. Jüngst, "Hat das Lukasevangelium paulinischen Charakter?" *TSK*, 69 (1896), 215-244.

292. Alexander Mair, "The Modern Overestimate of Paul's Relation to Christianity," *Exp*, 5th series, 6 (1897), 241-257.

293. W. F. Slater, "The Pauline 'Mystery' in the Apocalypse," *Exp*, 8th series, 1 (1911), 129-148.

294. E. C. Selwyn, "A Personal Reference to St. Paul in the Fourth Gospel," *Exp*, 8th series, 12 (1916), 229-236.

295. C. A. Ritchey, "Luther and Paul: Their Experiences and Doctrines of Salvation," *BW*, 50 (1917), 226-231.

296. G. E. French, "Is St. Paul in the Gospels?" *Exp*, 8th series, 22 (1921), 219-223.

297. J. M. Bover, "Fr. Luis de León traductor de San Pablo," *EE*, 7 (1928), 417-431.

298. E. Hirsch, "Petrus und Paulus," *ZNW*, 29 (1930), 63-76.

299. H. G. Wood, "Mark's Gospel and Paulinism," *ET*, 51 (1939-1940), 321-333.

300. Hannis Hirschberg, "Allusions to the Apostle Paul in the Talmud," *JBL*, 62 (1943), 73-89.

301. Campbell Bonner, "A Reminiscence of Paul on a Coin Amulet," *HTR*, 43 (1950), 165-168.

302. Johannes Munck, "Peter and Paul in the Apocalypse of St. John," *Nunt*, 4 (1950), cols. 25-26.

303. Panagiotos I. Bratsiotes, "'Ο 'Απόστολος Παῦλος καὶ ἡ 'Ορθόδοξος 'Εκκλησία," Θ, 25 (1954), 58-70.

304. Leslie Conrad, Jr., "Paul and Preaching to a Military-Minded America," *LQ*, 7 (1955), 44-47.

305. Elias Andrews, "The Relevance of Paul for Preaching," *CJT*, 2 (1956), 49-55.

306. Gerald Bonner, "The Scillitan Saints and the Pauline Epistles," *JEH*, 7 (1956), 141-146.

307. Arnold Ehrhardt, "An Unknown Orphic Writing in the Demosthenes Scholia and St. Paul," *ZNW*, 48 (1957), 101-110.

308. A. Salles, "La diatribe anti-paulinienne dans 'le Roman pseudo-clémentin' et l'origine des 'Kérygmes de Pierre,'" *RB*, 64 (1957), 516-551.

See also numbers 264, 375, and 2966.

O. Miscellaneous Studies

309. David Schulz, "Sollte der Apostel Paulus wirklich nicht in Colossa und Laodicea gewesen sein?" *TSK*, 2 (1829), 535-538.

310. [A.] Tholuck, "Die Reden des Apostels Paulus in der Apostelgeschichte, mit seinen Briefen verglichen," *TSK*, 12 (1839) 305-328.

311. F. W. C. Umbreit, "Die Veränderung des Namens Σαῦλος in Παῦλος: Eine exegetisch-kritische Vermuthung," *TSK*, 25 (1852), 377-378.

312. Max Krenkel, "Die Θηριομαχία des Apostels Paulus," *ZWT*, 9 (1866), 368-375.

313. E. H. Plumptre, "St. Paul as a Man of Business," *Exp*, 1st series, 1 (1875), 259-266.

314. G. Heinrici, "Zur Geschichte der Anfänge paulinischer Gemeinden," *ZWT*, 20 (1877), 89-129.

315. A. H. Blom, "Paulinische Studiën; I, Waar Paulus de Christenen heeft vervolgd," *TT*, 13 (1879), 337-343.

316. H. U. Meyboom, "Het Romeinsch burgerrecht van Paulus," *TT*, 13 (1879), 73-101, 239-267, 310-336.

317. H. U. Meyboom, "Het getuigenis van Paulus te Jerusalem," *TT*, 14 (1880), 395-421, 599-621; 15 (1881), 96-116, 224-247.

318. G. Heinrici, "Zum genossenschaftlichen Charakter der paulinischen Christengemeinden," *TSK*, 54 (1881), 505-524.

319. E. C. S. Gibson, "Sources of St. Paul's Teaching," *Exp*, 2nd series, 4 (1882), 33-45, 121-132, 209-220, 278-293, 343-355, 421-429.

320. A. Hilgenfeld, "Paulus und Korinth," *ZWT*, 31 (1888), 159-206.

321. A. Hilgenfeld, "Paulus von Damascus bis zum Briefe an die Galater," *ZWT*, 31 (1888), 1-29.

322. W. M. Ramsay, "St. Paul at Ephesus," *Exp*, 4th series, 2 (1890), 1-22.

323. W. J. Slater, "How Paul Preached the Gospel at Corinth," *ET*, 3 (1891-1892), 406-409.

324. W. J. Beecher, "Paul's Visit to Jerusalem," *BW*, 2 (1893), 434-443.

325. F. Rendale, "The Pauline Collection for the Saints," *Exp*, 4th series, 8 (1893), 321-336.

326. H. F. Burton, "Rome in Paul's Day," *BW*, 3 (1894), 87-96.

327. Gustav Volkmar, "Von Damascus bis zum Galaterbrief nach Paulus und Lukas," *STZ*, 1 (1894), 150-162.

328. A. H. Franke, "Die Stellung des Apostels Paulus zu seinem Volke," *TSK*, 68 (1895), 421-470, 733-773.

329. Meredith Hughes, "St. Paul before the Chiliarch," *ET*, 7 (1895-1896), 382-384.

330. W. M. Ramsay, "St. Paul's Handicraft," *ET*, 8 (1896-1897), 286.

331. Eberhard Nestle, "Requests and Replies," *ET*, 8 (1896-1897), 153-154 [σκηνοποιός, Acts 18 : 5].

332. J. H. Wilkinson, "Was St. Paul Married?" *Exp*, 5th series, 5 (1897), 436-442.

333. C. H. van Rhijn, "Σαῦλος ὁ καὶ Παῦλος," *TS*, 17 (1899), 82-84.

334. John Kelman, "St. Paul the Hebrew, the Greek and the Roman," *ET*, 12 (1900-1901), 247-252, 513-520; 13 (1901-1902), 76-81.

335. W. M. Ramsay, "Corroboration: The Census Lists of Quirinius and Augustus, and the Family and Rank of St. Paul," *Exp*, 6th series, 4 (1901), 321-335.

336. W. M. Ramsay, "The Cities of the Pauline Churches," *Exp*, 6th series, 4 (1901), 401-414.

337. E. Preuschen, "Paulus als Antichrist," *ZNW*, 2 (1901), 169-201.

338. E. C. Selwyn, "St. Paul Identified with Antichrist by the Jews," *Exp*, 6th series, 4 (1901), 115-121.

339. Eberhard Nestle, "The Aprons and Handkerchiefs of St. Paul," *ET*, 13 (1901-1902), 282.

340. W. M. Ramsay, "St. Paul," *Exp*, 6th series, 6 (1902), 81-92.

341. R. L. Collins, "St. Paul's Sojourn in Asia," *ET*, 15 (1903-1904), 382-383.

342. J. G. Gray, "Roman Houses, in which St. Paul Preached the Kingdom of God," *USR*, 15 (1903-1904), 310-319.

343. G. H. Davis, "St. Paul's Use of the 'Jus Gentium,'" *ET*, 16 (1904-1905), 477-488.

344. W. M. Ramsay, "The Tarsian Citizenship of St. Paul," *ET*, 16 (1904-1905), 18-21.

345. S. Krauss, "Die jüdischen Apostel," *JQR*, 17 (1905), 370-383.

346. W. M. Ramsay, "Tarsus," *Exp*, 7th series, 1 (1906), 258-277, 353-369, 453-470; 2 (1906), 29-47, 135-160, 268-288, 365-384.

347. P. P. Flournoy, "The Disappointment of Paul," *USR*, 20 (1908-1909), 206-211.
348. G. Hörnicke, "Paulus und Josephus," *NKZ*, 20 (1909), 650-664.
349. A. W. Lindenmuth, "Paul's Personal Apologetics," *LCR*, 28 (1909), 250-256.
350. Alexander Souter, "Did St. Paul Speak Latin?" *Exp*, 8th series, 1 (1911), 337-342.
351. C. W. Briggs, "The Apostle Paul in Arabia," *BW*, 4 (1913), 255-269.
352. A. B. Kinsey, "Saul, who is called Paul," *ET*, 25 (1913-1914), 427.
353. Rudolf Knopf, "Paul and Hellenism," *AJT*, 18 (1914), 497-520.
354. P. J. van Melle, "Het werk van Lucas: een historisch pleidooi voor het Romeinsche gerechtshof ten behoeve van de prediking van Paulus," *TS*, 33 (1915), 111-121.
355. L. M. Miller, "Why Did St. Paul Write Greek?" *BS*, 72 (1915), 23-33.
356. H. A. A. Kennedy, "St. Paul's Apostolic Consciousness and the Interpretation of the Epistles," *ET*, 27 (1915-1916), 8-13.
357. Rendel Harris, "Who sent Apollos to Corinth?" *Exp*, 8th series, 11 (1916), 175-183.
358. A. T. Robertson, "The Versatility of Paul," *Exp*, 8th series, 14 (1917), 389-396.
359. H. W. Julford, "St. Paul and Euripides," *ET*, 31 (1919-1920), 331 [Acts 21 : 39].
360. Rendel Harris, "Did St. Paul Quote Euripides?" *ET*, 31 (1919-1920), 36-37 [Acts 21 : 39].
361. A. M. Williams, "St. Paul's Speech at Lystra," *ET*, 31 (1919-1920), 189.
362. J. A. Gurney, "St. Paul the Co-operator," *Exp*, 8th series, 19 (1920), 439-444.
363. James Moffatt, "Paul and his First Critics," *Exp*, 8th series, 22 (1921), 69-80.
364. L. Murillo, "El ministerio de San Pablo en Antioquía," *EE*, 1 (1922), 273-296.
365. Dr. Bornhäuser, "Paulus und das Aposteldekret," *NKZ*, 34 (1923), 391-438.

366. C. R. Bowen, "Paul's Collection and the Book of Acts,"
     JBL, 42 (1923), 49-58.
367. W. W. Everts, "Paul and the Mystery Religions," *BS*,
     80 (1923), 357-359.
368. A. M. Pope, "Paul's Address before the Council at Jerusalem,"
     Exp, 8th series, 25 (1923), 426-446.
369. J. C. West, "The Martyrdom of St. Paul," *Th*, 6 (1923),
     257-260.
370. F. J. Badcock, "St. Paul's Apostolic Commission," *Th*,
     8 (1924), 13-20, 79-88.
371. A. T. Fowler, "Paul, Q, and the Jerusalem Church," *JBL*,
     43 (1924), 9-14.
372. E. M. Martinson, "Paul as Pastor," *BR*, 9 (1924), 350-370.
373. J. H. Michael, "Paul and Job: A Neglected Analogy," *ET*,
     36 (1924-1925), 67-73.
374. H. Offermann, "Paul and Hellenism," *LCR*, 43 (1924), 289-
     301.
375. W. T. Whitley, "The Insignificance of the Apostle Paul to
     his own Generation," *RE*, 21 (1924), 322-333.
376. J. A. Faulkner, "Paul as Church Organizer," *RE*, 22 (1925),
     202-215.
377. Th. Schlatter, "Gallio und Paulus in Korinth," *NKZ*,
     36 (1925), 500-540.
378. J. Jeremias, "War Paulus Witwer?" *ZNW*, 25 (1926), 310-
     312.
379. M. S. Enslin, "Paul and Gamaliel," *JR*, 7 (1927), 360-375.
380. W. K. L. Clarke, "Was St. Paul a Stammerer?" *ET*, 39 (1927-
     1928), 458-460.
381. W. E. P. Cotter, "St. Paul's Eucharist," *ET*, 39 (1927-1928),
     235 [Acts 20 : 6-12].
382. S. J. Case, "The Jewish Bias of Paul," *JBL*, 47 (1928), 20-31.
383. J. A. Faulkner, "Paul," *RE*, 25 (1928), 48-61.
384. A. F. Puukko, "Paulus und das Judentum," *SOr*, 2 (1928),
     1-87.
385. A. J. Richardson, "Was St. Paul Crucified at Perga?" *Th*,
     16 (1928), 42-46.
386. M. D. R. Willink, "Paul, a Slave of Jesus Christ," *Th*, 16
     (1928), 46-47.
387. D. W. Richardson, "Called of God to Know, to See, and to
     Hear," *USR*, 40 (1928-1929), 272-291.

388. J. Jeremias, "Nochmals: War Paulus Witwer?" *ZNW*, 28 (1929), 321-323.

389. Herbert Preisker, "Jerusalem und Damaskus — ein Beitrag zum Verständnis des Urchristentums," *TB*, 8 (1929), 49-54.

390. Raphael Tonneau, "Éphèse au temps de saint Paul," *RB*, 38 (1929), 5-34, 321-363.

391. James Williams, "The Rich Young Ruler and St. Paul." *ET*, 41 (1929-1920), 139-140.

392. W. Arndt, "Paul as Citizen," *CTM*, 2 (1931), 736-747.

393. A. Marmorstein, "Paulus und die Rabbinen," *ZNW*, 30 (1931), 271-285.

394. M. Goguel, "La vision de Paul à Corinthe et sa comparution devant Gallion," *RHPR*, 12 (1932), 321-333.

395. P. E. Kretzmann, "Words from the Mystery Religions in the New Testament?" *CTM*, 3 (1932), 536-537.

396. A. W. Meyer, "Saulus — Paulus," *CTM*, 3 (1932), 335-340.

397. A. Oepke, "Probleme der vorchristlichen Zeit des Paulus," *TSK*, 105 (1933), 387-424.

398. L. B. Radford, "St. Peter and St. Paul," *ET*, 45 (1933-1934), 300-305.

399. W. E. Henry, "Some Modern Aspects of Paul's World," *RE*, 31 (1934), 173-187.

400. F. A. Schilling, "Why Did Paul go to Damascus?" *ATR*, 16 (1934), 199-205.

401. Samuel Belkin, "The Religious Background of Paul," *JBL*, 54 (1935), 41-62.

402. Harvey Farmer, "The Apostle Paul," *BS*, 92 (1935), 328-338.

403. E. B. Allo, "La portée de la collecte pour Jérusalem dans les plans de saint Paul," *RB*, 45 (1936), 529-537.

404. H. Offermann, "The Historical Setting of Paul's Ministry," *LCQ*, 9 (1936), 165-183.

405. H. E. Dana, "Where Did Paul Persecute the Church?" *ATR*, 20 (1938), 16-26.

406. W. W. Moore, "The Chained Ambassador," *USR*, 50 (1938-1939) 103-111.

407. W. Grundmann, "Die Apostel zwischen Jerusalem und Antiochia," *ZNW*, 39 (1940), 110-137.

408. G. A. Harrer, "Saul who also is Called Paul," *HTR*, 33 (1940), 19-33.

409. T. Torrance, "St. Paul at Philippi," *EQ*, 13 (1941), 62-74.

410. W. A. McDonald, "Archaeology and St. Paul's Journeys in Greek Lands; Part III, Corinth," *BA*, 5 (1942), 36-48.
411. Erik Sjöberg, "Paulus och judendom," *STK*, 18 (1942), 19-33.
412. Andreas ab Alpe, "S. Paulus, 'praedicator, et Apostolus et magister,' " *VD*, 23 (1943), 199-206, 238-244.
413. D. W. Riddle, "The Jewishness of Paul," *JR*, 23 (1943), 240-244.
414. F. W. Beare, "Note on Paul's First Visit to Jerusalem," *JBL*, 63 (1944), 407-410.
415. F. V. Filson, "Ephesus and the New Testament," *BA*, 8 (1945), 73-80.
416. R. S. Kinsey, "Rome in the Time of St. Paul," *LCQ*, 18 (1945), 407-411.
417. O. Linton, "Paulus och juridiken," *STK*, 21 (1945), 173-192.
418. W. A. McDonald, "Archaeology and St. Paul's Journeys in Greek Lands; Part IV, Ephesus," *BA*, 8 (1945), 62-73.
419. J. R. Porter, "The 'Apostolic Decree' and Paul's Second Visit to Jerusalem," *JTS*, 47 (1946), 169-174.
420. W. Rees, "Corinth in St. Paul's Time," *Scr*, 2 (1947), 71-76, 105-111.
421. C. E. Cook, "Paul the Christian, a Preacher's Devotional Study," *ET*, 60 (1948-1949), 212-214.
422. H. Rosin, "Civis Romanus sum," *NedTT*, 3 (1948-1949), 16-27.
423. Alan Robinson, "Saints Peter and Paul in the New Testament," *Scr*, 4 (1949), 120-127.
424. F. R. M. Hitchcock, "The Trials of St. Paul and Apollonius," *Herm*, No. 75 (1950), 24-34.
425. G. J. D. Aalders, "Paulus in Europa," *GTT*, 51 (1951), 129-135.
426. Oscar Broneer, "Corinth, Center of St. Paul's Missionary Work in Greece," *BA*, 14 (1951), 78-96.
427. Lucien Cerfaux, "Saint Paul et sa succession," *RSR*, 41 (1953), 188-202.
428. S. E. Johnson, "Paul and the Manual of Discipline," *HTR*, 48 (1955), 157-166.
429. W. K. Prentice, "St. Paul's Journey to Damascus," *ZNW*, 46 (1955), 250-255.
430. W. Rees, "St. Paul's First Visit to Philippi," *Scr*, 12 (1955), 99-105.
431. G. S. Duncan, "Paul's Ministry in Asia — the Last Phase," *NTSt*, 3 (1957), 211-218.
See also number 2963.

SECTION III

CRITICAL STUDIES OF THE PAULINE LITERATURE

A. GENERAL STUDIES

432. A. Tholuck, "Einleitende Bemerkungen in das Studium der paulinischen Briefe; die Lebensumstände, den Charakter und die Sprache des Apostels betreffend," *TSK*, 8 (1835), 364-393.

433. J. C. M. Laurent, "Zur Kritik der Briefe des Apostels Paulus," *TSK*, 37 (1864), 487-515, 639-673.

434. A. Hilgenfeld, "Die Paulus-Briefe und ihre neuesten Bearbeitungen," *ZWT*, 9 (1866), 293-315, 337-367.

435. A. Hilgenfeld, "Paulinische Forschungen," *ZWT*, 16 (1873), 161-201.

436. A. D. Loman, "Quaestiones Paulinae. Prolegomena. I. Noodzakelijkheid eener herziening van de grondslagen onzer kennis van het oorspronkelijk Paulinisme," *TT*, 16 (1882), 141-163.

437. G. Volkmar, "Ein Gang durch die beiden Apostelgeschichten, des Paulus und des Lukas, im Bereiche des Apostelstreites," *STZ*, 2 (1885), 33-71.

438. A. D. Loman, "Quaestiones Paulinae. II," *TT*, 20 (1886), 42-113.

439. A. D. Loman, "Paulus en de Kanon," *TT*, 20 (1886), 387-406.

440. F. Godet, "General Review of St. Paul's Epistles," *Exp*, 3rd series, 8 (1888), 35-47.

441. D. Völter, "Ein Votum zur Frage nach der Echtheit, Integrität und Composition der vier Paulinischen Hauptbriefe," *TT*, 23 (1889), 265-325.

442. J. T. Marshall, "Did St. Paul Use a Semitic Gospel?" *Exp*, 4th series, 2 (1890), 69-80.

443. Theodor Zahn, "The Epistles of St. Paul in the Fires of Modern Criticism," *LCR*, 9 (1890), 212-231.

444. G. W. Gwilliam, "Is the Apostolic Liturgy Quoted by St. Paul?" *Exp*, 4th series, 3 (1891), 401-410.

445. C. M. Mead, "External Evidence as to Cicero's Writings and Paul's," *BS*, 48 (1891), 470-493.

446. Dr. Wandal, "Paulus, der Apostel Jesu Christi, vor dem Richterstuhl der neuesten Kritik," *NKZ*, 7 (1896), 693-718.

447. C. Clemen, "Die Reihenfolge der paulinischen Hauptbriefe," *TSK*, 70 (1897), 219-270.

448. Bernhard Weiss, "The Present Status of the Inquiry Concerning the Genuineness of the Pauline Epistles," *AJT*, 1 (1897), 328-403.

449. W. C. van Manen, "A Wave of Hypercriticism," *ET*, 9 (1897-1898), 205-211, 257-259, 314-319.

450. W. C. van Manen, "Uit den strijd over hoofdbrieven," *TT*, 32 (1898), 363-370.

451. J. H. Wilkinson, "Recent Theories as to the Composition and Date of the New Testament Epistles," *AJT*, 2 (1898), 118-123.

452. E. F. Williams, "Is Paul a Competent Witness?" *BS*, 56 (1899), 657-672.

453. H. U. Meyboom, "De Hypothese-Völter," *TT*, 41 (1907), 122-151.

454. Dr. Weber, "Das 'Alte' und das 'Neue' Paulusbild," *NKZ*, 20 (1909), 626-649.

455. A. J. Dickinson, "The Letters and Epistles of Paul," *RE*, 8 (1911), 567-584.

456. [A.] Freitag, "Kritische Anmerkungen zu den Pastoralen und zum Epheser- und zweiten Thessalonicherbrief," *ZNW*, 13 (1912), 91-94.

457. S. H. Hooke, "The Interpretation of St. Paul," *ET*, 25 (1913-1914), 326-331.

458. W. M. Ramsay, "Suggestions on the History and Letters of St. Paul," *Exp*, 8th series, 5 (1913), 127-145, 264-284, 347-371.

459. Maurice Jones, "The Epistles of the Captivity: Where were they Written?" *Exp*, 8th series, 10 (1915), 289-316.

460. C. W. Emmet, "The Fourth Book of Esdras and St. Paul," *ET*, 27 (1915-1916), 551-556.

461. Alfred Loisy, "Les épîtres de Paul," *RHLR*, N.S. 7 (1921), 76-125, 213-250.

462. Alfred Loisy, "Les épîtres attribuées à Paul et les épîtres catholiques," *RHLR*, N.S. 7 (1921), 289-348.

463. D. A. Penick, "Paul's Epistles Compared with one another and with the Epistle to the Hebrews," *AJP*, 42 (1921), 58-72.
464. E. E. Flack, "The Apostle Paul and the Old Testament," *LQ*, 53 (1923), 330-356.
465. P. I. Bratsiotes, "'Ο 'Απόστολος Παῦλος καὶ ἡ μετάφρασις τῶν Ο'," Θ, 3 (1925), 189-216.
466. E. von Dobschütz, "Zum paulinischen Schriftbeweis," *ZNW*, 24 (1925), 306-307.
467. Gunnar Rudberg, "Hellenistisk litteraturfoskning och Nya Testament," *Er*, 23 (1925), 193-205.
468. L. Murillo, "Paulus et Pauli scripta (Prologus)," *VD*, 6 (1926), 146-148.
469. D. Strömholm, "Was the Gospel Narrative Known to the Authors of the Epistles?" *HJ*, 26 (1927), 31-42.
470. P. E. Kretzmann, "The Place and Time of the Captivity Letters," *CTM*, 1 (1930), 426-433.
471. M. J. Lagrange, "Saint Paul ou Marcion," *RB*, 41 (1932), 5-30.
472. C. J. Cadoux, "The Dates and Provenance of the Imprisonment Epistles of St. Paul," *ET*, 45 (1933-1934), 471-473.
473. Olaf Linton, "Den paulinska forskningens båda huvudproblem," *STK*, 11 (1935), 115-141.
474. Denis Buzy, "Saint Paul et saint Matthieu," *RSR*, 28 (1938), 473-478.
475. R. C. Horn, "Classical Quotations and Allusions of St. Paul," *LCQ*, 11 (1938), 281-288.
476. Paul Schubert, "Form and Function of the Pauline Letters," *JR*, 19 (1939), 365-377.
477. J. J. Collins, "Rabbinic Exegesis and Pauline Exegesis," *CBQ*, 3 (1941), 15-26, 145-158.
478. D. W. Riddle, "A Fresh View of the Introduction to Paul's Letters," *CQ*, 18 (1941), 306-314.
479. C. J. Costello, "The Old Testament in Saint Paul's Epistles," *CBQ*, 4 (1942), 141-145.
480. Lyder Brun, "De paulinske fangenskapsbrev i ny ovesettelse," *NTT*, 44 (1943), 129-155.
481. S. E. Donlon, "The Form-Critics, the Gospels, and Saint Paul," *CBQ*, 6 (1944), 306-325.
482. E. J. Goodspeed, "The Editio Princeps of Paul," *JBL*, 64 (1945), 193-204.

483. J. W. Bailey, "Light from Paul on Gospel Origins," *ATR*, 28 (1946), 217-226.
484. A. Eschliman, "La rédaction des épîtres pauliniennes," *RB*, 53 (1946), 185-196.
485. C. H. Dodd, "Matthew and Paul," *ET*, 58 (1946-1947), 293-298.
486. A. W. Argyle, "Parallels between the Pauline Epistles and Q," *ET*, 60 (1948-1949), 318-320.
487. C. H. Buck, Jr., "The Early Order of the Pauline Corpus," *JBL*, 68 (1949), 351-357.
488. A. C. Cotter, "The Epistles of the Captivity," *CBQ*, 11 (1949), 370-380.
489. C. L. Mitton, "The Relationship between I Peter and Ephesians," *JTS*, N.S. 1 (1950), 67-73.
490. K. Prümm, "Gal. und 2 Kor. — Ein lehrgehaltlicher Vergleich," *B*, 31 (1950), 27-72.
491. K. Prümm, "Röm. 1-11 und 2 Kor. 3," *B*, 31 (1950), 164-203.
492. H. Wedell, "Is the Term 'Captivity Epistles' Justified?" *Th*, 50 (1947), 366-372.
493. D. Daube, "Jewish Missionary Maxims in Paul," *ST*, 1 (1947 [1948]), 158-169.
494. Eric F. F. Bishop, "Does Aretas Belong in 2 Corinthians or Galatians?" *ET*, 64 (1952-1953), 188-189.
495. K. L. Carroll, "The Expansion of the Pauline Corpus," *JBL*, 72 (1953), 230-237.
496. F. Gryglewicz, "Traces of I Macc. in the Epistles of St. Paul," *Scr*, 6 (1953), 149-152.
497. S. Lyonnet, "L'étude du milieu littéraire et l'exégèse du Nouveau Testament," *B*, 36 (1956), 1-38.
498. E. E. Ellis, "A Note on Pauline Hermeneutics," *NTSt*, 2 (1955), 127-133.
499. Jack Finegan, "The Original Form of the Pauline Collection," *HTR*, 49 (1956), 85-103.
500. Gerhard Friedrich, "Lohmeyers These über das paulinische Briefpräskript kritisch beleuchtet," *TLZ*, 81 (1956), 343-346.
501. Lewis Johnson, "The Pauline Letters from Caesarea," *ET*, 68 (1956-1957), 24-26.
502. John Knox, "A Note on the Format of the Pauline Corpus," *HTR*, 50 (1957), 311-314.
See also numbers1, 3, 8, 11, 13, 19, 44, 95, 519, 638, and 2109.

B. Textual Criticism

503. H. Rönsch, "Italafragmente des Römer- und Galater-briefes aus der Abtei Göttweig," *ZWT*, 22 (1879), 224-238.

504. H. Rönsch, "Die Doppelübersetzungen im lateinischen Texte des cod. Boernerianus der paulinischen Briefe," *ZWT*, 26 (1883), 73-98, 309-344.

505. F. Zimmer, "Der Codex Augiensis (F Paul), eine Abschrift des Boernerianus (G Paul)," *ZWT*, 30 (1887), 76-90.

506. W. B. Smith, "The Pauline Manuscripts F and G," *AJT*, 7 (1903), 452-482, 662-688.

507. Hugh Pope, "St. Jerome's Latin Version of St. Paul's Epistles," *ITQ*, 9 (1914), 413-445.

508. D. Thomson, "Pelagius and the Pauline Vulgate," *ET*, 27 (1915-1916), 425-427.

509. E. Diehl, "Zur Textgeschichte des lateinischen Paulus," *ZNW*, 20 (1921), 97-132.

510. [J. R. Harris], "Tatianic Reactions in the Pauline Epistles," *BBC*, 2 (1926), 12-14.

511. V. F. Büchner, "A Marcionite Reading in Ephraem's Commentary on the Pauline Epistles," *BBC*, 5 (1928), 37-38 [Eph. 2 : 14].

512. M. J. Lagrange, "Les papyrus Chester Beatty pour les épîtres de S. Paul et l'Apocalypse," *RB*, 31 (1934), 481-493.

513. Kirsopp and Silva Lake, "Some Recent Discoveries," *RL*, 5 (1936), 89-102.

514. D. Plooij, "The Latin Text of the Epistles of St. Paul," *BBC*, 11 (1936), 11-12.

515. P. Benoit, "Le Codex paulinien Chester Beatty," *RB*, 46 (1937), 58-82.

516. H. Seesemann, "Der Chester-Beatty-Papyrus 46 und der Paulustext des Clemens Alexandrinus," *ZNW*, 36 (1937), 90-97.

517. Heinrich Seesemann, "Die Bedeutung des Chester-Beatty-Papyrus für die Textkritik der Paulusbriefe," *TB*, 16 (1937), 92-97.

518. J. de Zwaan, "Licht uit de Pesjitta voor de exegese van Paulus en den text van het N.T.," *NTS*, 22 (1939), 248-252.

519. A. Eschliman, "La rédaction des épîtres pauliniennes," *RB*, 53 (1946), 185-196.

520. G. Zuntz, "Réflexions sur l'histoire du texte paulinien," *RB*, 59 (1952), 5-22.

521. A. F. J. Klijn, "A Note on Ephraem's Commentary on the Pauline Epistles," *JTS*, 5 (1954), 76-78.
522. R. V. G. Tasker, "The Text of the 'Corpus Paulinum,'" *NTSt*, 1 (1955), 180-191.
523. L. Delekat, "Die syropalästinische Übersetzung der Paulusbriefe und die Peschitta," *NTSt*, 3 (1957), 223-232.

C. PHILOLOGICAL STUDIES

1. Lexicography (Greek words arranged alphabetically)

524. N. Ya. Marr, "Слѣдъ ἀγάπη у армянъ," *KhV*, 1 (1912), 41-42; 2 (1913), 145-147.
525. Erik Peterson, "'Αγάπη," *BibZ*, 20 (1932), 378-382.
526. R. B. Willis, " 'Adokimos' — 'Castaway' — 'Rejected,'" *USR*, 32 (1920-1921), 315-325.
527. W. H. Cobb, "Αἰώνιος, II Cor. iv. 17 and v. 1," *JBL* (June and December, 1883), 61.
528. D. J. Theron, "'Αλήθεια in the Pauline Corpus," *EQ*, 26 (1954), 3-18.
529. R. M. Pope, "Studies in Pauline Vocabulary,' *ET*, 22 (1910-1911), 71-73 [ἀποκαραδοκία].
530. Louis Bouyer, "'Αρπαγμός," *RSR*, 39 (1951-1952), 280-288.
531. J. M. Furness, "'Αρπαγμός . . . ἑαυτὸν ἐκένωσε," *ET*, 69 (1957), 93-94.
532. Barnabas Ahern, "The Indwelling Spirit, Pledge of Our Inheritance," *CBQ*, 9 (1947), 179-189 [ἀρραβών].
533. R. M. Pope, "Studies in Pauline Vocabulary; 2. Of a Good Degree," *ET*, 21 (1909-1910), 112-114 [βαθμός].
534. L. G. da Fonseca, "Διαθήκη — Foedus an Testamentum," *B*, 9 (1928), 26-40.
535. G. W. Stemler, "De beteekenis der woorden δικαιοσύνη en δικαιοῦν bij Paulus," *TS*, 11 (1893), 371-376.
536. E. P. Gould, "St. Paul's Use of δικαιοῦν," *AJT*, 1 (1897), 149-158.
537. W. A. Stevens, "On the Forensic Meaning of δικαιοσύνη," *AJT*, 1 (1897), 443-450.
538. L. Jamison, "*Dikaiosyne* in the Usage of Paul," *JBR*, 21 (1953), 93-99.
539. W. R. Hutton, "δοκοῦντες = 'aspire,'" *ET*, 57 (1945-1946), 112.
540. G. Sass, "Zur Bedeutung von δοῦλος bei Paulus," *ZNW*, 40 (1941), 24-32.

541. J. M. Bover, " 'Imaginis' notio apud B. Paulum," *B*, 4 (1923), 174-179 [εἰκών].

542. E. Harmsen, "Über εἰς τό mit dem artikulirten Infinitif in den Briefen an die Römer und Korinther," *ZWT*, 17 (1874), 345-359.

543. H. A. A. Kennedy, "Two Exegetical Notes on St. Paul: I, A Special Use of ἐν," *ET*, 28 (1916-1917), 322-323.

544. K. W. Clark, "The Meaning of ἐνεργέω and κατεργέω in the New Testament," *JBL*, 54 (1935), 93-102.

545. C. Spicq, "'Ἐπιποθεῖν, désirer ou chérir?" *RB*, 64 (1957), 184-195.

546. R. M. Pope, "Studies in Pauline Vocabulary; Of Indwelling Power," *ET*, 22 (1910-1911), 312-313 [ἐπισκηνόω].

547. R. M. Pope, "Studies in Pauline Vocabulary; Of the Heavenly Places," *ET*, 23 (1911-1912), 365-368 [ἐπουράνιος].

548. E. Peterson, "'Ἔργον in der Bedeutung 'Bau' bei Paulus," *B*, 22 (1941), 439-441.

549. F. Märcker, "Über ἔργων νόμου in Römer- und Galaterbrief," *TSK*, 46 (1873), 707-721.

550. H. S. Nash, "Θειότης — Θεότης, Rom. 1 : 20, Col. 2 : 9," *JBL*, 18 (1899), 1-34.

551. G. F. Findlay, "St. Paul's Use of *Thriambeuo*," *Exp*, 1st series, 10 (1879), 403-421; 11 (1880), 78-79.

552. R. M. Pope, "Studies in Pauline Vocabulary; Of the Triumph-joy," *ET*, 21 (1909-1910), 19-21 [Θριαμβεύω].

553. L. W. Grensted, "2 Cor. 10 : 9; John 1 : 22," *ET*, 35 (1923-1924), 331 [ἵνα].

554. E. Stauffer, "'Ἵνα und das Problem des teleologischen Denkens bei Paulus," *TSK*, 102 (1930), 232-257.

555. Anton Fridrichsen, "'Ἰσόψυχος = ebenbürtig, solidarisch," *SO*, 18 (1938), 42-49.

556. Panayotis Christou, "'Ἰσόψυχος, Phil. 2 : 20," *JBL*, 70 (1951), 293-296.

557. D. R. Goodwin, "On the Use of לֵב and καρδία in the Old and New Testaments," *JBL* (June and December, 1881), 67-72.

558. Andrew Thorn, "Paul's Use of 'Katallage', Rom. 5 : 11, 11 : 15; 2 Cor. 5 : 18," *ET*, 4 (1892-1893), 335-336.

559. E. H. van Leeuwen, "De καταλλαγή," *TS*, 28 (1910), 159-171.

560. J. C. Stout, "Paul's Use of καταργέω," *BR*, 2 (1917), 447-452.

561. F. W. Mozley, "Two Words in Galatians," *Exp*, 8th series, 4 (1912), 143-146 [κατεγνωσμένος and δικαιοῦσθαι].

562. Dr. Senths, "Der Begriff des καύχημα bei Paulus," *NKZ*, 38 (1927), 501-521.

563. Ragnar Asting, "Kauchesis. Et bidrag til den religisøe selvføledse hos Paulus," *NTT*, 26 (1925), 129-203.

564. David Daube, "κερδαίνω as a Missionary Term," *HTR*, 40 (1947), 109-120.

565. Stephen Bedale, "The Meaning of κεφαλή in the Pauline Epistles," *JTS*, 5 (1954), 211-215.

566. J. Y. Campbell, "Κοινωνία and its Cognates in the New Testament," *JBL*, 51 (1932), 352-380.

567. W. H. G. Thomas, "Apostolic Arithmetic; a Pauline Word-Study," *ET*, 17 (1905-1906), 211-214 [λογίζομαι].

568. G. S. Baker, "A Note on the Meaning of λογικός in the New Testament," *Herm*, 74 (1949), 57-59.

569. F. C. Hill, "A Further Note on λογικός," *Herm*, 76 (1950), 25-27 [Rom. 12 : 1].

570. J. L. Davies, "Note on λογισμοί in 2 Corinthians 10," *Exp*, 4th series, 4 (1891), 298-302.

571. A. W. Slaten, "The Qualative use of νόμος in the Pauline Epistles," *AJT*, 23 (1919), 213-219.

572. C. F. D. Moule, "A Note on ὀφθαλμοδουλία," *ET*, 59 (1947-1948), 250.

573. Vinc. Iacono, "La Παλιγγενεσία in S. Paolo e nell' ambiente pagano," *B*, 15 (1934), 369-398.

574. R. M. Pope, "Studies in Pauline Vocabulary; of Boldness of Speech," *ET*, 21 (1909-1910), 236-238 [παρρησία].

575. J. M. Bover, "Uso del adjetivo singular πᾶς en San Pablo," *B*, 19 (1938), 411-434.

576. M. O. Massinger, "Paul's Use of the Word Faith," *BS*, 107 (1950), 181-194; 108 (1951), 434-446; 109 (1952), 353-357 [πίστις].

577. Gabriel Hebert, " 'Faithfulness" and 'Faith,' " *Th*, 58 (1955), 373-379.

578. John Macpherson, "The Use of the Word *Pleroma* in Ephesians and Colossians," *Exp*, 2nd series, 4 (1882), 462-472.

579. W. R. Schoemaker, "The Use of רוּחַ and of πνεῦμα," *JBL*, 23 (1904), 13-67.

580. Félix Puzo, "Significado de la palabro 'pneuma' en San Pablo," *EB*, 1 (1941-1942), 437-460.

581. R. R. Brewer, "The Meaning of *politeuesthe* in Philippians 1 : 27," *JBL*, 73 (1954), 76-83.

582. A. Tholuck, "Erneute Untersuchung über σάρξ als Quelle der Sünde," *TSK*, 28 (1855), 477-497.

583. Eberhard Nestle, "St. Paul's Handicraft: Acts xviii. 3," *JBL*, 11 (1892), 205-206 [σκηνοποιός].

584. J. de Finance, "La σοφία chez saint Paul," *RSR*, 25 (1935), 385-417.

585. A. Lemonnyer, "A propos des sens divers de στοιχεῖον," *RSPT*, 1 (1907), 505-506.

586. Joseph Huby, "Στοιχεῖα dans Bardesane et dans Saint Paul,", *B*, 15 (1934), 365-368.

587. Claes Blum, "The Meaning of στοιχεῖον and its Derivatives in the Byzantine Age; a Study in Byzantine Magic," *Er*, 44 (1946), 315-325.

588. P. Skok, "Στοιχεῖον," *ŽA*, 1 (1951), 18-24.

589. W. H. G. Thomas, " 'Together,' " *ET*, 22 (1910-1911), 523-524 [συν- compounds].

590. T. R. Glover, "A Preposition of St. Paul's," *Exp*, 8th series, 12 (1916), 292-299 [σύν].

591. Brendan McGrath, " 'Syn' Words in Saint Paul," *CBQ*, 14 (1952), 219-226.

592. J. G. Griffiths, "Romans 8 : 28," *ET*, 61 (1949-1950), 286 [συνεργεῖν].

593. K. Thieme, "Die ταπεινοφροσύνη, Phil. 2 und Röm. 12," *ZNW*, 8 (1907), 9-33.

594. D. J. Theron, " 'Adoption' in the Pauline Corpus," *EQ*, 28 (1956), 6-14 [υἱοθεσία].

595. Archdeacon Hendenson, "I Timothy 1 : 14," *ET*, 27 (1915-1916), 380-381 [ὑπερπλεονάζω].

596. [H.] Sladeczek, " Ἡ φιλαδελφία nach den Schriften des h. Apostels Paulus," *TQ*, 76 (1894), 272-295.

597. P. Thomson, "Φιλοτιμέομαι," *ET*, 27 (1915-1916), 427.

598. D. R. Goodwin, "On the use of ψυχή and πνεῦμα and Connected Words in Sacred Writings," *JBL* (June and December, 1881), 73-86.

See also numbers 605, 616, 619, 626, 760, 831, 877, and 879.

2. Paul's Literary Style

599. F. Köster, "Ob St. Paulus seine Sprache an der des Demosthenes gebildet habe ?" *TSK*, 27 (1854), 305-322.
600. Friederich Köster, "Did Paul Model His Language after
that of Demosthenes ?" *BS*, 11 (1854), 514-527.
601. Joel Swartz, "The Eloquence of St. Paul," *LQ*, 2 (1872),
418-434.
602. F. W. Farrar, "The Rhetoric of St. Paul," *Exp*, 1st series,
10 (1879), 1-27.
603. John Massie, "The Irony of St. Paul," *Exp*, 2nd series,
8 (1884), 92-107.
604. E. G. King, "St. Paul's Method of Quotation," *Exp*, 3rd
series, 10 (1889), 233-238.
605. W. P. Workman, "The Hapax Legomena of St. Paul," *ET*,
7 (1895-1896), 418-419.
606. E. E. Kellet, "St. Paul the Poet," *Exp*, 6th series, 9 (1904),
339-348.
607. C. F. Sanders, "St. Paul's Conception of Preaching," *LQ*,
34 (1904), 260-274.
608. E. E. Kellet, "St. Paul the Poet," *LCR*, 24 (1905), 316-318.
609. Marcus Dods, "Paul's Style of Preaching," *LCR*, 26 (1907),
28-30.
610. A. Marth, "Die Zitate des hl. Paulus aus der Profanliteratur,"
ZKT, 37 (1913), 889-894.
611. Frank Granger, "The Style of St. Paul," *Exp*, 8th series,
10 (1915), 326-340.
612. R. M. Pope, "Studies in Pauline Vocabulary; Hyperbole,"
ET, 27 (1915-1916), 182-184.
613. E. Strange, "Diktierpausen in den Paulusbriefen," *ZNW*,
18 (1917), 109-117.
614. O. Eger, "Rechtswörter und Rechtsbilder in den paulinischen Briefen," *ZNW*, 18 (1917), 84-108.
615. Maurice Jones, "The Style of St. Paul's Preaching," *Exp*,
8th series, 14 (1917), 241-258, 330-347.
616. C. H. Dodd, "Pauline Illustrations from Recently Published
Papyri," *Exp*, 8th series, 15 (1918), 291-296.
617. H. J. Rose, "The *Clausulae* of the Pauline Corpus," *JTS*,
25 (1923-1924), 17-43.
618. H. Windisch, "Das Problem des paulinischen Imperativs,'
ZNW, 23 (1924), 265-281.

619. W. W. Everts, "Paul's Contribution to the Vocabulary of the New Testament," *RE*, 22 (1925), 193-201.

620. Paul Joüon, "Notes de philologie paulinienne," *RSR*, 15 (1925), 531-535 [Rom. 2 : 16; 5 : 6; 2 Cor. 12 : 7; Eph. 2 : 20; and καταργεῖν].

621. Ray Knight, "Biblical Mistranslation," *HJ*, 30 (1932), 591-599.

622. Jaroslav Konopásek, "Les 'questions rhétoriques' dans le Nouveau Testament," *RHPR*, 12 (1932), 47-66, 141-161.

623. R. A. Moody, "The First Person Plural as used by St. Paul," *ET*, 43 (1931-1932), 379.

624. Ernst von Dobschütz, "Wir und Ich bei Paulus," *ZST*, 10 (1932-1933), 251-277.

625. E. B. Allo, "Le défaut d'éloquence et le style oral de Saint Paul," *RSPT*, 23 (1934), 29-39.

626. F. W. Gingrich, "The Words St. Paul Coined," *ATR*, 17 (1935), 234-236.

627. L. V. Lester-Garland, "The Sequence of Thought in the Pauline Epistles," *Th*, 33 (1936), 228-238.

628. R. M. Pope, "The Greek Style of St. Paul," *ET*, 49 (1937-1938), 534-536.

629. A. M. Vitti, "L'éloquenza di S. Paolo nelle sue lettere," *B*, 21 (1940), 413-425.

630. A. M. Vitti, "L'éloquenza di S. Paolo colta al vivo da S. Luca negli Atti," *B*, 22 (1941), 159-197.

631. S. Zedda, "Similitudines Evagelii et similitudines S. Pauli," *VD*, 24 (1944), 88-95, 112-119, 142-150.

632. W. F. Lofthouse, "Singular and Plural in St. Paul's Letters," *ET*, 58 (1946-1947), 179-182.

633. E. C. Malte, "Light from the Papyri on St. Paul's Terminology," *CTM*, 18 (1947), 499-517.

634. W. C. Wake, "The Authenticity of the Pauline Epistles — a Contribution from Statistical Analysis," *HJ*, 47 (1948), 50-55.

635. J. van Dodewaard, "Die sprachliche Übereinstimmung zwischen Markus-Paulus und Markus-Petrus," *B*, 30 (1949), 91-108, 218-238.

636. A. M. Perry, "Epistolary Form in Paul," *CQ*, 26 (1949), 48-53.

637. A. Schön, "Eine weitere metrische Stelle bei St. Paulus?" *B*, 30 (1949), 510-513.

638. R. L. Archer, "The Epistolary Form in the New Testament,"
ET, 63 (1951-1952), 296-298.

639. W. F. Lofthouse, " 'I' and 'We' in the Pauline Letters,"
ET, 64 (1952-1953), 241-245.

640. D. G. Bradley, "The *Topos* as a Form in the Pauline Pa-
raenesis," *JBL*, 72 (1953), 238-246.

641. John Reumann, "St. Paul's Use of Irony," *LQ*, 7 (1955),
140-145.

642. Gustav Karlsson, "Formelhaftes in Paulusbriefen?" *Er*,
54 (1956), 138-141.

643. Leon Morris, "Καὶ ἅπαξ καὶ δίς," *NT*, 1 (1956), 205-208
[Phil. 4 : 16 and I Thess. 2 : 18].

644. H. A. Musurillo, S. J., "The Style of St. Paul: Apropos of
Brunot's *Le génie littéraire de Saint Paul*," *ThSt*, 17 (1956),
219-223.
See also numbers 519, 684, 689, 1121, 1290, 1504, 1524
1810 ff., 2108, 2117, and 2215 ff.

D. INDIVIDUAL EPISTLES

1. The Epistle to the Romans

a. *Textual Criticism*

645. F. W. Farrar, "Various Readings in the Epistle to the
Romans," *Exp*, 1st series, 9 (1879), 202-220 [Rom. 1 : 7, 32;
2 : 17; 4 : 18-19; 5 : 1; 7 : 6, 25; 9 : 5; 11 : 6; 12 : 11; 13 : 5;
14 : 6; 16 : 5].

646. J. H. A. Michelsen, "Kritisch onderzoek naar den oudsten
tekst van 'Paulus' brief aan de Romeinen,' " *TT*, 20 (1886),
372-386; 473-490; 21 (1887), 163-203.

647. M. J. Lagrange, "La Vulgate latine de Saint Jérôme aux
Romains et le texte grec," *RB*, N.S. 13 (1916), 225-239.

648. Gustave Bardy, "Le texte de l'épître aux Romains, dans
le commentaire d'Origène-Rufin," *RB*, 17 (1920), 229-
241.

649. Rudolf Bultmann, "Glossen im Römerbrief," *TLZ*, 72
(1947), 197-202.

650. E. Brady, "The Position of Romans in P. 46," *ET*, 59 (1947-
1948), 249-250.

651. C. S. C. Williams, "P[46] and the Textual Tradition of Romans,"
ET, 61 (1949-1950), 125-126.

652. W. H. P. Hatch, "A Recently Discovered Fragment of the Epistle to the Romans," *HTR*, 45 (1952), 79-85.

653. Harald Sahlin, "Einige Textemendationen zum Römerbrief," *TZ*, 9 (1953), 92-100.

654. John Knox, "A Note on the Text of Romans," *NTSt*, 2 (1956), 191-193.

655. J. J. Prins, "Rom. I-VI volgens Tischendorf's Editio VIII," *TT*, 8 (1874), 510-520.

656. R. Steinmetz, "Textkritische Untersuchung zu Röm. 1, 7," *ZNW*, 9 (1908), 177-189.

657. Anton Fridrichsen, "Quatre conjectures sur le texte du Nouveau Testament," *RHPR*, 3 (1923), 439-442 [Includes Rom. 2 : 1; Gal. 2 : 10; and Phil. 2 : 5].

658. R. R. Williams, "A Note on Romans 4 : 1," *ET*, 63 (1951-1952), 91-92.

659. Alexander Souter, "Pelagius' Text of Romans 5 : 12 with Comment," *ET*, 28 (1916-1917), 42-43.

660. J. H. Michael, "The Text of Romans 6 : 13 in the Chester Beatty Papyrus," *ET*, 49 (1937-1938), 235.

661. J. P. Wilson, "Romans 8 : 28, Text and Interpretation," *ET*, 60 (1948-1949), 110-111.

662. C. Strömmer, "Röm. 9, 5," *ZNW*, 8 (1907), 319-320; 9 (1908), 80.

663. Cuthbert Lattey, "The Codex Vaticanus on Romans 9 : 5," *ET*, 34 (1922-1923), 331.

664. Cuthbert Lattey, "The Codex Ephraemi Rescriptus in Romans 9 : 5," *ET*, 35 (1923-1924), 42-43.

665. Eberhard Nestle, "A Parallel to Rom. 12 : 11," *ET*, 10 (1998-1999), 284.

666. R. G. Bury, "Romans 12 : 16; I Corinthians 13 : 7," *ET*, 49 (1937-1938), 430.

667. J. Dupont, "Pour l'histoire de la doxologie finale de l'épître aux Romains," *RBén*, 58 (1948), 3-22.
See also number 503.

b. *Historical and Literary Criticism*

668. [C. F.] Kling, "Über den historischen Charackter der Apostelgeschichte und die Aechtheit der beiden letzten Kapitel des Römerbriefs, mit Beziehung auf Hrn. Dr. Baur," *TSK*, 10 (1837), 290-327.

669. W. Beyschlag, "Das geschichtliche Problem des Römerbriefs," *TSK*, 40 (1867), 627-665.

670. W. Schmidt, "Zum Römerbrief," *TSK*, 71 (1898), 246-296.

671. E. Riggenbach, "Die Starken und Schwachen in der römischen Gemeinde," *TSK*, 66 (1893), 649-678.

672. Adolf Deissmann, "Prolegomena to the Epistle to the Romans — A Word to Students of Theology," *ET*, 11 (1899-1900), 109-111.

673. W. B. Smith, "Address and Destination of Romans," *JBL*, 20 (1901), 1-21.

674. W. B. Smith, "Did Paul Write Romans?" *HJ*, 1 (1903), 309-334.

675. P. W. Schmiedel, "Did Paul Write Romans? — A Reply," *HJ*, 1 (1903), 532-552.

676. W. A. Lambert, "Did Paul Write Romans?" *LCR*, 23 (1904), 58-66.

677. P. Corssen, "Zur Überlieferungsgeschichte des Römerbriefes," *ZNW*, 10 (1909), 1-45, 97-102.

678. Kirsopp Lake, "The Shorter Form of St. Paul's Epistle to the Romans," *Exp*, 7th series, 10 (1910), 504-525.

679. D. De Bruyne, "La finale marcionite de la lettre aux romains retrouvée," *RBén*, 28 (1911), 133-142.

680. A. J. Dickinson, "The Genesis of the Epistle to the Romans," *RE*, 10 (1913), 423-430.

681. James Drummond, "Occasion and Object of the Epistle to the Romans," *HJ*, 11 (1913), 787-804.

682. J. MacRory, "The Occasion and Object of the Epistle to the Romans," *ITQ*, 9 (1914), 21-32.

683. H. Pachali, "Der Römerbrief als historisches Problem. Bemerkungen zu W. Lütgerts gleichnamiger Abhandlung," *TSK*, 87 (1914), 481-505.

684. M. J. Lagrange, "Langue, style, argumentation dans l'épître aux Romains," *RB*, N.S. 12 (1915), 216-235.

685. Rendel Harris," St. Paul's Use of Testimonies in the Epistle to the Romans," *Exp*, 8th series, 17 (1919), 401-414.

686. A. M. Pope, "The Genesis of the Roman Epistle," *Exp*, 8th series, 21 (1921), 359-365.

687. W. Michaelis, "Kenchreä (Zur Frage des Abfassungsorte des Rm)," *ZNW*, 25 (1926), 144-154.

688. F. Bohn, "Die Verzahnung des Römerbriefes, Kapitel 1-8," *TSK*, 104 (1932), 439-448.

689. E. von Dobschütz, "Zum Wortschatz und Stil des Römerbriefs," *ZNW*, 33 (1934), 51-66.

690. R. H. Miller, "Life Situations in the Roman Church as Reflected in Paul's Letters," *RE*, 32 (1935), 170-180.

691. K. Prümm, "Zur Struktur des Römerbriefes," *ZKT*, 72 (1950), 333-349.

692. Stanislas Lyonnet, "Note sur le plan de l'épître aux Romains," *RSR*, 39 (1951-1952), 301-316.

693. W. F. Beck, "Paul Writes to the Romans," *CTM*, 26 (1955), 265-276.

694. Jacques Dupont, "Le problème de la structure littéraire de l'épître aux Romains," *RB*, 62 (1955), 365-397.

695. P. Suitbertus a S. Joanne a Cruce, "De structura idearum in ep. ad Romanos," *VD*, 34 (1956), 68-87.
See also numbers 491 and 2960.

c. *Theological Studies*

696. Connop Thirlwall, "Notes on the Epistle to the Romans," *Exp*, 1st series, 3 (1876), 1-10, 151-160, 215-223.

697. Franz Delitzsch, "Talmudic Notes on St. Paul's Epistle to the Romans," *LQ*, 11 (1881), 477-502.

698. Henry Wace, "On the Epistle to the Romans," *Exp*, 2nd series, 2 (1881), 427-437.

699. R. D. C. Robbins, "The Epistle to the Romans in the Revised Version," *BS*, 39 (1882), 722-751.

700. F. Godet, "Paul's Gospel to the Romans," *Exp*, 3rd series, 3 (1886), 241-259.

701. W. G. Blaikie, "Homiletical Features of the Epistle to the Romans," *Exp*, 3rd series, 6 (1887), 99-113.

702. J. Haussleiter, "Der Glaube Jesu Christi und der christliche Glaube. Ein Beitrag zur Erklärung des Römerbriefes," *NKZ*, 2 (1891), 109-145, 205-230.

703. A. Hilgenfeld, "Der Brief des Paulus an die Römer," *ZWT*, 35 (1892), 296-346, 385-406; 36 (1893), 129-162, 257-281, 407-432.

704. G. F. Wahle, "Paulus Römerbrief seinem Inhalt und Plan nach," *NKZ*, 4 (1893), 549-578.

705. Edward Hicks, "A Roman to Romans; Brief Notes on

Romans 3 : 4, 19; 5; 6 : 1-10; 7; 8 : 15-17," *ET*, 5 (1893-1894), 565-567.

706. A. C. Headlam, "The Theology of the Epistle to the Romans," *ET*, 6 (1894-1895), 57-60, 103-106, 152-155, 206-208, 263-268, 355-357, 491-494, 547-550.

707. Edward Hicks, "A Roman to Romans; Corrigenda," *ET*, 6 (1894-1895), 93-94.

708. J. Barmby, "The Meaning of 'Righteousness of God' in the Epistle to the Romans," *Exp*, 5th series, 4 (1896), 124-139.

709. J. A. Beet, "Difficult Passages in Romans," *Exp*, 5th series, 7 (1898), "1. The Son of David and of God," 20-34; "2. St. Paul's Theory of Ethics," 136-150; "3. Justification through Faith," 275-288; "4. The Death of Christ," 365-376; 8 (1898), "5. Faith and Peace with God," 62-73; "6. Through our Lord Jesus Christ," 143-158; "7. The New Life in Christ," 370-380; "8. The Reign of the Law," 448-459.

710. G. A. Hoog, "Over de rechtvaardiging uit het geloof naar den brief van de Romeinen," *TS*, 17 (1899), 386-391.

711. A. Robertson, "Studies in the Epistle to the Romans," *Exp*, 5th series, 9 (1899), 1-15, 187-204, 345-355.

712. James Denney, "The Theology of the Epistle to the Romans," *Exp*, 6th series, 3 (1901), "1. Introductory," 1-14; "2. The Doctrine of Sin," 172-181; "3. The Doctrine of Sin (cont.)," 283-295; "4. The Gospel, a Divine Righteousness," 433-450; 4 (1901), "5. Faith and Righteousness to the Romans," 81-95; "6. The Righteousness of God and the New Life," 299-311; "7. The New Life and the Spirit," 422-436.

713. Sally N. Roach, "The Epistle to the Romans," *RE*, 4 (1907), 555-572; 5 (1908), 83-94.

714. P. C., "El neo-paganismo anticristiano según la Epístola a los Romanos," *EB*, 4 (1932), 218-239, 291-316.

715. J. W. Buckham, "The Misunderstood Epistle," *RL*, 2 (1933), 110-118.

716. E. Tormählin, "Das Thema des Römerbriefes," *NKZ*, 44 (1933), 585-596, 619-627.

717. N. P. Williams, "The Message of the Epistles; Romans," *ET*, 45 (1933-1934), 6-10.

718. John McNicol, "The Righteousness of God in the Epistle to the Romans," *EQ*, 6 (1934), 302-311.

719. Thomas Houghton, "The Testimony of the Epistle to the Romans to the Old Testament," *EQ*, 7 (1935), 419-426.

720. J. F. Walvoord, "Law in the Epistle to the Romans," *BS*, 94 (1937), 15-30, 281-295.

721. G. A. Barton, "The Interpretation of the Epistle to the Romans," *ATR*, 21 (1939), 81-93.

722. R. L. Aldrich, "Grace in the Book of Romans," *BS*, 97 (1940), 217-228, 335-348.

723. R. M. Hawkins, "Romans: a Reinterpretation," *JBL*, 60 (1941), 129-140.

724. Anders Nygren, "Romarbrevet och förkunnelsen," *STK*, 17 (1941), 1-16.

725. R. J. Drummond, "A Comprehensive View of the Epistle to the Romans," *EQ*, 14 (1942), 241-249.

726. A. J. Martin, "The Sovereignty of Grace as Seen in Rom. 8 : 28-30," *BS*, 99 (1942), 453-468.

727. Cuthbert Lattey, "Relativity in Romans," *CBQ*, 5 (1943), 179-182.

728. G. O. Griffith, "The Apocalyptic Note in Romans," *ET*, 56 (1944-1945), 153-155.

729. S. Lyonnet, "De 'Iustitia Dei' in Epistola ad Romanos," *VD*, 25 (1947), 23-34, 118-121, 129-144, 193-203, 257-263.

730. T. W. Manson, "St. Paul's Letter to the Romans — and Others," *BJRL*, 31 (1948), 224-240.

731. C. A. Smith, "The Practical Psychology of Saint Paul in the Epistle to the Romans," *CBQ*, 10 (1948), 413-428.

732. A. Feuillet, "Le plan salvifique de Dieu d'après l'épître aux Romains," *RB*, 57 (1950), 336-387, 489-529.

733. Anders Nygren, "Objektives und Persönliches im Römerbrief," *TLZ*, 77 (1952), 591-596.

734. R. V. G. Tasker, "The Doctrine of Justification by Faith in the Epistle to the Romans," *EQ*, 24 (1952), 37-46.

735. Thomas Barrosse, "Death and Sin in Saint Paul's Epistle to the Romans," *CBQ*, 15 (1953), 438-459.

736. P. S. Minear, "The Truth about Sin and Death; the Meaning of Atonement in the Epistle to the Romans," *Interp*, 7 (1953), 142-155.

737. J. E. Bear, "The Epistle to the Romans," *Interp*, 9 (1955), 71-90.

738. K. B. Cully, "Grace and Justification Today; an Interpretation of the Theme of Romans," *Interp*, 11 (1957), 421-428.

739. William Hamilton, "A Theology for Modern Man; a Study of the Epistle to the Romans," *Interp*, 11 (1957), 387-404.

740. S. Lyonnet, "Notes sur l'exégèse de l'épître aux Romains," *B*, 38 (1957), 35-61.
    See also numbers 549, 2740, 2940, 2944, 2950, 2960, 2979 ff., and 2984.

d. *Exegesis of Individual Passages*

741. C. Willing, "Zur Erklärung des Römerbriefs (Cap. I-IV)," *ZWT*, 33 (1890), 270-302.

742. G. B. Stevens, "A Paraphrase of the Epistle to the Romans," *BW*, 8 (1896), 299-309, 390-395 [chapters 1-8].

743. Prosper Schepens, "Vocatus Apostolus (Rom. 1 : 1; 1 Cor. 1 : 1)," *RSR*, 16 (1926), 40-42.

744. Ernst Bröse, "Zur Auslegung von Röm. 1, 3-4," *NKZ*, 10 (1899), 562-573.

745. A. H. Blom, "Paulinische Studien. VI, Het belang van Jezus' opstanding, enz., naar Rom. 1, 4," *TT*, 14 (1880), 388-394.

746. Alexander Brown, "Declared or Constituted Son of God," *ET*, 5 (1893-1894), 308-309 [Rom. 1 : 4].

747. Walter Charlesworth, "The Spirit of Holiness, Romans 1 : 4," *ET*, 5 (1893-1894), 115.

748. Alfred Huddle, "Romans 1 : 4," *ET*, 5 (1893-1894), 116.

749. J. A. Selbie, "Romans 1 : 4," *ET*, 5 (1893-1894), 186-187.

750. W. S. Curzon-Siggers, "The Power of the Resurrection," *ET*, 6 (1894-1895), 44 [Rom. 1 : 4].

751. W. H. G. Thomas, "Romans 1 : 4," *ET*, 24 (1912-1913), 44-45.

752. R. W. Harding, "Romans 1 : 4," *ET*, 28 (1916-1917), 479.

753. Ioannes Trinidad, "Praedestinatus Filius Dei . . . ex resurrectione mortuorum (Rom. 1, 4)," *VD*, 20 (1940), 145-150.

754. M. E. Boismard, "Constitué fils de dieu," *RB*, 60 (1953), 5-17 [Rom. 1 : 4].

755. Thomas Fahy, "Exegesis of Romans 8 : 29; 1 : 4," *ITQ*, 23 (1956), 410-412.

756. [T.], "Romans 1 : 5; 16 : 26," *ET*, 5 (1893-1894), 567.

757. G. H. Parke-Taylor, "A Note on ἐις ὑπακοὴν πίστεως' in Romans 1 : 5 and 16 : 26," *ET*, 55 (1943-1944), 305-306.

758. F. W. Grosheide, "Rom. 1 : 6-7, 24 en 4 : 1," *TT*, 46 (1912), 402-410.

759. A. Harnack, "Zu Röm. 1, 7," *ZNW*, 3 (1902), 83-86.
760. E. H. van Leeuwen, "'Αγαπητοί," *TS*, 21 (1903), 139-151 [Rom. 1 : 7].
761. H. Kutter, "Über den Begriff δικαιοσύνη Θεοῦ in Röm. 1 : 17," *STZ*, 6 (1889), 183-187.
762. T. Häring, "Noch einmal δικαιοσύνη θεοῦ in Röm. 1, 17," *TSK*, 69 (1896), 139-141.
763. G. A. Chadwick, "The Just Shall Live by Faith," *Exp*, 7th series, 1 (1906), 178-182 [Hab. 2 : 4; Gal. 3 : 11; Heb. 10 : 38; Rom. 1 : 17].
764. Olaf Moe, "Luthers yndlingsord i Romerbrevet," *NTT*, 18 (1917), 129-147 [Rom. 1 : 17].
765. J. R. MacKay, "On the Meaning of the Phrase 'from Faith to Faith' in Rom. 1 : 17," *ET*, 30 (1918-1919), 378-379.
766. L. van den Eerenbeemt, " 'Iustitia enim Dei in eo revelatur ex fide in fidem' (Rom. 1, 17)," *VD*, 2 (1922), 120-124, 206-208.
767. A. Merk, " 'Iustus ex fide vivit' (Rom. 1, 17)," *VD*, 3 (1923), 193-198.
768. S. Lyonnet, "De 'Iustitia Dei' in Epistola ad Romanos," *VD*, 25 (1947), 23-34, 118-121, 129-144, 193-203, 257-263 [Rom. 1 : 17; 3 : 5, 21-22, 25-26; 10 : 3].
769. M. Michelsen, "Über einige sinnverwandte Aussprüche des Neuen Testaments: Röm. 1, 17 bis 2, 16," *TSK*, 46 (1873), 319-347.
770. P. C., "El neo-paganismo anticristiano según la Epístola a los Romanos (1, 18 y sig.)," *EB*, 4 (1932), 218-239, 291-316.
771. J. Y. Campbell, "Great Texts Reconsidered," *ET*, 50 (1938, 1939), 229-233 [Rom. 1 : 18].
772. T. C. Smith, "The Wrath of God," *RE*, 45 (1948), 193-208 [Rom. 1 : 18].
773. P. D. Schjött, "Eine religionsphilosophische Stelle bei Paulus (Röm. 1, 18-20)," *ZNW*, 4 (1903), 75-78.
774. C. Lattey, "Theses Paulinae: III, S. Paulus docet Dei existentiam per ea quae facta sunt naturali lumine rationis certo cognosci posse (Rom. 1, 18-32)," *VD*, 3 (1923), 311-314.
775. Felix Flückiger, "Zur Unterscheidung von Heiden und Juden in Röm. 1 : 18—2 : 3," *TZ*, 10 (1954), 154-158.
776. E. DeWitt Burton, "Sin, Guilt, Condemnation: the Argument of Rom. 1 : 18—3 : 20," *BW*, 31 (1908), 194-206.

777. E. de los Rios, "Animadversiones in doctrinam Paulinam de peccatis (Notulae in Rom. 1, 18-3, 20)," *VD*, 12 (1932), 89-93.

778. Käte Oltmanns, "Das Verhältnis von Röm. 1, 18-3, 20 zu Röm. 3, 21 ff.," *TB*, 8 (1929), 110-116.

779. A. Fridrichsen, "Zur Auslegung von Röm. 1, 19 f.," *ZNW*, 17 (1916), 159-168.

780. John Reith, "Romans 1 : 20," *ET*, 5 (1893-1894), 222-223.

781. John Reid, " 'Decensus Averni,' " *ET*, 5 (1893-1894), 187 [Rom. 1 : 21-32].

782. E. Klostermann, "Die adäquate Vergeltung in Röm. 1, 22-31," *ZNW*, 32 (1933), 1-6.

783. J. Jeremias, "Zu Röm. 1, 22-32," *ZNW*, 45 (1954), 119-121.

784. N. Hyldahl, "A Reminiscence of the Old Testament at Romans i. 23," *NTSt*, 2 (1956), 285-288.

785. M. J. Lagrange, "Le catalogue des vices dans l'épître aux Romains (1, 28-31)," *RB*, N.S. 8 (1911), 534-549.

786. P. C. S., "Inexcusabilidad de los creyentes, complices de los incrédulos (Rom. 2, 1-5)," *EB*, 7 (1935), 287-297.

787. F. Giesecke, "Zur Exegese von Röm. 2, 11-16," *TSK*, 59 (1886), 173-182.

788. James Morison, "St. Paul on the Heathen," *Exp*, 2nd series, 7 (1884), 454-466 [Rom. 2 : 12-16].

789. P. C. S., "La ley revelada en orden al juicio divino. Posición de los creyentes, judíos y gentiles (Rom. 2, 12-29)," *EB*, 7 (1935), 223-240.

799. Wilhelm Mundle, "Zur Auslegung von Röm. 2, 13 ff.," *TB*, 13 (1934), 249-256.

791. A. Lehmann, "Der Bibelvers Röm. 2, 14," *TSK*, 50 (1877), 514-518.

792. Felix Flückiger, "Die Werke des Gesetzes bei den Heiden (nach Röm. 2, 14 ff.)," *TZ*, 8 (1952), 17-42.

793. M. Kähler, "Auslegung von Kap. 2, 14-16 im Römerbrief," *TSK*, 47 (1874), 261-306.

794. Otto Kuss, "Die Heiden und die Werke des Gesetzes (nach Röm. 2, 14-16)," *MTZ*, 5 (1954), 77-98.

795. Bo Reicke, "Syneidesis in Röm. 2, 15," *TZ*, 12 (1956), 157-161.

796. E. Driessen, " 'Secundum Evangelium meum' (Rom. 2, 16; 16, 25; 2 Tim. 2, 8)," *VD*, 24 (1944), 25-32.

797. Olivo Olivieri, "Sintassi, senso e rapporto col contesto di Rom. 2, 17-24," *B*, 11(1930), 188-215.

798. W. R. Forrester, "Romans 2 : 18," *ET*, 36 (1924-1925), 285.

799. Vacher Burch, "Circumcision of the Heart," *ET*, 29 (1917-1918), 330-331 [Rom. 2 : 29].

800. Bernardin Schneider, "The Meaning of Saint Paul's Antithesis, 'The Letter and the Spirit,' " *CBQ*, 15 (1953), 163-207 [Rom. 2 : 29].

801. A. Fridrichsen, "Exegetisches zu den Paulusbriefen," *TSK*, 102 (1930), 291-301 [Rom. 3 : 1; 13 : 8; 1 Cor. 3 : 9; Phil. 3 : 1].

802. Olivo Olivieri, "Quid ergo amplius Iudaeo est ? etc. (Rom. 3, 1-8)," *B*, 10 (1929), 31-52.

803. P. C. S., "Los judíos y la Promesa (Rom. 3, 1-8)," *EB*, 7 (1935), 298-313.

804. J. G. Griffiths, "Romans 3 : 3," *ET*, 53 (1941-1942), 118.

805. H. J. Botschuyver, "Proeve eener vertaling van Rom. 3 : 4-8," *GTT*, 27 (1926-1927), 316-327.

806. H. J. Botschuyver, "Iets over Rm. 3 : 7," *NTS*, 2 (1919), 208-209.

807. H. Ljungvik, "Zum Römerbrief 3, 7-8," *ZNW*, 32 (1933), 207-210.

808. A. Fridrichsen, "Nochmals Römer, 3, 7-8," *ZNW*, 34 (1935), 306-308.

809. W. O. Fitch, "Note on Romans 3 : 8b, ὧν τὸ κρίμα ἔνδικόν ἐστι," *ET*, 59 (1947-1948), 26.

810. W. F. Beck, "Φόβος, Rom. 3 : 18," *CTM*, 22 (1951), 511-512.

811. J. Louw, "De wijze van de openbaring der δικαιοσύνη τοῦ Θεοῦ, Rom. 3 : 21-24," *NTS*, 2 (1919), 72-76.

812. W. Bleibtreu, "Der Abschnitt Röm. 3, 21-26, unter namentlicher Berücksichtigung des Ausdrucks ἱλαστήριον," *TSK*, 56 (1883), 548-568.

813. G. Kittel, "Zur Erklärung von Röm. 3, 21-26," *TSK*, 80 (1907), 217-233.

814. J. M. Bover, "El pensamiento generador de la teología de S. Pablo sugerido por Rom. 3, 21-26," *B*, 20 (1939), 142-172.

815. A. T. Robertson, "Expositions," *RE*, 30 (1933), 424-433 [Rom. 3 : 21-31].

816. D. Völter, "Die Verse Röm. 3, 22b-26 und ihre Stellung innerhalb der ersten Kapitel des Römerbriefs," *ZNW*, 10 (1909), 180-183.

817. F. W. Christie, "The Judicial and Mystic Idea of Religion: An Exposition of Rom. 3 : 24 and Gal. 2 : 20," *BW*, 31 (1908), 445-447.

818. E. Käsemann, "Zum Verständnis von Röm. 3, 24-26," *ZNW*, 43 (1950-1951), 150-154.

819. J. F. K. Gurlitt, "Studien zur Erklärung der ἔνδειξις τῆς δικαιοσύνης τοῦ Θεοῦ, Röm. 3, 25," *TSK*, 13 (1840), 930-1000.

820. W. F. Rinck, "Über Römer 3, 25," *TSK*, 15 (1842), 791-794.

821. I. M. Bover, "Quem proposuit Deus 'propitiatorum,'" *VD*, 18 (1938), 137-142 [Rom. 3 : 25].

822. J. M. Creed, "Πάρεσις in Dionysius of Halicarnassus and in St. Paul," *JTS*, 41 (1940), 28-30 [Rom. 3 : 25].

823. L. Moraldi, "Sensus vocis ἱλαστήριον in Rom. 3, 25," *VD*, 26 (1948), 257-276.

824. S. Lyonnet, "Propter remissionem praecedentium delictorum (R. 3, 25)," *VD*, 28 (1950), 282-287.

825. R. R. Nicole, "C. H. Dodd and the Doctrine of Propitiation," *WTJ*, 17 (1954-1955), 142-143 [Rom. 3 : 25].

826. L. Morris, "The Meaning of ἱλαστήριον in Romans iii. 25," *NTSt*, 2 (1955), 33-43.

827. G. Funke, "Bezieht sich die Versöhnung allein auf den Menschen oder auf Gott und den Menschen? Ein dogmatisch-exegetischer Versuch über Röm. 3, 25 und 26," *TSK*, 15 (1842), 297-328.

828. R. D. C. Robbins, "Notes on Acts 14 : 16, 17; 17 : 30; and Rom. 3 : 25, 26," *BS*, 36 (1879), 61-71.

829. D. P. Brown, "Romans 3 : 25, 26," *Exp*, 5th series, 6 (1897), 158-160.

830. W. E. Wilson, "Romans 3 : 25, 26," *ET*, 29 (1917-1918), 472-473.

831. H. G. Meecham, "Romans 3 : 25 f.; 4 : 25 — the Meaning of διά c. acc.," *ET*, 50 (1938-1939), 564.

832. Vincent Taylor, "Great Texts Reconsidered," *ET*, 50 (1938-1939), 295-300 [Rom. 3 : 25].

833. Thomas Fahy, "Exegesis of Rom. 3 : 25 f.," *ITQ*, 23 (1956), 69-73.

834. J. R. Mackay, "Romans 3 : 26," *ET*, 32 (1920-1921), 329-330.

835. Gerhard Friedrich, "Das Gesetz des Glaubens, Röm. 3, 27," *TZ*, 10 (1954), 401-417.

836. S. Lyonnet, "De Rom. 3, 30 et 4, 3-5 in Concilio Tridentino et apud S. Robertum Bellarminum," *VD*, 29(195 1), 88-97.
837. W. Feyerabend, "Über den Schluss des 3. Kapitals im Briefe an die Römer," *NKZ*, 3 (1892), 409-420.
838. M. D. R. Willink, " 'Imputed Righteousness,' " *Th*, 15 (1927), 221-222 [Rom. 4].
839. G. Volkmar, "Über Röm. 4, 1 und dessen Zusammensetzung," *ZWT*, 5 (1862), 221-224.
840. J. A. Bain, "Romans 4 : 1," *ET*, 5 (1893-1894), 430.
841. [G.] Küssner, "Studien über Röm. IV, 1 sqq.," *ZWT*, 34 (1891), 450-463.
842. [L.] Kraussold, "Über Römer 4, 2," *TSK*, 15 (1842), 783-790.
843. W. Spohn, "Über Röm. 4, 2," *TSK*, 16 (1843), 429-436.
844. F. X. Porporato, "De Paulina pericopa Rom. 4, 11-12," *VD*, 17 (1937), 173-179.
845. F. W. Kölbing, "Biblische Erörterungen: 2. Über die κληρονομία τοῦ κόσμου, Röm. 4, 13," *TSK*, 18 (1845), 694-696.
846. Basilius Haensler, "Nochmals zu Röm. 4, 19 (Gn. 25, 1 f.)," *BibZ*, 14 (1916-1917), 164-169.
847. Prebendarius, "Romans 4 : 25," *ET*, 5 (1893-1894), 117.
848. R. A. Mitchell, "Note on Romans 4 : 25," *ET*, 5 (1893-1894), 187.
849. D. M. Stanley, "Ad historiam exegeseos Rom. 4, 25," *VD*, 29 (1951), 257-274.
850. B. B. Warfield, "St. Paul's Use of the Argument from Experience," *Exp*, 5th series, 1 (1895), 226-236 [Rom. 5].
851. W. E. Wilson, "The Relation of Sin and Death in Romans 5," *ET*, 39 (1927-1928), 476-478.
852. N. A. Dahl, "Two Notes on Romans 5," *ST*, 5 (1951 [1952]), 37-48.
853. G. T. Thomson, "Exegesis of Romans V-VIII," *EQ*, 15 (1943), 247-251; 16 (1944), 4-8, 81-87.
854. Thomas Barrosse, "Death and Sin in Saint Paul's Epistle to the Romans," *CBQ*, 15 (1953), 438-459 [Rom. 5-8].
855. A. R. Crabtree, "Translation of Romans 5 : 1 in the Revised Standard Version of the N.T.," *RE*, 43 (1946), 436-439.
856. J. M. Bover, " 'Gloriamur,' " *B*, 22 (1941), 41-45 [Rom. 5 : 2].
857. F. Ruffenach, " 'Caritas Dei diffusa est in cordibus nostris per Spiritum Sanctum, qui datus est nobis' (Rom. 5, 5)," *VD*, 12 (1932), 303-304.

858. J. A. Kunze, "Versuch einer Erklärung der Stelle Röm. 5, 6 ff.," *TSK*, 23 (1850), 407-410.

859. Ragnar Leivestad, "Rom. 5, 7," *NTT*, 57 (1956), 245-248.

860. Anonymous, "Über ἐφ' ᾧ, bei Röm. 5, 12," *TQ*, 13 (1831), 397-444.

861. C. M. Esbjörn, "Romans 5 : 12," *LQ*, 12 (1882), 453-455.

862. S. Lyonnet, "Le sens de ἐφ' ᾧ en Rom. 5, 12 et l'exégèse des pères grecs," *B*, 36 (1955), 436-456.

863. S. Hoekstra, "Proeve van verklaring van Rom. 5 : 12b," *TT*, 2 (1868), 63-74.

864. [M. V.] Aberle, "Exegetische Studien 1, über Römer 5, 12-14," *TQ*, 36 (1854), 453-470.

865. William Hamilton, "The Punctuation and Rendering of Romans 5 : 12-14," *ET*, 24 (1912-1913), 234.

866. Stanislas Lyonnet, "Le péché originel et l'exégèse de Rom. 5, 12-14," *RSR*, 44 (1956), 63-84.

867. W. M. L. de Wette (tr. M. Stuart), "DeWette's Commentary on Romans 5 : 12-19," *BS*, 5 (1848), 263-283.

868. John Murray, "The Imputation of Adam's Sin," *WTJ*, 18 (1955-1956), 146-162; 19 (1956-1957), 25-44, 141-169; 20 (1957), 1-25 [Rom. 5 : 12-21].

869. [A.] Klöpper, "Die Bedeutung und der Zweck des Abschnitts Röm. 5, 12-21," *TSK*, 42 (1869), 496-514.

870. D. T. Fiske, "Dr. Forbes on Rom. 5 : 12-21," *BS*, 27 (1870), 697-721.

871. J. Forbes, "Reply to Dr. Fiske on Rom. 5 : 12-21," *BS*, 28 (1871), 739-751.

872. Isaiah Dole, "Paraphrase of Rom. 5 : 12-21," *BS*, 45 (1888), 518-520.

873. Gerhard Friedrich, "'Αμαρτία οὐκ ἐλλογεῖται, Röm. 5, 13," *TLZ*, 77 (1952), 523-528.

874. F. Godet, "The Logical Arrangement of Romans 5 : 15-17," *Exp*, 4th series, 1 (1890), 285-295.

875. J. M. Bover, "In Rom. 5, 15: exegesis logica," *B*, 4 (1923), 94-96.

876. Ghislain Lafont, "Sur l'interprétation de Romains V, 15-21," *RSR*, 45 (1957), 481-513.

877. Owen Street, "On the Use of the Preposition εἰς in the Phrases εἰς κατάκριμα and εἰς δικαίωσιν ζωῆς in Rom. 5 : 18," *BS*, 10 (1853), 522-527.

878. H. H. B. Ayles, "Romans 5 : 18," *ET*, 20 (1908-1909), 189-190.
879. J. de Zwaan, "Rom. 5 : 19, Jacobus 3 : 6, 4 : 4 en de κοινή," *TS*, 31 (1913), 85-94.
880. D. M. Henry, "Romans 5 : 20," *ET*, 5 (1893-1894), 426-427.
881. A. H. Blom, "De betrekking van de zonde tot den Christen, naar Rom. VI," *TT*, 14 (1880), 373-388.
882. J. A. Beet, "On Romans 6 : 1," *Exp*, 2nd series, 1 (1881), 387-400.
883. Thomas Howat, "Romans 6 : 1-4," *ET*, 5 (1893-1894), 310.
884. J. C. Jacoby, "An Exegetical Study of Romans 6 : 1-6," *LQ*, 39 (1909), 582-592.
885. Rudolf Schnackenburg, "Todes- und Lebensgemeinschaft mit Christus — Neue Studien zu Röm. 6, 1-11," *MTZ*, 6 (1955), 32-53.
886. John Murray, "Christian Baptism," *WTJ*, 13 (1950-1951), 132-136 [Rom. 6 : 2-6].
887. J. H. Goodhue, "Exposition of Rom. 6 : 2, 8 and 10, 11," *BS*, 14 (1857), 538-555.
888. Florentinus Ogara, " 'Complantati similitudini mortus eius simul et resurrectionis erimus': Notae in Rom. 6, 3-11 et Rom. 6, 19-23," *VD*, 15 (1935), 194-203.
889. S. A. Repass, "Discursus on Romans 6 : 4," *LCR*, 10 (1891), 308-316.
890. George Farmer, "Romans 6 : 4," *ET*, 5 (1893-1894), 223-224.
891. A. E. Garvie, "Romans 6 : 4," *ET*, 13 (1901-1902), 350.
892. P. Gächter, "Zur Exegese von Röm. 6, 5," *ZKT*, 54 (1930), 88.
893. Conatus, "Romans 6 : 7," *ET*, 5 (1893-1894), 381-382.
894. K. G. Kuhn, "Röm. 6, 7," *ZNW*, 30 (1931), 305-310.
895. Conatus, "Romans 6 : 8, 9," *ET*, 5 (1893-1894), 524-525.
896. H. P. Berlage, "Rom. 6 : 10," *TT*, 29 (1895), 585-595.
897. R. A. Mitchell, "Christ's Death to Sin," *ET*, 5 (1893-1894), 265-267 [Rom. 6 : 16].
898. J. Moffatt, "The Interpretation of Romans 6 : 17-18," *JBL*, 48 (1929), 233-238.
899. A. E. Garvie, "The Wages and the Gift," *ET*, 5 (1893-1894), 428-429 [Rom. 6 : 23].
900. F. W. C. Umbreit, "Des Apostel Paulus Selbstbekenntnis im siebenten Kapitel des Briefes an die Römer," *TSK*, 24 (1851), 633-645.

901. E. W. Krummacher, "Über das Subject in Röm. 7. Eine exegetisch-psychologische Untersuchung," *TSK*, 35 (1862), 119-136.

902. E. Achelis, "Über das Subject in Röm. 7. Eine biblisch-theologische Untersuchung," *TSK*, 36 (1863), 670-704.

903. J. M. Bover, "Valor de los terminos 'Ley', 'Yo', 'Pecado', en Rom. 7," *B*, 5 (1924), 192-196.

904. A. F. N. Lekkerkerker, "Romeinen 7, een belijdenis der gemeente," *NTS*, 23 (1940), 99-109.

905. André Rétif, "A propos de l'interprétation du chapitre VII des *Romains* par saint Augustin," *RSR*, 33 (1946), 368-371.

906. D. M. Davies, "Free from the Law; an Exposition of the Seventh Chapter of Romans," *Interp*, 7 (1953), 156-162.

907. C. L. Mitton, "Romans 7 Reconsidered," *ET*, 65 (1953-1954), 78-81, 99-103, 132-135.

908. Eduard Ellwein, "Das Rätsel von Römer 7," *KD*, 1 (1955), 247-268.

909. John Murray, "Divorce," *WTJ*, 11 (1948-1949), 105-122 [Rom. 7 : 1-3].

910. Bernardin Schneider, "The Meaning of Saint Paul's Antithesis, 'The Letter and the Spirit,' " *CBQ*, 15 (1953), 163-207 [Rom. 7 : 6].

911. W. A. Jarrell, "Romans 7 : 7-25: The Experience of Sinners," *RE*, 5 (1908), 586-597.

912. E. de los Rios, "Peccatum et Lex: Animadversiones in Rom. 7, 7-25." *VD*, 11 (1931), 23-28.

913. Dr. Bonwetsch, "Römer 7, 14 ff. in der alten Kirche und in Luthers Vorlesungen über den Römerbrief," *NKZ*, 30 (1919), 135-156.

914. Paul Althaus, "Zur Auslegung von Röm. 7, 14 ff. Antwort an Anders Nygren," *TLZ*, 77 (1952), 475-480.

915. John Tomlinson, "Interpretation of Romans 7 : 14-25," *LQ*, 11 (1881), 558-564.

916. Ludvig Selmer, "Rom. 7, 14-25," *NTT*, 26 (1925), 88-104.

917. H. B. Searight, "Rom. 7 : 17: A Short Study in Religious Psychology," *USR*, 23 (1911-1912), 144-149.

918. Wilfrid Browning, "Studies in Texts — Rom. 7 : 18 f.," *Th*, 52 (1949), 22-25.

919. M. L. Culler, "Exposition of Rom. 7 : 19," *LQ*, 33 (1903), 98-105.

920. F. Müller, "Zwei Marginalien im Brief des Paulus an die Römer," ZNW, 40 (1941), 249-254 [Rom. 7 : 22; 8 : 3].

921. K. J. Kapteijn, "Het lichaam dezes doods," GTT, 10 (1909), 113-126 [Rom. 7 : 24].

922. John Wilson, "Romans 7 : 24-8 : 2, a Rearrangement," ET, 4 (1892-1893), 192.

923. Joseph Huby, "La vie dans l'esprit d'après saint Paul (Romains, ch. 8)," RSR, 30 (1940), 5-39.

924. M. L. Loane, "The Eighth Chapter of the Epistle to the Romans," EQ, 13 (1941), 214-218.

925. F. L. Anderson, "How God Gets the Law Fulfilled: Rom. 8 : 1-4," BW, 30 (1907), 118-122.

926. F. Overbeck, "Über ἐν ὁμοιώματι σαρκὸς ἁμαρτίας, Röm. 8, 3," ZWT, 12 (1869), 178-212.

927. E. Zeller, "Zu Röm. 8, 3: ἐν ὁμοιώματι σαρκὸς ἁμαρτίας," ZWT, 13 (1870), 301-307.

928. R. M. Spence, "Romans 8 : 3," ET, 9 (1897-1898), 479-480.

929. P. I. Bratsiotes, "'Ερμηνευτικὸν σημείωμα εἰς τὰ χωρία Παύλου, 'Ρωμ. Θ'3 καὶ I' 1," Θ, 12 (1934), 85.

930. N. R. Haskins, "Romans 8 : 11," ET, 6 (1894-1895), 190.

931. Fl. Ogara, " 'Ipse Spiritus testimonium reddit spiritu nostro, quod sumus filii Dei,'" VD, 16 (1936), 200-208 [Rom. 8 : 12- 17].

932. J. C. James, "'Αββὰ ὁ πατήρ," ET, 26 (1914-1915), 428-429 [Rom. 8 : 15].

933. A. Roosen, "Testimonium Spiritus (R. 8, 16)," VD, 28 (1950), 214-226.

934. [M. J]. Mack, "Über das Elend, die Sehnsucht und Hoffnung der Creatur. Erklärung der Stelle Röm. VIII, 16-25," TQ, 15 (1833), 601-638.

935. Thomas Fahy, "Exegesis of Romans 8 : 16-25," ITQ, 23 (1956), 178-181.

936. J. M. Rupprecht, "Betrachtung der Stelle Röm. 8, 18-23, mit besonderer Rücksicht auf die Erklärung derselben von Prof. Zyro," TSK, 24 (1851), 214-236.

937. Fl. Ogara, " 'Expectatio creaturae revelationem filiorum Dei expectat,' " VD, 18 (1938), 193-201 [Rom. 8 : 18-23].

938. [F. Fr.] Zyro, "Neue Erklärung von Röm. 8, 18-25," TSK, 18 (1845), 403-416.

939. F. Fr. Zyro, "Neue Erörterung der Stelle Röm. 8, 18-25," TSK, 24 (1851), 645-666.

940. Edwin Lewis, "A Christian Theodicy; an Exposition of Romans 8 : 18-39," *Interp*, 11 (1957), 405-420.

941. George Mackenzie, " 'The Earnest Expectation of the Creature,' " *ET*, 5 (1893-1894), 333-334 [Rom. 8 : 19].

942. Robert Scott, "The Earnest Expectation of the Creature," *ET*, 5 (1893-1894), 265 [Rom. 8 : 19].

943. L. Usteri, "Beitrag zur Erklärung der κτίσις, Röm. 8, 19 u. f.," *TSK*, 5 (1832), 835-840.

944. George Philip, "Creation Waiting for Redemption, an Expository Study of Romans 8 : 19-22," *ET*, 5 (1893-1894), 315-319, 415-416, 509-512.

945. A. Viard, "Expectatio creaturae," *RB*, 59 (1952), 337-354 [Rom. 8 : 19-22].

946. A. Dubarle, "Le gémissement des créatures dans l'ordre divin du cosmos (Rom. 8, 19-22)," *RSPT*, 38 (1954), 445-465.

947. F. R. M. Hitchcock, " 'Every creature,' not 'all creation,' in Romans 8 : 22," *Exp*, 8th series, 11 (1916), 372-383.

948. C. H. van Rhijn, "Rom. 8 : 23," *TS*, 23 (1905), 377-378.

949. Pierre Benoit, " 'Nous gémissons, attendant la délivrance de notre corps' (Rom. viii, 23)," *RSR*, 39 (1951-1952), 267-280.

950. C. C. Oke, "A Suggestion with Regard to Romans 8 : 23," *Interp*, 11 (1957), 455-460.

951. J. J. Murray, "The Anchor of Hope. Romans 8 : 24; Hebrews 6 : 19," *Exp*, 2nd series, 5 (1883), 435-442.

952. W. H. Weeda, "Rm. 8 : 24a. Want wij zijn in hope zalig geworden," *NTS*, 1 (1918), 169-170.

953. W. Grimm, "Über die Stelle Röm. 8, 26-27," *ZWT*, 26 (1883), 456-459.

954. R. F. Boyd, "The Work of the Holy Spirit in Prayer; an Exposition of Romans 8 : 26, 27," *Interp*, 8 (1954), 35-42.

955. K. G. Manz, "Συνεργεῖ εἰς ἀγαθόν," *CTM*, 6 (1935), 615 [Rom. 8 : 28].

956. J. G. Griffiths, "Romans 8 : 28," *ET*, 49 (1937-1938), 474-476.

957. E. C. Blackman, "A Further Note on Romans 8 : 28," *ET*, 50 (1938-1939), 378-379.

958. E. H. Daniell, "Romans 8 : 28," *ET*, 61 (1949-1950), 59.

959. F. V. McFatridge, "The Called According to His Purpose," *RE*, 48 (1951), 416-423. [Rom. 8 : 28].

960. E. B. Allo, "Versets 28-30 du chap. VIII *ad Rom.* (La question de la prédestination dans l'ép. aux Romains)," *RSPT*, 7 (1913), 263-273.

961. E. B. Allo, "Encore *Rom.* VIII, 28-30," *RSPT*, 13 (1924), 503-505.

962. L. Poellot, "The Doctrine of Predestination in Rom. 8 : 28-39," *CTM*, 23 (1952), 342-353.

963. Alfred Durand, "Le Christ 'Premier-né,'" *RSR*, 1 (1910), 56-66 [Rom. 8 : 29 and Col. 1 : 15 ff.].

964. Th. Laetsch, "Sermon Study on Rom. 8 : 29-32," *CTM*, 13 (1942), 40-51.

965. A. W. Argyle, "Romans 8 : 32," *JTS*, 4 (1953), 214-215.

966. A. Roberts, "Interpretation of Romans 8 : 33, 34," *Exp*, 5th series, 3 (1896), 380-391.

967. J. P. Lilley, "The Invincible Love," *ET*, 5 (1893-1894), 518-521 [Rom. 8 : 35].

968. Carpus, "Life and Death as Antagonists of Love," *Exp*, 1st series, 3 (1876), 119-133 [Rom. 8 : 38-39].

969. J. M. Simcock, "Note on Romans VIII. 39," *Exp*, 2nd series, 8 (1884), 239-240.

970. E. P. Gould, "Romans IX-XI," *JBL* (June and December, 1883), 22-41.

971. K. Buhl, "Der Gedankengang von Röm. 9-11," *TSK*, 60 (1887), 295-320.

972. C. Lattey, "Theses Paulinae: VIII. De reiectione Iudaeorum (Rom. 9-11)," *VD*, 5 (1925), 20-26.

973. R. M. Hawkins, "The Rejection of Israel: An Analysis of Romans IX-XI," *ATR*, 23 (1941), 329-335.

974. J. M. Bover, "La reprobación de Israel en Rom. 9-11," *EE*, 25 (1951), 63-82.

975. Erich Dinkler, "The Historical and the Eschatological Israel in Romans, chapters 9-11; a Contribution to the Problem of Predestination and Individual Responsibility," *JR*, 36 (1956), 109-127.

976. C. B. Caird, "Expository Problems: Predestination — Romans ix-xi," *ET*, 68 (1957), 324-326.

977. W. J. Goedbloed, "Een moeilijk hoofdstuck uit den Romeinenbrief," *GTT*, 31 (1930-1931), 228-241 [Rom. 9].

978. S. Lyonnet, "De doctrina praedestinationis et reprobationis in Rom 9," *VD*, 34 (1956), 193-201, 257-271.

979. A. van Veldhuizen, "Rom. 9 : 2: ὅτι λύπη μοί ἐστιν μεγάλη καὶ ἀδιάλειπτος ὀδύνη τῇ καρδίᾳ μου," *TS*, 28 (1910), 130.

980. James Morison, "Anathema from Christ," *Exp*, 1st series, 6 (1877), 177-185 [Rom. 9 : 3].

981. W. H. Davis, "Anathema — Romans 9 : 3," *RE*, 31 (1934), 205-207.

982. W. Grimm, "Über die Doxologie in Röm. 9, 5," *ZWT*, 12 (1869), 311-321.

983. Ernst Harmsen, "Über die Doxologie in Röm. 9, 5," *ZWT*, 15 (1872), 510-520.

984. E. Abbot, "Remarks on Rom. ix. 5," *JBL* (June and December, 1881), 87-154.

985. Timothy Dwight, "On Romans ix. 5," *JBL* (June and December, 1881), 22-55.

986. Ezra Abbot, "Recent Discussions on Rom. IX. 5," *JBL* (June and December, 1883), 90-112.

987. Ernst Bröse, "Wird Christus Röm. 9, 5 Θεός genannt?" *NKZ*, 10 (1899), 645-657.

988. E. Günther, "Zur Exegese von Röm. 9, 5," *TSK*, 73 (1900), 636-644.

989. A. Durand, "La divinité de Jésus-Christ dans St. Paul, Rom. IX, 5," *RB*, 12 (1903), 550-570.

990. J. M. S. Baljon, "Rom. IX : 5b," *TS*, 4 (1886), 232-234.

991. J. H. L. Roozemeyer, "Rom. IX : 5b," *TS*, 4 (1886), 397-399.

992. E. H. Plumptre, "The Potter and the Clay," *Exp*, 1st series, 4 (1876), 469-480 [Rom. 9 : 19-24].

993. v. d. W. te G., "Eene afgesnedere zaak doen op aarde. Rom. 9 : 28," *GTT*, 4 (1903), 173-175.

994. A. van Veldhuizen, "Rom. 9 : 30-33," *TS*, 29 (1911), 439.

995. E. H. van Leeuwen, "Zelotisme naar de beschrijving van Paulus," *TS*, 8 (1890), 75-88 [Rom. 10 : 2].

996. Felix Flückiger, "Christus des Gesetzes τέλος," *TZ*, 11 (1955), 153-157 [Rom. 10 : 4].

997. J. F. Genung, "The Righteousness which is of Faith," *JBL*, (June and December, 1884), 29-36 [Rom. 10 : 4-11].

998. M. J. Hughes, "Romans 10 : 6-8," *ET*, 19 (1907-1908), 524-525.

999. G. H. Whitaker, "Hebrews 4 : 2 and Romans 10 : 16 ff.," *Exp*, 8th series, 23 (1922), 239-240.

1000. [G. W.] Matthias, "Der Oelbaum des Römerbriefes," *TSK*, 39 (1866), 520-532 [Rom. 11].

1001. P. E. Hughes, "The Olive Tree of Romans XI," *EQ*, 20 (1948), 22-45.

1002. V. Bartling, " 'All Israel Shall Be Saved,' Rom. 11 : 26," *CTM*, 12 (1941), 641-657.

1003. F. W. Grosheide, "Romeinen 11, 26," *GTT*, 53 (1953), 49-52.

1004. R. Cölle, "Zur Exegese und homiletischen Behandlung der Epistel für das Trinitatisfest: Röm. 11, 33-36," *TSK*, 82 (1909), 458-470.

1005. Florentinus Ogara, " 'Ex ipso et per ipsum et in ipso sunt omnia': Notae in Rom. 11, 33-36," *VD*, 15 (1935), 164-171.

1006. G. H. Whitaker, "The Twelfth Chapter of Romans," *ET*, 27 (1915-1916), 475-477.

1007. M. D., "Twenty Misused Scripture Texts; VI. Rom. 12 : 1," *ET*, 6 (1894-1895), 568.

1008. J. B. Weatherspoon, "The Conservation of Life," *RE*, 23 (1926), 129-136 [Rom. 12 : 1].

1009. Florentinus Ogara, " 'Rationabile obsequium vestrum': Notae in Rom. 12, 1-5," *VD*, 15 (1935), 5-14.

1010. S. T. Lowrie, "Romans XII. 1-8 — Translation and Interpretation," *PTR*, 17 (1919), 627-643.

1011. B. Hennen, "Ordines sacri. Ein Deutungs-Versuch zu I Cor. 12, 1-31 und Röm. 12, 3-8," *TQ*, 119 (1938), 427-469.

1012. Florentinus Ogara, " 'Habentes . . . donationes . . . differentes,' " *VD*, 16 (1936), 5-13 [Rom. 12 : 6].

1013. L. Lindeboom, "De analogia fidei en Rom. 12 : 6 (7)," *GTT*, 17 (1916-1917), 448-457, 511-526.

1014. C. Spicq, "Φιλόστοργος (à propos de Rm. 12.10)," *RB*, 62 (1955), 497-510.

1015. R. P. Ashe, "Romans 12 : 13, 14," *ET*, 39 (1927-1928), 46.

1016. T. K. Cheyne, "The Rendering of Romans xii. 16," *Exp*, 2nd series, 6 (1883), 469-472.

1017. [F. Fr.] Zyro, "Über Röm. 12, 19: δότε τόπον τῇ ὀργῇ," *TSK*, 18 (1845), 887-892.

1018. E. R. Smothers, "Give Place to the Wrath," *CBQ*, 6 (1944), 205-215 [Rom. 12 : 19].

1019. J. E. Yonge, "Heaping Coals of Fire on the Head," *Exp*, 3rd series, 2 (1885), 158-159 [Rom. 12 : 20].

1020. John Steele, "Heaping Coals on the Head (Pr. 25 : 22; Ro. 12 : 20)," *ET*, 44 (1932-1933), 141.

1021. A. Škrinjar, " 'Carbones ignis congeres super caput eius,' " *VD*, 18 (1938), 143-150 [Rom. 12 : 20].

1022. M. J. Dahood, "Two Pauline Quotations from the Old Testament," *CBQ*, 17 (1955), 19-24 [Rom. 12 : 20].

1023. Florentinus Ogara, " 'Noli vinci a malo, sed vince in bono malum' (Rom. 12, 21)," *VD*, 19 (1939), 11-17.

1024. Spencer Roberton, "A Note on Romans 12 : 21: μὴ νικῶ ὑπὸ τοῦ κακοῦ," *ET*, 60 (1948-1949), 322.

1025. C. H. van Rhijn, "Rom. XIII en Openb. XIII. Over en naar aanleiding van een rectorale oratie," *TS*, 25 (1907), 287-297.

1026. W. J. Grant, "Citizenship and Civil Obedience; Romans 13," *ET*, 54 (1942-1943), 180-181.

1027. August Strobel, "Zum Verständnis von Rm 13," *ZNW*, 47 (1956), 67-92.

1028. Oscar Cullmann, "Zur neuesten Diskussion über die ἐξουσίαι in Röm. 13 : 1," *TZ*, 10 (1954), 321-336.

1029. Robert Morgenthaler, "Roma, sedes Satanae. Röm. 13 : 1 ff. im Lichte von Luk 4 : 5-8," *TZ*, 12 (1956), 289-304.

1030. F. W. Grosheide, "Bijdrage tot de verklaring van Rom. 13 : 1-7," *GTT*, 48 (1948), 135-149.

1031. H. M. Gale, "Paul's View of the State; a Discussion of the Problem in Romans 13 : 1-7," *Interp*, 6 (1952), 409-414.

1032. K. H. Schelkle, "Staat und Kirche in der patristischen Auslegung von Rom. 13, 1-7," *ZNW*, 44 (1952-1953), 223-236.

1033. A. M. Brouwer, "Christen en overheid volgens Rom. 13 : 1-10," *NTS*, 23 (1940), 150-163.

1034. J. Héring, " 'Serviteurs de Dieu.' Contributions à l'exégèse de Romains 13 : 3-4," *RHPR*, 30 (1950), 31-40.

1035. J. de Zwaan, "Een trekje van Paulus' karakter," *TT*, 47 (1913), 468-471 [Rom. 13 : 6].

1036. A. van Veldhuizen, "Wie zijn λειτουργοὶ Θεοῦ in Rom. 13 : 6," *TS*, 32 (1914), 312-314.

1037. Willi Marxsen, "Der ἕτερος νόμος, Röm. 13 : 8," *TZ*, 11 (1955), 230-237.

1038. F. W. Grosheide, "Romans 13 : 8b," *TS*, 31 (1913), 345-348.

1039. D. G. Hughes, "Nota breve," *EB*, N.S. 2 (1943), 307-309 [Rom. 13 8b].

1040. Florentinus Ogara, " 'Nemini quidquam debeatis nisi ut invicem diligatis': Notae in Rom. 13, 8-10," *VD*, 15 (1935), 41-47.

1041. Florentinus Ogara, " 'Hora est iam nos de somno surgere' (Rom. 13, 11-14)," *VD*, 14 (1934), 353-360.

1042. W. M. L. de Wette, "Exegetische Bemerkungen — 2. Über Röm. 14," *TSK*, 3 (1830), 351-352.

1043. John Murray, "The Weak and the Strong," *WTJ*, 12 (1949-1950), 136-153 [Rom. 14].

1044. C. A. Gaertner, "Instructions to the Weak and the Strong According to Romans 14," *CTM*, 21 (1950), 659-673.

1045. [K. F.] Nösgen, "Eine kleine paulinische Studie über Römer 14, 17-18," *NKZ*, 16 (1905), 546-561.

1046. C. Lindeboom, "Hoe moeten zij wederlegd worden, die zeggen, dat Matth. 10 : 32 en Rom. 14 : 22 met elkander in strijd zijn?" *GTT*, 5 (1904), 28-29.

1047. M. D., "Twenty Misused Scripture Texts; VII. Rom. 14 : 23," *ET*, 6 (1894-1895), 568.

1048. M. A. N. Rovers, "Nog iets over de laatste hoofdstukken van Paulus' brief aan de Romeinen," *TT*, 2 (1868), 310-325 [Rom. 15-16].

1049. J. W. Straatman, "Het slot van den brief van Paulus aan de Romeinen," *TT*, 2 (1868), 24-57 [Rom. 15-16].

1050. H. Holtzmann, "Der Stand der Verhandlungen über die beiden letzten Capitel des Römerbriefes," *ZWT*, 17 (1874), 504-518.

1051. J. H. Scholten, "Rom. XV en XVI," *TT*, 10 (1876), 1-33.

1052. W. H. Ryder, "The Authorship of Romans xv. xvi," *JBL*, 17 (1898), 184-198.

1053. W. B. Smith, "Unto Romans: XV and XVI," *JBL*, 20 (1901), 129-151; 21 (1902), 117-169.

1054. D. De Bruyne, "Les deux derniers chapitres de la lettre aux Romains," *RBén*, 25 (1909), 423-430.

1055. C. W. Emmet, "Romans 15 and 16: A New Theory," *Exp*, 8th series, 11 (1916), 275-288.

1056. A. T. Hanson, "The Interpretation of the Second Person Singular in Quotations from the Psalms in the New Testament: A Note on Romans XV, 3," *Herm*, No. 73 (1949), 69-72.

1057. F. Spitta, "Zu Röm. 15, 4.7.8," *TSK*, 86 (1913), 109-112.

1058. G. R. Wynne, "Mercy and Truth," *ET*, 21 (1909-1910), 405-407 [Rom. 15 : 9 and Eph. 2 : 17].

1059. Ludwig Gaugusch, "Untersuchungen zum Römerbrief; der Epilog (15, 14-16, 27); eine exegetische Studie," *BibZ*, 24 (1938-1939), 165-184, 252-266.

1060. M. Michelsen, "Über einige sinnverwandte Aussprüche des Neuen Testaments: Röm. 15, 16," *TSK*, 46 (1873), 128-135.

1061. L. Radermacher, "Σφραγίζεσθαι: Röm. 15, 28," *ZNW*, 32 (1933), 87-89.

1062. Alexander Mair, "Apologetic Argument from the Names in Romans 16," *Exp*, 4th series, 7 (1893), 75-80.

1063. E. G. Sihler, "A Note on the First Christian Congregation at Rome," *CTM*, 3 (1932), 180-184 [Rom. 16].

1064. F. M. Young, "Romans 16: A Suggestion," *ET*, 47 (1935-1936), 44.

1065. A. Spaeth, "Phebe, the Deaconess," *LCR*, 4 (1885), 21-222, 260-281 [Rom. 16 : 1].

1066. Margaret D. Gibson, "Phoebe," *ET*, 23 (1911-1912), 281 [Rom. 16 : 1].

1067. K. Erbes, "Zeit und Ziel der Grüsse Röm. 16, 3-15 und der Mitteilungen 2 Tim. 4, 9-21," *ZNW*, 10 (1909), 128-147, 195-218.

1068. C. H. van Rhijn, "Rom. 16 : 4," *TS*, 23 (1905), 378-378.

1069. B. W. Bacon, "Andronicus," *ET*, 42 (1930-1931), 300-304 [Rom. 16 : 7].

1070. P. E. Kretzmann, "Zu Röm. 16, 17 f.," *CTM*, 4 (1933), 413-424.
    On Rom. 1 : 20 see number 550; 3 : 24-26, number 2546; chapters 5 to 8, number 2933; 5 : 11, number 558; 8 : 28, number 592; 8 : 28-30, number 726; 11 : 15, number 558; 11 : 36, number 2557; 12 : 13, number 2260; and chapter 14, number 1211.

2. The Corinthian Correspondence

1071. [F.] Bleek, "Erörterungen in Beziehung auf die Briefe Pauli an die Korinther," *TSK*, 3 (1830), 614-632.

1072. [C. F.] Kling, "Biblisch-theologische Erörterungen über einige Abschnitte der Korintherbriefe," *TSK*, 12 (1839), 431-513.

1073. [W.] Beyschlag, "Über die Christuspartei zu Korinth," *TSK*, 38 (1865), 217-276.

1074. A. Hilgenfeld, "Die Christus-Leute in Korinth," *ZWT*, 8 (1865), 242-265.
1075. A. Hilgenfeld, "Paulus und die korinthischen Wirren," *ZWT*, 14 (1871), 99-119.
1076. A. Hilgenfeld, "Die Christus-Leute in Korinth und die Nikolaiten in Asien," *ZWT*, 15 (1872), 200-225.
1077. G. Heinrici, "Die Christengemeinde Korinths und die religiösen Genossenschaften der Griechen," *ZWT*, 19 (1876), 465-525.
1078. H. Holtzmann, "Das gegenseitige Verhältniss der beiden Korintherbriefe," *ZWT*, 22 (1879), 455-492.
1079. H. Holtzmann, "Der Streit über die Christus-Partei in Korinth," *ZWT*, 28 (1885), 233-245.
1080. Oberkonsistorialrat Kühn, "Zur Einleitung in die beiden Korintherbriefe," *NKZ*, 6 (1895), 981-990.
1081. Anonymous, "The Four Epistles of Paul to the Corinthians," *ET*, 9 (1897-1898), 21-25.
1082. V. Ermoni, "Les épîtres aux Corinthiens et la critique," *RB*, 8 (1899), 283-289.
1083. J. H. Kennedy, "St. Paul's Correspondence with Corinth," *Exp*, 5th series, 10 (1899), 182-195.
1084. W. M. Ramsay, "Historical Commentary on the Epistles to the Corinthians," *Exp*, 6th series, 1 (1900), 19-31, 91-111, 203-217, 273-289, 380-387; 2 (1900), 81-105, 287-302, 368-381, 429-444; 3 (1901), 93-110, 220-240, 343-360.
1085. W. M. Ramsay, "Historical Commentary on the Epistles to the Corinthians," *LCR*, 19 (1900), 344-355.
1086. K. Hoss, "Zu den Reiseplänen des Apostels Paulus in Kor. I und II," *ZNW*, 4 (1903), 268-270.
1087. Robert Mackintosh, "Corinth and the Tragedy of St. Paul," *Exp*, 7th series, 6 (1908), 77-83.
1088. Robert Mackintosh, "The Brief Visit to Corinth," *Exp*, 7th series, 6 (1908), 226-234.
1089. S. E. Chandler, "The Corinthian Correspondence," *BW*, 34 (1909), 198-208.
1090. R. Perdelwitz, "Die sogenannte Christuspartei in Korinth," *TSK*, 84 (1911), 180-204.
1091. A. J. Dickinson, "The Genetic History of 1 and 2 Corinthians; Studies Constructive and Critical," *RE*, 14 (1917), 32-39.
1092. Mary E. Andrews, "The Party of Christ in Corinth," *ATR*, 19 (1937), 17-29.

1093. T. W. Manson, "St. Paul in Ephesus: (3) The Corinthian Correspondence," *BJRL*, 26 (1941), 101-120.
1094. J. Haspecker, "Vestigia Evangelii oralis in S. Pauli ad Corinthios Epistulis," *VD*, 27 (1949), 129-142, 206-213.
1095. Patrick Cleary, "The Epistles to the Corinthians," *CBQ*, 12 (1950), 10-33.
See also numbers 103, 104, 106, 112, 124, 284, 323, 410, 420, and 426.

3. The First Epistle to the Corinthians

a. *Textual Criticism*

1096. C. G. C[orbet], "Pauli locus in Epistola I ad Cor. II. 4 ex Origene reconstitutus," *Mn*, 9 (1860), 315-318 [πειθοισσοφιας for πειθοισοφιας].
1097. Joseph Huby, "Comment lire I Corinthiens II, 4a?" *SR* (= *RSR*, 32) (1944), 245-247.
1098. H. G. Meecham, "The Anarthrous Θεός in John 1 : 1 and 1 Corinthians 3 : 16," *ET*, 63 (1951-1952), 126.
1099. W. F. Howard, "1 Corinthians 4 : 6 (Exegesis or Emendation)," *ET*, 33 (1921-1922), 479-480.
1100. J. T. Hudson, "I Cor. 4 : 6," *ET*, 35 (1923-1924), 32.
1101. N. Herz, "A Hebrew Word in Greek Disguise," *ET*, 7 (1895-1896), 48 [I Cor. 7 : 3, ὀφειλομένην εὔνοιαν = עוֹנָתָהּ, Ex. 21 : 10].
1102. J. E. L. Oulton, "A Variant Reading in I Corinthians vii. 5," *Herm*, No. 72 (1948), 20 [ἐπιχαρῇ ὑμῖν in Origen *On Prayer*, II. 2].
1103. Eberhard Nestle, "I Corinthians 10 : 9," *ET*, 19 (1907-1908), 429.
1104. W. D. Morris, "I Corinthians 11 : 10," *ET*, 39 (1927-1928), 139.
1105 J. P. Wilson, "I Corinthians 11 : 10," *ET*, 39 (1927-1928), 283-284.
1106. A. W. Tyler, "Paul's Panegyric of Love — A New Critical Text, Translation, and Digest," *BS*, 30 (1873), 128-143 [I Cor. 12 : 27-13 : 13].
1107. E. Nestle, "1 Kor. 13, 3," *ZNW*, 7 (1906), 280.
1108. R. G. Bury, "Romans 12 : 16; I Corinthians 13 : 7," *ET*, 49 (1937-1938), 430.

1109. F. W. Grosheide, "I Kor. 15 : 33," *GTT*, 16 (1915), 79-84.

1110. A. Vaccari, "Il testo 1 Cor. 15, 51," *B*, 13 (1932), 73-76.

1111. A. Romeo, " 'Omnes quidem resurgemus' seu 'Omnes quidem nequaquam dormiemus' (I Cor. 15, 51)," *VD*, 14 (1934), 142-148, 250-255, 267-275, 313-320, 328-336, 375-378.

1112. P. Brandhuber, "Die sekundären Lesarten bei 1 Kor. 15,51. Ihre Verbreitung und Entstehung," *B*, 18 (1937), 303-333, 418-438.

1113. A. Jones, "The Vulgate Text of I Cor. 15, 51 and the Greek Text," *Scr*, 2 (1947), 45-48.

b. *Historical and Literary Criticism*

1114. F. Godet, "The First Epistle to the Corinthians," *Exp*, 3rd series, 2 (1885), 70-80, 161-177.

1115. Gust. Wahle, "Paulus erster Brief an die Korinther, seinem Inhalt und Plan nach," *NKZ*, 9 (1898), 540-553.

1116. A. van Veldhuizen, "De crisis in de gemeente van Korinthe op het einde der eerste eeuw," *TS*, 22 (1904), 1-22.

1117. Dawson Walker, "The Epistle of St. Paul to the Corinthians," *RE*, 4 (1907), 71-85, 352-366, 514-533.

1118. G. G. Findlay, "Paul's First Letter to the Corinthians," *Exp*, 8th series, 9 (1915), 289-325.

1119. A. van Veldhuizen, "Een vertaling van Paulus' 1en Brief aan de Korinthiërs," *TS*, 34 (1916), 174-208.

1120. F. W. Grosheide, "De leidende gedachte in Paulus' 1en Brief aan de Korinthiërs," *GTT*, 18 (1917-1918), 353-376.

1121. T. S. Duncan, "The Style and Language of Saint Paul in his First Letter to the Corinthians," *BS*, 83 (1926), 129-143.

1122. V. D. Melconian, "First Corinthians," *Interp*, 7 (1953), 62-77.

c. *Theological Studies*

1123. J. A. Bruins, "De parousie in den eersten Corinther brief," *TT*, 26 (1892), 381-415, 471-513.

1124. N. J. D. White, "A Point in the Christology of First Corinthians," *Exp*, 6th series, 2 (1900), 15-24.

1125. G. Schläger, "Der Abendmahls-, der Auferstehungsbericht und die Herrenworte im 1 Brief an die Korinther," *TT*, 46 (1912), 136-157.

1126. Everett Henry, "Outstanding Features of 1 Corinthians," *RE*, 25 (1928), 355-369.

1127. T. W. Manson, "The Message of the Epistles; I Corinthians," *ET*, 44 (1932-1933), 500-504.
1128. E. B. Allo, "Sagesse et pneuma dans la première épître aux Corinthiens," *RB*, 43 (1934), 321-346.

d. *Exegesis of Individual Passages*

1129. N. A. Dahl, "Paulus apostel og menigheter i Korinth (1 Kor. 1-4)," *NTT*, 54 (1953), 1-24.
1130. J. Weiss, "Der Eingang des ersten Korintherbriefes," *TSK*, 73 (1900), 125-130 [I Cor. 1 : 1 ff.].
1131. C. H. van Rhijn, "Het opschrift van den Eersten Brief aan de Korinthiërs," *TS*, 18 (1900), 357-362 [I Cor. 1 : 1-3].
1132. B. Hapig, "Quam doceat S. Paulus I Cor. 1, 4 apostolici muneris dignitatem et obligationem," *VD*, 6 (1926), 112-115, 129-135.
1133. Florentinus Ogara, " 'In omnibus divites facti estis in illo,' " *VD*, 16 (1936), 225-232 [I Cor. 1 : 4-8].
1134. J. F. M'Fadyen, "Old Texts in Modern Translation; I Corinthians 1 : 10 (Moffatt)," *ET*, 49 (1937-1938), 72-76.
1135. Florentinus Ogara, " 'Ut id ipsum dicatis omnes et non sint in vobis schismata,' " *VD*, 16 (1936), 257-266, 289-294, 321-329 [I Cor. 1 : 10 ff.].
1136. W. J. Jobling, "Is Christ Divided? I Corinthians 1 : 11 ff.," *ET*, 56 (1944-1945), 54-55.
1137. J. M. S. Baljon, "De verschillende partijen in de Korinthische gemeente; 1 Kor. 1 : 12," *TS*, 5 (1887), 256-259.
1138. U. Holzmeister, "Enthalten die Verse I Kor. 1, 14 u. 16 einen Widerspruch?" *ZKT*, 24 (1910), 500-525.
1139. E. Peterson, "1 Cor. 1, 18 f. und die Thematik des jüdischen Busstages," *B*, 32 (1951), 97-103.
1140. Heinrich Frick, "Meditation on I Cor. 1 : 21-25," *Th*, 17 (1928), 256-257.
1141. Josef Bohatec, "Inhalt und Reihenfolge der 'Schlagworte der Erlösungsreligion,' I Kor. 1 : 26-31," *TZ*, 4 (1948), 252-271.
1142. W. M. Nicolson, "I Corinthians 1 : 30," *ET*, 9 (1897-1898), 524.
1143. Dr. Wiesinger, "Die Predigt des Apostels Paulus als Vorbild aller Predigt nach I Kor. 2," *NKZ*, 70 (1899), 687-702.
1144. D. W. Martin, " 'Spirit' in the Second Chapter of First Corinthians," *CBQ*, 5 (1943), 381-395.

1145. M. Ginsburger, "La 'gloire' et l'"autorité' de la femme dans I Cor. 2, 1-10," *RHPR*, 12 (1932), 245-248.

1146. M. D., "Twenty Misused Scripture Texts; VIII. I Cor. 2 : 2,"' *ET*, 6 (1894-1895), 568.

1147. W. J. P. Boyd, "I Corinthians 2 : 8," *ET*, 68 (1956-1957), 158.

1148. Trevor Ling, "A Note on I Corinthians 2 : 8," *ET*, 68 (1956-1957), 26.

1149. M. D., "Twenty Misused Scripture Texts; I. I Cor. 2 : 9," *ET*, 6 (1894-1895), 201.

1150. v. d. W., "I Cor. 2 : 9," *GTT*, 1 (1900), 134-136.

1151. D. John, "St. Paul and Empedocles," *ET*, 39 (1927-1928), 237-238 [I Cor. 2 : 9].

1152. Rendel Harris, "A Quotation from Judith in the Pauline Epistles," *ET*, 27 (1915-1916), 13-15 [I Cor. 2 : 10 parallels Judith 8 : 14].

1153. Geoffrey Carlisle, "Studies in Texts," *Th*, 12 (1926), 103-104 [I Cor. 2 : 14].

1154. A. G. Jones, "The Power is of God," *USR*, 22 (1910-1911), 245-252 [I Cor. 3 : 5].

1155. Artur Landgraf, "I Cor. 3, 10-17 bei den lateinischen Vätern und in der Frühscholastik," *B*, 5 (1924), 140-172.

1156. Anton Fridrichsen, "Themelios, I Kor. 3, 11," *TZ*, 2 (1946), 316.

1157. Hugh Pope, "He shall be Saved, yet so as by Fire," *ITQ*, 4 (1909), 441-456 [I Cor. 3 : 15].

1158. F. Ruffenach, "Nescitis quia templum Dei estis, et Spiritus Dei habitat in vobis? (I Cor. 3, 16) — An nescitis quoniam membra vestra templum sunt Spiritus Sancti? (I Cor. 6, 19) — Vos enim estis templum Dei vivi (2 Cor. 6, 16)," *VD*, 13 (1933), 37-40.

1159. T. H. Bindley, "A Note on I Corinthians 4 : 1," *ET*, 30 (1918-1919), 184-185.

1160. G. H. Whitaker, "I Cor. 4 : 1," *ET*, 30 (1918-1919), 426.

1161. F. Giesekke, "Zur Exegese von Kor. I. 4, 2," *TSK*, 65 (1892), 763-769.

1162. L. Brun, "Noch einmal die Schriftnorm I Kor. 4, 6," *TSK*, 103 (1931), 453-456.

1163. Anton Fridrichsen, "Exegetisches zum Neuen Testament," *SO*, 13 (1934), 38-46 [I Cor. 5 : 1; Phil. 3 : 13].

1164. S. Cox, "That Wicked Person," *Exp*, 1st series, 3 (1876), 355-368 [I Cor. 5 : 1-5, 13, and II Cor. 2 : 5-11].

1165. J. M. Bover, "Paschale sacrificium sincere celebrandum (I Cor. 5, 7-8)," *VD*, 6 (1926), 97-103.

1166. G. G. Findlay, "The Letter of the Corinthian Church to St. Paul," *Exp*, 6th series, 1 (1900), 401-407 [I Cor. 5 : 9].

1167. U. Holzmeister, "Quid in epistula praecanonica S. Pauli ad Corinthios contentum fuerit," *VD*, 17 (1937), 313-316 [I Cor. 5 : 9].

1168. H. Koch, "Zu I Cor. 5, 9 f., 11, 5 ff., und Felix culpa," *ZNW*, 21 (1922), 137-140.

1169. J. H. Bernard, "The Connexion between the Fifth and Sixth Chapters of I Corinthians," *Exp*, 7th series, 3 (1907), 433-443.

1170. H. H. B. Ayles, "I Corinthians 6 : 1," *ET*, 27 (1915-1916), 334.

1171. Marcus Dods, "St. Paul on Going to Law," *Exp*, 1st series, 1 (1875), 142-155 [I Cor. 6 : 1-7].

1172. A. H. Forster, "I Corinthians 6 : 2," *ET*, 25 (1913-1914), 285-286.

1173. B. v. d. Werff, "Hoe moeten we I Cor. 6 : 3a verstaan, waar Paulus zegt, dat wij de engelen zullen oordelen?" *GTT*, 7 (1906), 143-144.

1174. A. Vitti, " 'Angelos iudicabimus' (1 Cor. 6, 3)," *VD*, 2 (1928), 225-233.

1175. A. van Veldhuizen, "I Kor. 6 : 7," *TS*, 24 (1906), 67-68.

1176. A. d'Alès, "I Cor., vi, 11, καὶ ταῦτά τινες ἦτε," *RSR*, 1 (1910), 269.

1177. Marcus Dods, "St. Paul on Marriage," *Exp*, 1st series, 1 (1875), 237-248 [I Cor. 7].

1178. R. Mackintosh, "Marriage Problems at Corinth," *Exp*, 7th series, 4 (1907), 349-363 [I Cor. 7].

1179. E. Fascher, "Zur Witwerschaft des Paulus und der Auslegung von I Cor. 7," *ZNW*, 28 (1929), 62-69.

1180. F. W. Grosheide, "I Kor. 7 en 8-10," *GTT*, 33 (1932-1933), 481-491.

1181. Heinz Kruse, "Matrimonia 'Josephina' apud Corinthios?" *VD*, 26 (1948), 344-350 [I Cor. 7].

1182. Emanuel Hirsch, "Eine Randglosse zu 1 Kor. 7 [vs. 10 f.]," *ZST*, 3 (1925-1926), 50-62.

1183. John Murray, "Divorce," *WTJ*, 10 (1947-1948), 168-191 [I Cor. 7 : 10-15].

1184. J. Biedersack, S. J., "Über das sogenannte Paulinische Privilegium," *ZKT*, 7 (1883), 304-322 [I Cor. 7 : 12-15].

1185. [W. M. L.] de Wette, "Zur Geschichte der Kindertaufe," *TSK*, 3 (1830), 669-671 [I Cor. 7 : 14].

1186. J. A. Beet, "Sanctified in the Wife," *Exp*, 1st series, 10 (1879), 321-331 [I Cor. 7 : 14].

1187. D. W. Simon, "I Corinthians 7 : 14, a Reply to a Request," *ET*, 2 (1890-1891), 221-223.

1188. Adhémar d'Alès, "Tertullien sur I Cor., vii, 14," *RSR*, 2 (1911), 54-56.

1189. John Murray, "Christian Baptism," *WTJ*, 14 (1951-1952), [I Cor. 7 : 14].

1190. E. P. Gould, "Note on I Cor. vii. 15," *JBL* (June and December, 1881), 20-21.

1191. J. MacRory, "The Teaching of the New Testament on Divorce," *ITQ*, 4 (1909), 80-95 [I Cor. 7 : 15].

1192. Pierre Dulau, "The Pauline Privilege, Is it Promulgated in the First Epistle to the Corinthians?" *CBQ*, 13 (1951), 146-152 [I Cor. 7 : 15].

1193. Günther Harder, "Miszelle zu 1 Kor. 7, 17," *TLZ*, 79 (1954), 367-372.

1194. J. W. Straatman, "Bijdragen tot de kritiek en exegese van het N. Testament; I Cor. VII : 17-22," *TT*, 11 (1877), 24-62.

1195. E. J. Goodspeed, "The Syntax of I Cor. 7 : 18,27," *AJT*, 12 (1908), 249-250.

1196. E. J. Goodspeed, "A Patristic Parallel to I Cor. 7 : 18, 21," *JBL*, 36 (1917), 150.

1197. J. W. Straatman, "Bijdragen tot de kritiek en exegese des N. Testaments; I Cor. VII : 36, 37," *TT*, 8 (1874), 400-409.

1198. R. Steck, "Geistliche Ehen bei Paulus?" *STZ*, 34 (1917), 177-189 [I Cor. 7 : 36-37].

1199. W. C. van Manen, "De verloofden te Korinthe (I Kor. VII: 36-38)," *TT*, 8 (1874), 607-616.

1200. Joseph Sickenberger, "Syneisaktentum im ersten Korinther-briefe?" *BibZ*, 3 (1905), 44-68 (cf. 6 [1908], 377) [I Cor. 7 : 36-38].

1201. Carl Weyman, "Zu I Kor. 7, 36 ff.," *BibZ*, 6 (1908), 377.

1202. A. van Veldhuizen, "De raadselachtige παρθένοι in 1 Kor. 7 : 36-38." *TS*, 24 (1906), 185-202.

1203. Franz Fahnenbruch, "Zu 1 Kor. 7, 36-38," *BibZ*, 12 (1914), 391-401.

1204. Franz Herklotz, "Zu 1 Kor. 7, 36 ff.," *BibZ*, 14 (1916-1917), 344-345.

1205. Eric Bishop, "1 Cor. 7 : 36-38," *CBQ*, 10 (1948), 458.

1206. Richard Kugelman, "1 Cor. 7 : 36-38," *CBQ*, 10 (1948), 63-71.

1207. W. F. Beck, "Brief Studies: I Corinthians 7 : 36-38," *CTM*, 25 (1954), 370-372.

1208. J. Leal, " 'Super virgine sua' (I C. 7, 37)," *VD*, 35 (1957), 97-102.

1209. J. M. Hantz, "A Meditation on 1 Cor. 8 : 1," *LCR*, 39 (1920), 488-497.

1210. Walter Lock, "1 Corinthians 8 : 1-9; a Suggestion," *Exp*, 5th series, 6 (1897), 65-74.

1211. B. Wambacq, "Quid S. Paulus de usu carnium docuerit (1 Cor. 8, 10; Rom. 14)," *VD*, 19 (1939), 18-21, 60-64.

1212. W. Arndt, "The Meaning of 1 Cor. 9 : 9, 10," *CTM*, 3 (1932), 329-335.

1213. Georges Didier, "Le salaire du désintéressement (I Cor. ix, 14-27)," *RSR*, 43 (1955), 228-251.

1214. H. Chadwick, " 'All Things to All Men' (I Cor. ix. 22)," *NTSt*, 1 (1955), 261-295.

1215. Florentinus Ogara, " 'Bibebant . . . de spiritali consequente eos petra,' " *VD*, 16 (1936), 33-40 [I Cor. 9 : 24-10 : 5].

1216. B. B. Warfield, "Paul's Buffeting his Body," *ET*, 31 (1919-1920), 520-521 [I Cor. 9 : 26-27].

1217. D. R. Fotheringham, " 'I Buffet my Body,' " *ET*, 34 (1922-1923), 140 [I Cor. 9 : 27].

1218. H. R. Moxley, " 'I Buffet my Body,' " *ET*, 34 (1922-1923), 235 [1 Cor. 9 : 27].

1219. G. Schlaeger, "Kritische Bemerkungen zu 1 Korinther 10, besonders zur Erwaehnung des Abendmahls," *TT*, 47 (1913), 483-490.

1220. J. Hulsebos, "I Cor. 10 : 1-6," *GTT*, 1 (1900), 52-55.

1221. Gustave Martelet, "Sacrements, figures et exhortation en I Cor. X, 1-11," *RSR*, 44 (1956), 323-359, 515-559.

1222. John Murray, "Christian Baptism," *WTJ*, 13 (1950-1951), 128-129 [I Cor. 10 : 2].

1223. G. Gander, "I Cor. 10.2 parle-t-il du baptême?" *RHPR*, 37 (1957), 97-102.

1224. J. Dalmer, "Bemerkungen zu 1 Kor. 10, 3.4 und Eph. 4, 8-10," *TSK*, 63 (1890), 569-592.

1225. S. R. Driver, "Notes on Three Passages in St. Paul's Epistles," *Exp*, 3rd series, 9 (1889), 15-23 [I Cor. 10 : 4; Gal. 3 : 16; Eph. 4 : 8].

1226. E. Hampden-Cook, " 'The Rock was Christ' (1 Cor. 10 : 4)," *ET*, 18 (1906-1907), 142.

1227. E. E. Ellis, "A Note on First Corinthians 10 : 4," *JBL*, 76 (1957), 553-56.

1228. Florentinus Ogara, " 'Haec . . . in figura contingebant illis': Notae in I Cor. 10, 6-13," *VD*, 15 (1935), 227-232.

1229. R. N. Young, "Requests and Replies," *ET*, 2 (1890-1891), 43-44 [I Cor. 10 : 9].

1230. R. Macpherson, "τὰ τέλη τῶν αἰώνων, I Corinthians 10 : 11," *ET*, 55 (1943-1944), 222.

1231. M. M. Bogle, "τὰ τέλη τῶν αἰώνων, I Corinthians 10 : 11, a Suggestion," *ET*, 67 (1955-1956), 246-247.

1232. R. J. Foster, "The Meaning of I Cor. 10, 13," *Scr*, 2 (1947), 45.

1233. R. Kern, "Die Auffassung des heiligen Abendmahls bei Paulus nach I Kor. 10, 14 ff. und 11, 23 ff.," *TSK*, 75 (1902), 555-596.

1234. L. van den Eetenbeemt, " 'Calix benedictionis . . . nonne communicatio sanguinis Christi est ?' (I Cor. 10, 16)," *VD*, 4 (1924), 178-182.

1235. Edwin Johnson, "The Table of Demons," *Exp*, 2nd series, 8 (1884), 241-250 [I Cor. 10 : 21].

1236. C. Lindeboom, "De drinkbeker en de tafel des Heeren, en de drinkbeker en de tafel der duivelen, of de onvereenigbaarheid van Avondmaalsviering en werelddienst," *GTT*, 6 (1905), 137-139, 152-153 [I Cor. 10 : 21].

1237. Eduard Lohse, "Zu I Cor. 10, 26.31," *ZNW*, 47 (1956), 277-280.

1238. S. T. Lowrie, "1 Corinthians XI and the Ordination of Women as Ruling Elders," *PTR*, 19 (1921), 113-130.

1239. Othoniel Motta, "The Question of the Unveiled Woman (I Cor. 11 : 2-16)," *ET*, 44 (1932-1933), 139-141.

1240. Stefan Lösch, "Christliche Frauen in Corinth," *TQ*, 127 (1947), 216-261 [I Cor. 11 : 2-16].

1241. F. C. Synge, "Studies in Texts — I Cor. 11 : 2-16," *Th*, 56 (1953), 143.

1242. T. Gallus, " 'Non est creatus vir propter mulierem, sed mulier propter virum' (I Cor. 11, 9)," *VD*, 22 (1942), 141-151.

1243. [K. R.] Hagenbach, "Über die ἐξουσία I Cor. 11, 10," *TSK*, 1 (1828), 401-402.

1244. Dr. Lücke, "Einige Bemerkungen gegen Herrn Prof. Hagenbach's Erklärung der ἐξουσία I Kor. xi, 10," *TSK*, 1 (1828), 568-572.

1245. F. Düsterdieck, "Ein feiner Zug paulinischer Mystik," *TSK*, 36 (1863), 707-711 [I Cor. 11 : 10].

1246. J. A. Beet, "Because of the Angels," *Exp*, 1st series, 11 (1880), 20-33 [I Cor. 11 : 10].

1247. A. Roberts, "Power on the Head," *Exp*, 4th series, 10 (1894), 139-149 [I Cor. 11 : 10].

1248. E. E. Kellett, "A Note on 'Power on the Head,' " *ET*, 23 (1910-1911), 39 [I Cor. 11 : 10].

1249. P. Rose, " 'Power on the Head,' " *ET*, 23 (1911-1912), 183-184 [I Cor. 11 : 10].

1250. [F.] Herklotz, "Zu I Kor. 11, 10," *BibZ*, 10 (1912), 154.

1251. R. Perdelwitz, "Die ἐξουσία auf dem Haupt der Frau, I Kor. 11, 10," *TSK*, 86 (1913), 611-613.

1252. Dr. Jirku, "Die 'Macht' auf dem Haupte (I Kor. 11, 10)," *NKZ*, 32 (1921), 710-711.

1253. Dr. Bornhäuser, "Um der Engel willen, I Kor. 11, 10," *NKZ*, 41 (1930), 475-504.

1254. W. Foerster, "Zu I Cor 11, 10," *ZNW*, 30 (1931), 185-186.

1255. S. Mezzacasa, " 'Propter angelos' (I Cor. 11, 10)," *VD*, 11 (1931), 39-42.

1256. K., "Miscellanea," *CTM*, 3 (1932), 213-214 [I Cor. 11 : 10].

1257. J. A. Fitzmyer, "A Feature of Qumrân Angelology and the Angels of I Cor. xi. 10," *NTSt*, 4 (1957), 48-58.

1258. M. Stuart, "The Lord's Supper in the Corinthian Church," *BS*, (1843), 499-532 [I Cor. 11 : 17-34].

1259. W. K. L. Clarke, "Studies in Texts: I Cor. 11 : 20-21," *Th*, 7 (1923), 283-284.

1260. R. E. Gosse, "The Lord's Supper in First Corinthians," *CJRT*, 9 (1932), 292-297 [I Cor. 11 : 20 ff.].

1261. John Massie, "I Have Received of the Lord," *Exp*, 3rd series, 2 (1885), 206-211 [I Cor. 11 : 23].

1262. E. Bröse, "Die Präposition ἀπό, I Kor. 11, 23," *TSK*, 71 (1898), 351-360.

1263. A. N. Bogle, "I Corinthians 11 : 23-34," *ET*, 12 (1900-1901), 479.

1264. L. H. Bunn, "Symbol and Sacrament," *ET*, 53 (1941-1942), 149-150 [I Cor. 11 : 23-25].

1265. M. Goguel, "La relation du dernier repas de Jésus dans I Cor. 11, et la tradition historique chez l'apôtre Paul," *RHPR*, 10 (1930), 61-89 [I Cor. 11 : 23-26].

1266. T. A. Burkill, "The Last Supper," *Num*, 3 (1956), 161-177 [I Cor. 11 : 23-26].

1267. J. de Zwaan, "Verba sacramenti in Paulo ad Corinthios I, cap. xi : 24," *Mn*, N.S., 48 (1920), 321-323.

1268. U. Z. Rule, "Studies in Texts," *Th*, 19 (1929), 337-338 [I Cor. 11 : 24].

1269. K. Goetz, "Das vorausweisende Demonstrativum in Lc 22, 19-20 und I Cor 11, 24," *ZNW*, 38 (1939), 188-190.

1270. J. M. M'Queen, "Note on I Corinthians 11 : 24, 25," *ET*, 44 (1932-1933), 384.

1271. F. X. Porporato, " 'Hoc facite in meam commemorationem' (Lc. 22, 19; I Cor. 11, 24.25)," *VD*, 13 (1933), 264-270.

1272. A. H. Blom, "Aanteekeningen op eenige plaatsen in de brieven van Paulus," *TT*, 13 (1879), 358-364 [I Cor. 11 : 25; Gal 2 : 11, 13; 3 : 16, 20].

1273. Douglas Jones, "'Ανάμνησις in the LXX and the Interpretation of I Cor. xi. 25," *JTS*, 6 (1955), 183-191.

1274. B. Hennen, "Ordines sacri. Ein Deutungsversuch zu 1 Cor. 12, 1-31 und Röm. 12, 3-8," *TQ*, 119 (1938), 427-469.

1275. Guy de Broglie, "Le texte fondamental de saint Paul contre la foi naturelle (I Cor. xii, 3)," *RSR*, 39 (1951-1952), 253-266.

1276. Fr. Bleek, "Über die Gabe des γλώσσαις λαλεῖν in der ersten christlichen Kirche," *TSK*, 2 (1829), 1-79 [I Cor. 12 : 10].

1277. [H.] Olshausen, "Nachträgliche Bemerkungen über das Charisma des γλώσσαις λαλεῖν," *TSK*, 2 (1829), 538-549 [I Cor. 12 : 10].

1278. [Fr.] Bleek, "Noch ein paar Worte über die Gabe des γλώσσαις λαλεῖν," *TSK*, 3 (1830), 45-64 [I Cor. 12 : 10].

1279. Anonymous, "Über die Gabe des γλώσσαις λαλεῖν in der christlichen Gemeinde zu Corinth," *TQ*, 13 (1831), 43-76 [I Cor. 12 : 10].

1280. [H.] Olshausen, "Erklärung über die Bemerkungen des Herrn Prof. Bleek über die Sprachengabe," *TSK*, 4 (1831), 566-580 [I Cor. 12 : 10].

1281. J. G. Davies, "Pentecost and Glossolalia," *JTS*, 3 (1952), 228-231 [I Cor. 12 : 10 ff.].

1282. J. G. Tasker, "Harnack on I Corinthians 13," *ET*, 23 (1911-1912), 259-263.

1283. A. Harnack, "The Apostle Paul's Hymn of Love (I Cor. 13), and its Religious-Historical Significance," *Exp*, 8th series, 3 (1912), 385-408, 481-503.

1284. F. R. M. Hitchcock, "The Structure of St. Paul's Hymn of Love," *ET*, 34 (1922-1923), 488-492 [I Cor. 13].

1285. E. Lehmann und A. Fridrichsen, "I Kor. 13. Eine christlich-stoische Diatribe," *TSK*, 94 (1922), 55-95.

1286. F. R. Tennant, "Faith, Hope, and Knowledge in 1 Corinthians 13," *Exp*, 9th series, 2 (1924), 108-128.

1287. Pr. Dovydaitis, "Kuri yra viso I Cor. 13-jo shyrians problema?" Σ, 6 (1929), 215-216.

1288. A. Vitti, "Excellentior via: caritas (I Cor. 13)," *VD*, 9 (1929), 43-52.

1289. N. W. DeWitt, "Notes on I Cor. 13," *CJRT*, 7 (1930), 216-219.

1290. N. W. Lund, "The Literary Structure of Paul's Hymn to Love," *JBL*, 50 (1931), 266-297 [I Cor. 13].

1291. F. R. M. Hitchcock, "St. Paul's Hymn of Love," *Th*, 26 (1933), 65-75 [I Cor. 13].

1292. N. A. Dahl, "Apostelen Paulus' høisang om kjaerligheten," *NTT*, 37 (1936), 1-36 [I Cor. 13].

1293. R. Kroner, "A Meditation on 1 Cor. XIII," *ATR*, 30 (1948), 216-218.

1294. Allan Barr, "Love in the Church, a Study of First Corinthians, chapter 13," *SJT*, 3 (1950), 416-425.

1295. I. J. Martin, 3rd, "I Corinthians 13 Interpreted by its Context," *JBR*, 18 (1950), 101-105.

1296. Harald Riesenfeld, "Note bibliographique sur I Cor. XIII," *Nunt*, 6 (1952), cols. 47-48.

1297. James Brennan, "The Exegesis of 1 Cor. 13," *ITQ*, 21 (1954), 270-278.

1298. Pr. Dovydaitis, "Kaip suprast ir išverst κύμβαλον ἀλαλάζον (cymbalum tinniens) 1 Cor. 13, 1," Σ, 6 (1929), 212-215.

1299. E. Preuschen, " 'Und liesse meinen Leib brennen' 1 Kor. 13, 3," *ZNW*, 16 (1915), 127-138.

1300. J. H. Michael, "The Gift of Tongues at Corinth," *Exp*, 7th series, 4 (1907), 252-266 [I Cor. 13 : 8; 12 : 10,28; 14 : 6, 14].

1301. E. Preuschen, "Das Rätselwort im Spiegel 1 Cor. 13, 12," *ZNW*, 1 (1900), 180-181.

1302. S. E. Bassett, "I Cor. 13 : 12, βλέπομεν γὰρ ἄρτι δι' ἐσόπτρου ἐν αἰνίγματι," *JBL*, 47 (1928), 232-236.

1303. J. Beumer, " 'Tunc . . . cognoscum, sicut et cognitus sum' (I Cor. 13, 12)," *VD*, 22 (1942), 166-173.

1304. A. S. Perry, "I Corinthians 13 : 12a: βλέπομεν γὰρ ἄρτι δι' ἐσόπτρου ἐν αἰνίγματι," *ET*, 58 (1946-1947), 279.

1305. Henry Wace, "The Supremacy of Love," *Exp*, 2nd series, 1 (1881), 62-74 [I Cor. 13 : 13].

1306. Caldemeyer, "1 Kor. 13, 13," *TSK*, 69 (1896), 114-128.

1307. W. K. L. Clarke, "Studies in Texts: I Cor. 13 : 13," *Th*, 6 (1923), 222-223.

1308. R. J. Drummond, "The Greatest of These is — What ?" *EQ*, 23 (1951), 5-7 [I Cor. 13 : 13b].

1309. H. Pope, "Prophecy and Prophets in New Testament Times," *ITQ*, 7 (1912), 383-400 [I Cor. 14 : 1].

1310. v. d. W. te G., "Bidden met den geest en met het verstand; 1 Cor. 14 : 15a," *GTT*, 5 (1904), 12-14.

1311. L. Hirtzel, "Wer sind die ἰδιῶται ἢ ἄπιστοι 1 Kor. 14, 23.24?" *TSK*, 13 (1840), 120-127.

1312. M. Ulrich, "Nachtrag über die ἰδιῶται ἢ ἄπιστοι 1 Kor. XIV, 23.24," *TSK*, 16 (1843), 415-422.

1313. Joh. de Groot, "1 Kor. 14 : 35b," *TS*, 32 (1914), 245-247.

1314. W. M. L. de Wette, "Doctrine of the Resurrection of the Dead," *BS*, 6 (1849), 26-47 [I Cor. 15].

1315. J. A. Beet, "The Corinthian Saducees," *Exp*, 2nd series, 1 (1881), 33-43, 147-157 [1 Cor. 15].

1316. George Matheson, "No-Resurrection Impossible," *Exp*, 2nd series, 8 (1884), 128-138 [1 Cor. 15].

1317. J. W. Nott, "'Εγήγερται in I Cor. XV," *JBL* (June and December, 188), 41.

1318. W. Milligan, "The Resurrection of the Dead," *Exp*, 4th series, 1 (1890), 161-176; 2 (1890), 35-50, 101-115, 275-287; 4 (1891), 15-33, 191-207 [I Cor. 15].

1319. J. H. Bernard, "St. Paul's Doctrine of the Resurrection; a Study of 1 Cor. 15," *Exp*, 7th series, 5 (1908), 403-416, 491-504.

1320. T. H. Bindley, "A Study in 1 Cor. 15," *Exp*, 8th series, 7 (1914), 174-183.

1321. Canon Bindley, "A Study in 1 Corinthians 15," *ET*, 41 (1929-1930), 503-507.

1322. Ernst Bammel, "Herkunft und Funktion der Traditions-elemente in 1 Kor. 15 : 1-11," *TZ*, 11 (1955), 401-419.

1323. A. E. Morris, "A Note on 1 Corinthians 15 : 3-4," *ET*, 45 (1933-1934), 43-44.

1324. Paul Winter, "1 Corinthians XV, 3b-7," *NT*, 2 (1957), 142-150.

1325. B. M. Metzger, "A Suggestion Concerning the Meaning of 1 Cor. xv. 4b," *JTS*, N.S. 8 (L957), 118-123.

1326. R. E. Lee, "I Cor. 15 : 5-8," *ET*, 27 (1915-1916), 383-384.

1327. B. B. Warfield, "The Appearance of the Risen Jesus to All the Apostles," *Exp*, 3rd series, 1 (1885), 474-475 [I Cor. 15 : 7].

1328. Prebendary Huxtable, "The Sense in Which St. Paul Calls Himself an *Ectroma* — 1 Corinthians 15 : 8," *Exp*, 2nd series, 3 (1882), 268-280, 364-380.

1329. J. Holl, "Die Lehre von der Auferstehung des Fleisches nach 1 Cor. 15 : 13-53," *TQ*, 65 (1883), 234-270.

1330. J. C. Bowmer, "A Note on ἀποθνήσκω and κοιμάω in I Co-rinthians 15 : 20, 22," *ET*, 53 (1941-1942), 355-356.

1331. J. M. Bover, "Christus novus Adam (I Cor. 15, 20-23)," *VD*, 4 (1924), 299-305.

1332. R. D. Culver, "A Neglected Millennial Passage from St. Paul," *BS*, 113 (1956), 141-152 [I Cor. 15 : 20-24].

1333. Wilibald Grimm, "Über die Stelle 1 Kor. 15, 20-28," *ZWT*, 16 (1873), 380-410.

1334. A. C. Kendrick, "First Corinthians 15 : 20-28," *BS*, 47 (1890), 68-83.

1335. Anonymous, "Exposition of I Cor. 15 : 22," *LQ*, 2 (1872), 448-456.

1336. M. D., "A Misused Scripture Text," *ET*, 8 (1896-1897), 567-568 [I Cor. 15 : 22].

1337. J. W. Black, "1 Corinthians 15 : 22," *ET*, 9 (1897-1898), 382-383.

1338. C. Schmitt, "Versuch einer Erklärung von 1 Cor. xv, 22-28," *TQ*, 58 (1876), 60-84.

1339. R. Eckermann, "Exegetische Behandlung des Abschnitts I Kor. 15, 22-28," *CTM*, 3 (1932), 578-593.

1340. F. L. H. Millara, "Brevia — 1 Cor. 15 : 29," *Exp*, 4th series, 1 (1890), 238-240.

1341. E. Rust, "Baptized for the Dead," *ET*, 5 (1893-1894), 525-526 [I Cor. 15 : 29].

1342. P. Dürfelen. "Die Taufe für die Toten, 1 Kor. 15,29," *TSK*, 76 (1903), 291-238.

1343. H. Preisker, „Die Vicariatstaufe I C 15.29 — ein eschatologischer, nicht sakramentaler Brauch," *ZNW* 23 (1924), 298-304.

1344. [Th.] E[ngelder], "An Exegetical Curiosity," *CTM*, 3 (1932), 622-624 [1 Cor. 15 : 29].

1345. A. B. Oliver, "Why Are they Baptized for the Dead?" *RE*, 34 (1937), 48-53 [I Cor. 15 : 29].

1346. K. van Dijk, "I Cor. 15 : 29," *GTT*, 40 (1939), 213-223.

1347. P. J. Heawood, "Baptism for the Dead," *ET*, 54 (1942-1943), 330 [I Cor. 15 : 29].

1348. H. V. Martin, "Baptism for the Dead," *ET*, 54 (1942-1943), 192-193 [I Cor. 15 : 29].

1349. F. F. Bruce, "Baptism for the Dead," *ET*, 55 (1943-1944), 110-111 [I Cor. 15 : 29].

1350. P. J. Heawood, "Baptism for the Dead," *ET*, 55 (1943-1944), 278 [I Cor. 15 : 29].

1351. J. R. Thomson, "Baptism for the Dead," *ET*, 55 (1943-1944), 54 [I Cor. 15 : 29].

1352. C. S. C. Williams, "Baptism for the Dead," *ET*, 55 (1943-1944), 110 [I Cor. 15 : 29].

1353. B. M. Foschini, " 'Those Who are Baptized for the Dead,' I Cor. 15 : 29; An Exegetical Historical Dissertation," *CBQ*, 12 (1950), 260-276, 379-388; 13 (1951), 46-78, 172-198, 276-283.

1354. A. G. Moseley, "Baptized for the Dead," *RE*, 49 (1952), 57-61 [I Cor. 15 : 29].

1355. Otto Kuss, "Zur Frage einer vorpaulinischen Todestaufe," *MTZ*, 4 (1953), 1-17 [I Cor. 15 : 29].

1356. Maria Raeder, "Vikariatstaufe in I Cor. 15, 29?" *ZNW*, 46 (1955), 258-261.

1357. Anonymous, "1 Kor. 15, 29 und 30," *TSK* 33 (1860) 135-141.
1358. J. M. S. Baljon, "I Cor. 15 : 29-30," *TS*, 8 (1890), 208-212.
1359. S. Hoekstra, "Proeve van verklaring van 1 Cor. XV: 29, 30," *TT*, 24 (1890), 135-142.
1360. Arthur Carr, "1 Corinthians 15 : 29-34; an Argument and an Appeal," *Exp*, 6th series, 4 (1901), 185-193.
1361. C. P. Coffin, "The Meaning of 1 Cor. 15 : 32," *JBL*, 43 (1924), 172-176.
1362. J. W. Hunkin, "I Corinthians 15 : 32," *ET*, 39 (1927-1928), 281-282.
1363. Edward Hitchcock, "Exegesis of 1 Cor. 15 : 35-44, as illustrated by Natural History and Chemistry," *BS*, 17 (1860), 303-312.
1364. William Clifford, "1 Cor. 15 : 42," *ET*, 28 (1916-1917), 326.
1365. C. M. Mead, "A Query respecting the Translation of I Cor. xv. 42-44," *JBL*, 14 (1895), 89-91.
1366. Churchill Babington, "St. Paul and Philo Judaeus," *JCSP*, 1 (1854), 47-51 [I Cor. 15 : 44-47].
1367. A. H. Blom, "Verklaring van een paar loci Paulini," *TT*, 15 (1881), 628-634 [I Cor. 15 : 45 and II Cor. 10 : 7].
1368. M. D., "Misused Scripture Texts," *ET*, 9 (1897-1898), 239-240 [I Cor. 15 : 47].
1369. [A.] Rohling, "Die Überlebenden 1 Korinth. 15, 51," *TQ*, 81 (1899), 580-591.
1370. J. H. Burn, "I Corinthians 15 : 51," *ET*, 37 (1925-1926), 236-237.
1371. Philippus Oppenheim, "I Kor. 15, 51," *TQ*, 112 (1931), 92-135.
1372. D. R. Goodwin, "Πάντες οὐ and ἡμεῖς in I Cor. xv. 51 and 52," *JBL* (June and December, 1888), 121-125.
1373. A. Vitti, "Animadversiones in 1 Cor. 16, 1-13," *VD*, 6 (1926), 202-210.
1374. L. Hertling, "I Kor. 16, 15 und I Clem. 42," *B*, 20 (1939), 276-283.
1375. J. A. T. Robinson, "Traces of a Liturgical Sequence in 1 Cor. 16 : 20-24," *JTS*, 4 (1953), 38-41.
1376. C. Spicq, "Comment comprendre φιλεῖν dans I Cor. xvi, 22?" *NT*, 1 (1956), 200-204.

On 1 Cor. 1 : 1, see number 743; 2 : 6-8, number 2546; 3 : 9,

number 801; 8 : 6, number 2557; 11 : 23 ff., numbers 2904 ff.;
12 : 1-31, number 1011; 12 :27, number 2627; 13 : 7, number
666; 14 : 40, number 2260; and 15 : 3-8, number 2831.

4. The Second Epistle to the Corinthians

a. *Textual Criticism*

1377. J. M. S. Baljon, "Iets over den tekst van den tweeden brief
van Paulus aan de Korinthiërs (naar aanleiding van Georg
Heinrici, *Das zweite Sendschreiben des Ap. P. an die Korinthier
erklärt*)," *TT*, 21 (1887), 432-440.
1378. John Hennig, "The Measure of Man: A Study of 2 Cor.
10 : 12," *CBQ*, 8 (1946), 332-343.

b. *Historical and Literary Criticism*

1379. W. Beyschlag, "Zur Streitfrage über die Paulusgegner des
zweiten Korintherbriefs," *TSK*, 44 (1871), 635-676.
1380. A. H. Franke, "2 Kor. 6, 14-7, 1 und der erste Brief des
Paulus an die korinthische Gemeinde, 1 Kor. 5, 9-13," *TSK*,
57 (1884), 544-553.
1381. D. C. Thijm, "De tweede Brief aan de Corinthiërs en de
'Verisimilia' van Prof. A. Pierson en Prof. S. A. Naber,"
TS, 5 (1887), 95-141, 526-566.
1382. R. Drescher, "Der zweite Korintherbrief und die Vorgänge
in Korinth seit Abfassung des ersten Korintherbriefs," *TSK*,
70 (1897), 43-111.
1383. J. H. Kennedy, "Are there Two Epistles in 2 Corinthians?"
Exp, 5th series, 6 (1897), 231-238, 285-304.
1384. M. R. Vincent, "The Composition of Second Corinthians,"
ET, 9 (1897-1898), 42-44.
1385. N. J. D. White, "Are there Two Epistles in 2 Corinthians?
A Reply," *Exp*, 5th series, 7 (1898), 113-123.
1386. G. T. Purves, "The Unity of Second Corinthians," *USR*, 11
(1899-1900), 233-244.
1387. Dawson Walker, "The Second Epistle to the Corinthians,"
RE, 5 (1908), 373-396.
1388. Allan Menzies, "The Integrity of 2 Corinthians," *Exp*, 8th
series, 6 (1913), 366-375.
1389. R. A. Beardslee, "Second Corinthians," *BR*, 2 (1918),
89-111.

1390. Hugh Pope, "The Second Epistle to the Corinthians," *ITQ*, 15 (1920), 43-52.
1391. R. V. G. Tasker, "The Unity of 2 Corinthians," *ET*, 47 (1935-1936), 55-58.
1392. J. T. Dean, "The Great Digression. 2 Corinthians 2 : 14-7 : 4," *ET*, 50 (1938-1939), 86-89.
1393. Elis Malmeström, " 'Vi bedja å Kristi vögnar: låten försona eder med Gud,' " *STK*, 17 (1941), 197-205.

c. *Theological Studies*

1394. F. Godet, "The Second Epistle to the Corinthians," *Exp*, 3rd series, 2 (1885), 370-380, 415-425.
1395. G. A. J. Ross, "The Epistle of the Torn Heart; a Note on 2 Corinthians," *Exp*, 8th series, 25 (1923), 130-133.
1396. James Reid, "The Message of the Epistles; Second Corinthians," *ET*, 44 (1932-1933), 535-538.
1397. R. V. G. Tasker, "St. Paul and the Earthly Life of Jesus; a Study in the Second Epistle to the Corinthians," *ET*, 46 (1934-1935), 557-562.
    See also numbers 490, 491, and 494.

d. *Exegesis of Individual Passages*

1398. B. B. Warfield, "Some Difficult Passages in the First Chapter of Second Corinthians," *JBL* (December, 1886), 27-39.
1399. A. L. Tritton, "The Greeting in 2 Corinthians," *ET*, 23 (1911-1912), 181.
1400. F. V. Filson, " 'The God of All Comfort,' II Corinthians 1 : 3-7," *TTod*, 8 (1951-1952), 498-501.
1401. V. Bartling, "God's Triumphant Captive, Christ's Aroma for God (2 Cor. 2 : 12-17)," *CTM*, 22 (1951), 883-894.
1402. v. d. W. te G., "Eene dreivoudige tegenstelling. 2 Cor. 2 : 16-18," *GTT*, 6 (1905), 111-112, 131-134.
1403. v. d. W. te G., "De Gemeente een brief van Christus," *GTT*, 5 (1904), 81-89, 119-123, 141-144, 153-156, 177-184 [II Cor. 3].
1404. Johannes Goettsberger, "Die Hülle des Moses nach Ex 34 und 2 Kor 3," *BibZ*, 16 (1922-1924), 1-17.
1405. K. Prümm, "Der Abschnitt über die Doxa des Apostolats 2 Kor. 3, 1-4, 6 in der Deutung des hl. Johannes Chrysostomus," *B*, 30 (1949), 161-196, 377-400.

1406. H. Liese, "De Spiritu et littera (2 Cor. 3, 4-9)," VD, 11 (1931), 225-229.
1407. Florentinus Ogara, " 'Fiduciam talem habemus per Christum ad Deum' 2 Cor. 3, 4-11," *VD*, 18 (1938), 227-234.
1408. G. G. Findlay, "The Ministry of Reconciliation; a Study in 2 Cor. 3 : 5," *Exp*, 8th series, 12 (1916), 81-104.
1409. J. H. Bernard, "The Letter and the Spirit," *ET*, 5 (1893-1894), 302-307 [II Cor. 3 : 6].
1410. M. D., "A Misused Scripture Text," *ET*, 11 (1899-1900), 336 [II Cor. 3 : 6].
1411. Bernardin Schneider, "The Meaning of Saint Paul's Antithesis, 'The Letter and the Spirit,' " *CBQ*, 15 (1953), 163-207 [II Cor. 3 : 6].
1412. Boaz Cohen, "Note on Letter and Spirit in the New Testament," *HTR*, 47 (1954), 197-203 [II Cor. 3 : 6].
1413. A. van Veldhuizen, "2 Kor. 3 : 15 vv," *TS*, 29 (1911), 440-443.
1414. J. B. Nisius, "Zur Erklärung von 2 Kor. 3, 16 ff.," *ZKT*, 40 (1916), 617-675.
1415. K. Prümm, "Die katholische Auslegung von 2 Kor. 3, 17a in den letzten vier Jahrzehnten nach ihren Hauptrichtungen," *B*, 31 (1950), 316-345, 459-482; 32 (1951), 1-24.
1416. K. Prümm, "Israels Kehr zum Geist (2 Kor. 3 : 17a)," *ZKT*, 72 (1950), 385-442.
1417. L. Krummel, "Exegetische und dogmatische Erörterung der Stelle 2 Kor. 3, 17: der Herr ist der Geist," *TSK*, 32 (1859), 39-100.
1418. H. H. B. Ayles, "2 Corinthians 3 : 17," *ET*, 21 (1909-1910), 90-91.
1419. H. M. Hughes, "2 Cor. 3 : 17: ὁ δὲ κύριος τὸ πνεῦμα ἐστιν," *ET*, 45 (1933-1934), 235-236.
1420. Cuthbertus Lattey, " 'Dominus autem Spiritus est' (II Cor. 3, 17)," *VD*, 20 (1940), 187-189.
1421. S. Lyonnet, "S. Cyrille d'Alexandrie et 2 Cor. 3, 17," *B*, 32 (1951), 25-31.
1422. Prosper Grech, "2 Corinthians 3, 17 and the Pauline Doctrine of Conversion to the Holy Spirit," *CBQ* 17 (1955), 420-437.
1423. P. Galletto, " 'Dominus autem Spiritus est' (II Cor. 3, 17)," *RivB*, 5 (1957), 254-281.
1424. Gerard Ball, "Studies in Texts; 2 Cor. 3 : 17-18," *Th*, 6 (1923), 166-169.

1425. D. R. Griffiths, " 'The Lord is the Spirit' (2 Corinthians 3 : 17, 18)," *ET*, 55 (1943-1944), 81-83.
1426. P. Corssen, "Paulus und Porphyrios. (Zur Erklärung von 2 Kor. 3, 18)," *ZNW*, 19 (1919-1920), 2-11.
1427. Rendel Harris, "Enoch and 2 Corinthians," *ET*, 33 (1921-1922), 423-424 [II Cor. 3 : 18].
1428. K. G. Idema, "Ons spiegelend in de heerlijkheid des Heeren," *GTT*, 47 (1947), 140-144 [II Cor. 3 : 18].
1429. J. Dupont, "Le chrétien, miroir de la glorie divine, d'après II Cor. 3, 18," *RB*, 56 (1949), 392-411.
1430. James Iverach, "The Ministry of Light," *Exp*, 4th series, 3 (1891), 92-103 [II Cor. 4 : 1-6].
1431. Samuel Davies, "Remarks on the Second Epistle to the Corinthians 4 : 3, 4," *BS*, 25 (1868), 23-30.
1432. J. A. Bain, "2 Cor. 4 : 3-4," *ET*, 18 (1906-1907), 380.
1433. Hildebrand Höpfl, "2 Cor. 4 : 3, 4," *ET*, 18 (1906-1907), 428.
1434. W. Müllensiefen, "Satan der Θεὸς τοῦ αἰῶνος τούτου, 2 Kor. 4, 4?" *TSK*, 95 (1923-1924), 295-298.
1435. F. Zorell, " 'Deus huius saeculi' (2 Cor. 4, 4)," *VD*, 8 (1928), 54-57.
1436. v. d. W. te G., "Predikers niet van onszelven, naar van Christus Jezus, en in Zijne gemeenschap; 2 Cor. 4 : 4-10," *GTT*, 6 (1905), 57-59, 76-79.
1437. Claude Chavasse, "Studies in Texts — 2 Cor. 4 : 7," *Th*, 54 (1951), 99-100.
1438. v. d. W. te G., "Christus' kracht in èn door het lijden der Zijnen verheerlijkt; 2 Cor. 4 : 11, 12," *GTT*, 6 (1905), 105-108.
1439. M. J. Dahood, "Two Pauline Quotations from the Old Testament," *CBQ*, 17 (1955), 19-24 [II Cor. 4 : 13].
1440. v. d. W. te G., "De kracht des geloofs, 2 Cor. 4 : 13-15," *GTT*, 6 (1905), 108-111.
1441. C. Lindeboom, "De uitwendige Mensch en de inwendige Mensch, 2 Cor. 4 : 16b," *GTT*, 7 (1906), 111-114.
1442. J. B. Miles, "The Resurrection of the Body," *BS*, 26 (1869), 593-609 [II Cor. 5 : 1].
1443. v. d. W. te G., "Des christens hoop voor de toekomst, 2 Cor. 5 : 1-3," *GTT*, 6 (1905), 134-137.
1444. L. Wetzel, "Über 2 Kor. 5, 1-4," *TSK*, 59 (1886), 303-333.
1445. F. W. Grosheide, "Enkele opmerkingen over 2 Kor. 5 : 1-4," *TS*, 27 (1909), 253-288.

1446. S. T. Lowrie, "An Exegesis of 2 Corinthians v. 1-5," *PTR*, 1 (1903), 51-61.

1447. L. Brun, "Zur Auslegung von II Cor. 5, 1-10," *ZNW*, 28 (1929), 207-229.

1448. A. Feuillet, "La demeure céleste et la destinée des chrétiens (II Cor. V, 1-10)," *RSR*, 44 (1956), 161-192, 360-402.

1449. R. F. Hettlinger, "2 Corinthians 5 : 1-10," *SJT*, 10 (1957), 174-194.

1450. v. d. W. te G., "Het zuchten in dezen tabernakel, 2 Cor. 5 : 4-10," *GTT*, 6 (1905), 153-159, 173-174.

1451. Samuel Cox, "The Earnest of the Spirit," *Exp*, 2nd series, 7 (1884), 416-426 [II Cor. 5 : 5].

1452. T. H. Rice, "The Ministry of Reconciliation," *USR*, 20 (1908-1909), 1-6 [II Cor. 5 : 8].

1453. Carpus, "Heaven," *Exp*, 1st series, 1 (1875), 267-279 [2 Cor. 5 : 10].

1454. T. C. Johnson, "The Judgment as Disclosed in 2 Cor. 5 : 10," *USR*, 28 (1916-1917), 1-13.

1455. B. v. d. Werff, "Paulus' ijver in den arbeid zijner bediening (2 Cor. V, 11-21)," *GTT*, 7 (1906), 14-16, 30-34.

1456. W. S. C. Otis, "Exposition of 2 Cor. 5 : 14," *BS*, 27 (1870), 545-564.

1457. M. S. Enslin, "The Constraint of Christ," *CQ*, 11 (1934), 315-322 [2 Cor. 5 : 14].

1458. G. S. Hendry, "ἡ γὰρ ἀγάπη τοῦ Χριστοῦ συνέχει ἡμᾶς — 2 Corinthians 5 : 14," *ET*, 59 (1947-1948), 82.

1459. C. Spicq, "L'étreinte de la Charité (II Cor. V, 14)," *ST*, 8 (1954 [1955]), 123-132.

1460. H. P. Berlage, "2 Cor. 5 : 14-17," *TT*, 32 (1898), 343-362.

1461. H. F. Perry, "Knowing Christ after the Flesh (2 Cor. 5 : 16)," *BW*, 18 (1901), 284-286.

1462. Valentin Weber, "Wann und wie hat Paulus 'Christum nach dem Fleische gekannt' (2 Kor. 5, 16)" *BibZ*, 2 (1904), 178-187.

1463. A. D. Martin, "Knowing Christ κατὰ σάρκα," *ET*, 24 (1912-1913), 334-335 [II Cor. 5 : 16].

1464. A. M. Pope, "Paul's Previous Meeting with Jesus," *Exp*, 8th series, 26 (1923), 38-48 [II Cor. 5 : 16].

1465. F. C. Porter, "Does Paul Claim to have Known the Historical Jesus?" *JBL*, 47 (1928), 257-275 [II Cor. 5 : 16].

1466. S. T. Lowrie, "Exegetical Note on 2 Cor. V. 16, 17," *PTR*, 4 (1906), 236-241.

1467. Andrew Thom, "The Service of the Katallage, I Cor. 5 : 18," *ET*, 4 (1892-1893), 524-526.

1468. Th. Engelder, "Objective Justification," *CTM*, 4 (1933), 507-517, 564-577, 664-675 [II Cor. 5 : 18-20].

1469. F. Forster, " 'Reconcile,' II Cor. 5 : 18-20," *CTM*, 21 (1950), 296-298.

1470. H. P. Berlage, "2 Cor. 5 : 18-21," *TT*, 33 (1899), 319-331.

1471. B. v. d. Werff, "De Bediening der Verzoening, 2 Cor. V, 18-21," *GTT*, 7 (1906), 67-71.

1472. Andrew Thom, "The Law of the Katallage, 2 Cor. 5 : 19," *ET*, 4 (1892-1893), 267-268.

1473. A. M. Williams, "Reconciliation with God," *ET*, 31 (1919-1920), 280-282 [II Cor. 5 : 20].

1474. Dr. Hausleiter, "Die Stelle 2 Kor. 5, 21 in den Predigten Novatians," *NKZ*, 13 (1902), 270-275.

1475. B. v. d. Werff, "Tevergeefs ontvangen Genade, 2 Cor. VI, 1, 2," *GTT*, 7 (1906), 114-116.

1476. Florentinus Ogara, "Dominica I. Quadragesimae (Notae homileticae in 2 Cor. 6, 1-10)," *VD*, 13 (1933), 65-74.

1477. B. v. d. Werff, "Her Beeld van een waar Evangeliedienaar (2 Cor. VI, 3-10)," *GTT*, 7 (1906), 116-121, 139-140.

1478. B. v. d. Werff, "Des dienaars liefde vraagt wederliefde (2 Cor. VI, 11-13)," *GTT*, 7 (1906), 140-144.

1479. B. v. d. Werff, "Geen ander juk met de ongeloovigen aan- trekken (2 Cor. VI, 14-18)," *GTT*, 7 (1906), 142-143, 178-183.

1480. H. J. Schouten, "De Pericope II Cor. 6 : 14-7 : 1," *TS*, 18 (1900), 436-439.

1481. James Moffatt, "2 Corinthians 6 : 14-7 : 1," *ET*, 20 (1908-1909), 428-429.

1482. B. v. d. Werff, "Laat on ons zelven reinigen, 2 Cor. VII," *GTT*, 7 (1906), 183-185.

1483. B. v. d. Werff, "Des Apostels bede om de liefde der Corin- thiërs en de betuiging zijner liefde tot hen, 2 Cor. VII, 2-4," *GTT*, 7 (1906), 185-187.

1484. John Moncure, "Second Corinthians 7 : 8-10," *RE*, 16 (1919), 476-477.

1485. S. Datema, "Wat is de droefheid naar God?" *GTT*, 1 (1900), 85-87 [II Cor. 7 : 10].

1486. B. v. d. Werff, "Paulus' ijver voor en blijdschap over de gemeente (2 Cor. VII, 12-16)," *GTT*, 8 (1907), 261-266.

1487. B. v. d. Werff, "Een treffend voorbeeld van milddadigheid (2 Cor. 8 : 1-5)," *GTT*, 9 (1908), 1-9.

1488. B. v. d. Werff, "Opwekking tot milddadigheid (2 Cor. VIII, 6-15)," *GTT*, 8 (1907), 147-154.

1489. Henri Bois, "Exegetical and Homiletical Notes," *ET*, 4 (1892-1893), 502-504 [II Cor. 8 : 8].

1490. Alexander Ross, "The Grace of Our Lord Jesus Christ," *EQ*, 13 (1941), 219-225 [II Cor. 8 : 9].

1491. B. v. d. Werff, "De ware gelijkheid (2 Cor. VIII, 13-15)," *GTT*, 8 (1907), 187-190.

1492. B. v. d. Werff, "Over de broeders, aan wie het werk der inzameling is toebetrouwd (2 Cor. VIII, 16-24)," *GTT*, 8 (1907), 228-235.

1493. B. v. d. Werff, "Waarom Paulus de drie broeders naar Corinthe heeft gezonden (2 Cor. IX, 1-5)," *GTT*, 8 (1907), 350-354.

1494. H. J. Wicks, "St. Paul's Teaching as to the Rewards of Liberality," *ET*, 29 (1917-1918), 424-425 [II Cor. 9 : 6-11].

1495. Robert Mackintosh, "The Four Perplexing Chapters (2 Cor. 10-13)," *Exp*, 7th series, 6 (1908), 336-344.

1496. Valentin Weber, "Erklärung von 2 Kor. 10, 1-6," *BibZ*, 1 (1903), 64-78.

1497. Prebendary Whitefoord, "The Captivity of the Mind of Christ," *ET*, 6 (1894-1895), 488-490 [II Cor. 10 : 5].

1498. C. Molenaar, "Bij de exegese van II Corinthe 10 : 12-18," *GTT*, 52 (1952), 129-142.

1499. C. Holsten, "Zur Erklärung von II Kor. 11, 4-6," *ZWT*, 16 (1873), 1-56.

1500. J. P. Mozley, "2 Corinthians 11 : 12," *ET*, 42 (1930-1931), 212-214.

1501. A. Vitti, "Signa apostolatus Pauli; Animadversiones in 2 Cor. 11, 19-12, 9," *VD*, 8 (1928), 75-80, 106-110, 176-184.

1502. Florentinus Ogara, " 'Ministri Christi sunt? ut minus sapiens dico: plus ego,' " *VD*,18 (1938), 33-42 [II Cor. 11: 9—12: 9].

1503. C. Holsten, "Über 2 Kor. XI, 22-23," *ZWT*, 17 (1874) 388-406.

1504. Anton Fridrichsen, "Zum Stil des paulinischen Peristasen-katalogs, 2 Cor. 11, 23 ff.," *SO*, 7 (1928), 25-29.

1505. E. Schürer, "Der Ethnarch des Königs Aretas, 2 Kor. 11, 32," *TSK*, 72 (1899), 95-99.

1506. J. H. A. Michelsen, " 't Verhaal van Paulus' vlucht uit Damaskus, 2 Kor. XI : 32,33; XII : 1, 7a, een interpolatie," *TT*, 7 (1873), 421-429.

1507. J. A. Mazzeo, "Dante and the Pauline Modes of Vision," *HTR*, 50 (1957), 275-306 [II Cor. 12 : 2-4].

1508. H. Foschiani, " 'Datus est mihi stimulus' (2 Cor. 12, 7)," *VD*, 5 (1925), 26-29.

1509. Edward Beecher, "Dispensation of Divine Providence toward the Apostle Paul," *BS*, 12 (1855), 499-527 [II Cor. 12 : 7-10].

1510. Carpus, "The Strength of Weakness," *Exp*, 1st series, 3 (1876), 161-184 [II Cor. 12 : 9].

1511. C. S. Ward, "2 Cor. 12 : 9 in the Revised Version," *ET*, 23 (1911-1912), 39.

1512. M. A. N. Rovers, "Is 2 Cor. XII, 12 geïnterpoleerd?" *TT*, 4 (1870), 606-620.

1513. H. A. A. Kennedy, " 'Weakness and Power,' " *ET*, 13 (1901-1902), 349-350 [II Cor. 13 : 3-4].

1514. George Johnston, "2 Corinthians 13 : 8," *ET*, 5 (1893-1894), 68-69.

1515. R. Müllensiefen, "Wie sind 2 Kor. 13, 13 die drei Teile des Segenswunsches inhaltlich auseinanderzuhalten und miteinander zu verbinden?" *TSK*, 72 (1899), 254-266.

On II Cor. 2 : 5-11, see number 1164; 3 : 6, numbers 2726, 2728, 2731, and 2985; 3 : 17, number 2729; 4 : 17, number 527; 5 : 1, number 527; 5 : 1-5, number 2663; 5 : 18, number 558; 6 : 16, number 1158; 10 : 7, number 1367; 10 : 9, number 553.

5. The Epistle to the Galatians

a. *Textual Criticism*

1516. J. J. Prins, "De brief aan de Galatiërs in de Edit. N.T. VIII van Tischendorf," *TT*, 6 (1872), 615-627.

1517. F. Zimmer, "Zur Textkritik des Galaterbriefes," *ZWT*, 24 (1881), 481-493; 25 (1882), 327-343; 26 (1883), 294-308.

1518. M. J. Lagrange, "La Vulgate latine de l'épître aux Galates et le texte grec," *RB*, N.S. 14 (1917), 424-450.

1519. J. M. Bover, "Textus Codicis Claromontani (D) in Epistula ad Galatas," *B*, 12 (1931), 199-218.
1520. B. W. Bacon, "The Reading οἷς οὐδέ in Gal. 2 : 5," *JBL*, 42 (1923), 69-80.
1521. R. M. Spence, "The Diverse Punctuation of Gal. 2 : 20," *ET*, 11 (1899-1900), 381.
1522. W. R. W. Gardner, "Galatians 4 : 31-5 : 1," *ET*, 23 (1911-1912), 330.
See also numbers 503, 657, and 1641.

b. *Historical and Literary Criticism*

1523. M. Ulrich, "Über die Zeit der Abfassung des Galaterbriefes," *TSK*, 9 (1836), 448-465.
1524. J. B. Lightfoot, "On the Style and Character of the Epistle to the Galatians," *JCSP*, 3 (1857), 289-327.
1525. A. Hilgenfeld, "Die Unvereinbarkeit von Gal. 2 mit Apostel-geschichte 15, gegen Hrn. Diaconus E. Rauch in Arnstadt dargethan," *ZWT*, 1 (1858), 317-320.
1526. H. B. Hackett, "Remarks on Renderings of the Common Version (In the Epistle to the Galatians)," *BS*, 19 (1862), 211-225; 22 (1865), 138-149.
1527. W. Grimm, "Über die Nationalität der kleinasiatischen Galater," *TSK*, 49 (1876), 199-221.
1528. A. D. Loman, "Quaestiones Paulinae. Prolegomena. II. Uitgangspunt van het vernieuwde onderzoek: de echtheid van den brief aan de Galatiërs," *TT*, 16 (1882), 163-185.
1529. A. D. Loman, "Quaestiones Paulinae, 2de stuk. Onderzoek naar de echtheid van den brief aan de Galatiërs; 1ste hoofd-stuk: de uitwendige bewijsmiddelen voor en tegen de echt-heid," *TT*, 16 (1882), 302-328.
1530. A. D. Loman, "Quaestiones Paulinae, 3de stuk. De uit-wendige bewijzen voor en tegen de echtheid van den brief aan de Galatiërs," *TT*, 16 (1882), 452-487.
1531. [A. H.] Franke, "Die galatischen Gegner des Apostels Paulus," *TSK*, 56 (1883), 133-153.
1532. A. D. Loman, "Quaestiones Paulinae, 4e stuk. Tweede Vervolg en Slot van het eerste Hoofdstuk, behelzende: De uitwendige bewijzen voor en tegen de echtheid van den brief aan de Galatiërs," *TT*, 17 (1883), 14-51.
1533. J. J. Prins, "Hand. XV en Gal. II," *TT*, 17 (1883), 440-449.

1534. A. Hilgenfeld, "Zur Vorgeschichte des Galaterbriefes," *ZWT*, 27 (1884), 303-343.

1535. B. B. Warfield, "The Date of the Epistle to the Galatians," *JBL* (June and December, 1884), 50-64.

1536. W. C. van Manen, "Bezwaren tegen de echtheid van Paulus' brief aan de Galatiërs," *TT*, 20 (1886), 318-349.

1537. W. C. van Manen, "Marcions brief van Paulus aan de Galatiërs," *TT*, 21 (1887), 382-404, 451-533.

1538. J. J. Prins, "De brief aan de Galatiërs met zich zelven gebracht," *TT*, 21 (1887), 65-91.

1539. G. W. Stemler, "Marcion's doorhalingen in den brief van Paulus aan de Galatiërs," *TS*, 6 (1888), 209-234.

1540. A. H. Franke, "Galaterbrief und Apostelgeschichte," *TSK*, 63 (1890), 659-687.

1541. C. H. van Rhijn, "De Brief aan de Galatiërs en de Handelingen der Apostelen volgens R. Steck," *TS*, 8 (1890), 363-380, 421-449.

1542. H. U. Meyboom, "Aan de Galaten. (Naar aanleiding van geschriften van Baljon, Cramer en Völter)," *TT*, 25 (1891), 241-258.

1543. C. Clemen, "Die Adressaten des Galaterbriefs," *ZWT*, 37 (1894), 396-423.

1544. E. H. Gifford, "The Churches of Galatia — Notes on a Recent Controversy," *Exp*, 4th series, 10 (1894), 1-20.

1545. F. Rendall, "The Galatians of St. Paul and the Date of the Epistle," *Exp*, 4th series, 9 (1894), 254-264.

1546. Oberkonsistorialrat Kühn, "An wen ist der Galaterbrief gerichtet und wann ist er geschrieben?" *NZK*, 6 (1895), 156-162.

1547. Q. Zöckler, "Wo lag das biblische Galatien?" *TSK*, 68 (1895), 51-102.

1548. G. G. Findlay, "The Galatians of St. Paul's Epistle," *ET*, 7 (1895-1896), 235-236.

1549. W. M. Ramsay, "The Galatia of St. Paul's Letters," *ET*, 7 (1895-1896), 142-143.

1550. W. M. Ramsay, "The Galatians of St. Paul's Epistle," *ET*, 7 (1895-1896), 285-286.

1551. W. M. Ramsay, "The Epistle to the Galatians," *Exp*, 5th series, 7 (1898), 401-413.

1552. W. M. Ramsay, "A Historical Commentary on the Epistle

to the Galatians," *Exp*, 5th series, 8 (1898), 17-32, 118-135, 191-206, 290-303, 321-336, 433-448; 9 (1899), 57-63, 97-109; 10 (1899), 16-31, 104-118, 195-210.

1553. Alfred Kappeler, "Der Galaterbrief nach seiner Echtheit untersucht nebst kritischen Bemerkungen zu den paulinischen Hauptbriefen von Rud. Steck," *STZ*, 6 (1889), 11-19.

1554. W. M. Ramsay, "A New Theory as to the Date of the Epistle to the Galatians," *ET*, 12 (1900-1901), 157-160.

1555. W. A. Shedd, "The Date of the Epistle to the Galatians upon the South Galatian Theory," *ET*, 12 (1900-1901), 568.

1556. S. A. Fries, "Was meint Paulus mit Ἀραβία, Gal 1, 17?" *ZNW*, 2 (1901), 150-151.

1557. F. Rendall, "The First Galatian Ministry," *Exp*, 6th series, 3 (1901), 241-256.

1558. Dawson Walker, "The South Galatian Theory," *ET*, 13 (1901-1902), 511-514.

1559. B. W. Bacon, "Acts versus Galatians," *AJT*, 11 (1907), 454-474.

1560. Max Meinertz, "Apg. 15, 34 und die Möglichkeit des antiochenischen Streitfalles (Gal. 2, 11 ff.) nach dem Apostelkonzil," *BibZ*, 5 (1907), 392-401.

1561. J. I. Vance, "An Apostolic Fortnight," *USR*, 20 (1908-1909), 101-113.

1562. C. W. Emmet, "Galatians, the Earliest of the Pauline Epistles," *Exp*, 7th series, 9 (1910), 242-254.

1563. Alphons Steinmann, "Nordgalatien," *BibZ*, 8 (1910), 274-277.

1564. V. Weber, "Abfassungszeit und Leserkreis des Galaterbriefs," *TQ*, 92 (1910), 327-338.

1565. Alphons Steinmann, "Schlusswort zur Galaterfrage," *TQ*, 94 (1912), 511-526.

1566. Valentin Weber, "Die Frage der Identität von Gal. 2, 1-10 und Apg. 15," *BibZ*, 10 (1912), 155-167.

1567. C. W. Emmet, "Acts 15 : 3 and the Early Date of Galatians," *ET*, 24 (1912-1913), 475-476.

1568. Maurice Jones, "Acts 15 : 3 and the Early Date of Galatians," *ET*, 24 (1912-1913), 382-383.

1569. Maurice Jones, "Acts 15 : 3 and the Early Date of Galatians," *ET*, 24 (1912-1913), 566-567.

1570. W. M. Ramsay, "What were the Churches of Galatia?"
ET, 24 (1912-1913), 19-22, 61-63, 122-125, 219-223, 280-283,
331-333, 378-379, 471-473, 563-566.

1571. T. W. Crafer, "The Stoning of St. Paul at Lystra and the
Epistle to the Galatians," *Exp*, 8th series, 6 (1913), 375-384.

1572. A. J. Dickinson, "How Paul's Epistle to the Galatians
Grew Out of Letters to the Galatians," *BW*, 41 (1913), 172-177.

1573. Maurice Jones, "The Date of the Epistle to the Galatians,"
Exp, 8th series, 6 (1913), 193-208.

1574. Allan Menzies, "The Epistle to the Galatians," *Exp*, 8th
series, 7 (1914), 137-147.

1575. C. A. Scott, "The Early Date of Galatians: A Reply," *Exp*,
8th series, 7 (1914), 183-192.

1576. B. H. Tower, "St. Paul's Epistle to the Galatians: A Paraphrase," *Exp*, 8th series, 11 (1916), 231-240, 464-472.

1577. T. E. Bird, "The First Epistle of St. Paul," *ITQ*, 14 (1919),
356-365.

1578. Ernest DeW. Burton, "Those Trouble-Makers in Galatia,"
BW, 53 (1919), 555-560.

1579. J. J. Conway, "The Galatian Churches," *ITQ*, 14 (1919), 15-28.

1580. J. M. Bover, "Repetición de frases en la epístola a los Gálatas," *EE*, 14 (1935), 310-317.

1581. L. Fürbringer, "Kleine Studien aus dem Galaterbrief," *CTM*,
6 (1935), 501-511, 580-591, 650-660.

1582. Albert Greene, "The North-South Galatia Theory Controversy," *BS*, 92 (1935), 478-485.

1583. Florentinus Ogara, " 'Quae sunt per allegoriam dicta':
Notae in Gal. 4, 22-31," *VD*, 15 (1935), 67-76.

1584. A. E. Travis, "Date of Galatians — A Fresh Discussion of an
Old Problem," *RE*, 34 (1937), 476-486.

1585. F. F. Bruce, "The Date of the Epistle to the Galatians,"
ET, 51 (1939-1940), 396-397.

1586. L. G. Buckingham, "The Date of the Epistle to the Galatians," *ET*, 51 (1939-1940), 157-158.

1587. H. E. Dana, "Light from the Greek Text on the Date of
Galatians," *CQ*, 18 (1941), 160-163.

1588. D. B. Knox, "The Date of the Epistle to the Galatians,"
EQ, 13 (1941), 262-268.

1589. F. R. Crownfield, "The Singular Problem of the Dual
Galatians," *JBL*, 64 (1945), 491-500.

1590. Bernard Orchard, "The Problem of Acts and Galatians," *CBQ*, 7 (1945), 377-397.
1591. T. E. Bird, "The Problem of Acts and Galatians," *CBQ*, 8 (1946), 259.
1592. Martin Dibelius, "Das Apostelkonzil," *TLZ*, 72 (1947), 193-198.
1593. J. S. Callaway, "Paul's Letter to the Galatians and Plato's Lysis," *JBL*, 67 (1948), 353-355.
1594. C. H. Buck, Jr., "The Date of Galatians," *JBL*, 70 (1951), 113-122.
See also numbers 199, 490, 494, and 2970.

c. *Theological Studies*

1595. H. B. Hackett, "Analysis of the Argument in the Epistle to the Galatians," *BS*, 5 (1848), 97-102.
1596. F. Godet, "The Struggle for Christian Liberty in Galatia," *Exp*, 3rd series, 1 (1885), 283-303.
1597. F. Rendall, "St. Paul and the Galatian Judaizers," *Exp*, 3rd series, 10 (1889), 51-64, 107-122.
1598. E. DeW. Burton, "Redemption from the Curse of the Law," *AJT*, 11 (1907), 624-646.
1599. G. H. Robinson, "Galatians, the Epistle of Protestantism," *PTR*, 15 (1917), 604-622.
1600. J. M. Bover, "La epístola a los Gálatas, 'Carta magna de la libertad cristiana,'" *EE*, 5 (1926), 362-372.
1601. H. G. Wood, "The Message of the Epistles; the Letter to the Galatians," *ET* 44 (1932-1933), 453-457.
1602. L. Fuerbringer, "Kleine Studien aus dem Galaterbrief," *CTM*, 6 (1935), 650-660.
1603. Wm. Dallmann, "Lectures on Galatians," *CTM*, 11 (1940), 589-598, 828-838, 887-893; 12 (1941), 13-23.
1604. Carmelus Lo Giudice, "De unione fidelium cum Christo in epistola ad Galatas," *VD*, 20 (1940), 44-52, 81-84.
1605. R. M. Hawkins, "The Galatian Gospel," *JBL*, 59 (1940), 141-146.
1606. Wm. Arndt, "Galatians — A Declaration of Christian Liberty," *CTM*, 27 (1956), 673-692.
1607. Walter Grundmann, "Die Häretiker in Galatien," *ZNW*, 47 (1956), 25-66.
See also number 549.

d. *Exegesis of Individual Passages*

1608. Th. Vargha, " 'Paulus Apostolus non ab hominibus neque per hominem,' " *VD*, 8 (1928), 147-151 [Gal. 1 : 1].

1609. [E.] Moske, "Gal. 1, 1-17 und die Ananiasepisode," *TQ*, 92 (1910), 531-537.

1610. J. C. Lambert, " 'Another Gospel that is not Another' — Galatians 1 : 6,7," *ET*, 12 (1900-1901), 89-93.

1611. H. Zeydner, "Galatians 1 : 10," *TS*, 18 (1900), 363-364.

1612. M. Meinertz, "Zur Bekehrung des hl. Paulus (Gal. 1, 15 ff.)," *TQ*, 93 (1911), 223-229.

1613. A.-M. Denis, "L'investiture de la fonction apostolique par 'Apocalypse'. Étude thématique de Gal. 1, 16," *RB*, 64 (1957), 335-362, 492-515.

1614. G. A. Simcox, "*Brevia* — Secret History of St. Paul," *Exp*, 3rd series, 4 (1886), 156-158 [Gal. 1 : 17].

1615. Otto Bauernfeind, "Die erste Begegnung zwischen Paulus und Kephas Gal. 1, 18," *TLZ*, 81 (1956), 343-344.

1616. Otto Bauernfeind, "Die Begegnung zwischen Paulus und Kephas Gal. 1 : 18-20," *ZNW*, 47 (1956), 268-276.

1617. Bernard Orchard, "A New Solution of the Galatians Problem," *BJRL*, 28 (1944), 154-174 [Gal. 1 : 18-2 : 14].

1618. J. S. Purton, "A Biblical Note," *Exp*, 1st series, 10 (1879), 162-164 [Gal. 1 : 19].

1619. H. Koch, "Zur Jakobusfrage, Gal. 1, 19," *ZNW*, 33 (1934), 204-209.

1620. P. E. Kretzmann, "Zur Jakobusfrage, Gal. 1, 19," *CTM*, 6 (1935), 378.

1621. A. H. Blom, "Jacobus en Petrus. Bijdrage tot verklaring van Gal. II," *TT*, 4 (1870), 465-486.

1622. F. W. Grosheide, "De Synode der Apostelen," *GTT*, 11 (1910), 1-16 [Gal. 2].

1623. W. Foerster, "Die δοκοῦντες in Gal. 2," *ZNW*, 36 (1937), 286-292.

1624. Karl Heussi, "Galater 2 und der Lebensausgang der jerusalemischen Urapostel," *TLZ*, 77 (1952), 67-72.

1625. John Knox, "Fourteen Years Later," *JR*, 16 (1936), 341-349 [Gal. 2 : 1].

1626. W. M. Ramsay, "On the Interpretation of Two Passages in the Epistle to the Galatians," *Exp*, 5th series, 2 (1895), 103-118 [Gal 2 : 1-10; 1 : 6-7].

1627. Robert Mackintosh, "The Tone of Galatians 2 : 1-10," *ET*, 21 (1909-1910), 327-328.

1628. P. Boylan, "The Visit of Paul to Jerusalem in Galatians 2 : 1-10," *ITQ*, 17 (1922), 293-304.

1629. A. B. Bruce, "Was Titus Circumcized?" *Exp*, 1st series, 11 (1880), 201-205 [Gal. 2 : 3-5].

1630. Kirsopp Lake, "Galatians 2 : 3-5," *Exp*, 7th series, 1 (1906), 236-245.

1631. P. Tag, "Zur Exegese von Luk. 18, 7 und Gal. 2, 3-6," *TSK*, 57 (1884), 167-172.

1632. David Warner, "Galatians 2 : 3-8: as an Interpolation," *ET*, 62 (1950-1951), 380.

1633. Burk, "Versuch einer Erklärung von Gal. 2, 6," *TSK*, 38 (1865), 734-740.

1634. F. Märcker, "Über Gal. 2, 6," *TSK*, 39 (1866), 532-544.

1635. Burk, "Nochmals über Galater 2, 6," *TSK*, 41 (1868), 527-534.

1636. M. Brunec, "'Ἀπὸ δὲ τῶν δοκούντων (Gal 2, 6)," *VD*, 25 (1947), 280-288.

1637. R. Eisler, "The Meeting of Paul and the 'Pillars' in Galatians and in the Acts of the Apostles," *BBC*, 12 (1937), 58-64 [Gal. 2 : 9].

1638. Rupert Annand, "Note on the Three 'Pillars,'" *ET*, 67 (1955-1956), 178 [Gal. 2 : 9].

1639. Dawson Walker, "Galatians 2 : 10," *ET*, 11 (1899-1900), 190.

1640. Christian Pesch, S.J., "Über die Person des Kephas, Gal. II, 11," *ZKT*, 7 (1883), 456-490.

1641. J. Donovan, "Iota or Epsilon: A Suggested Reading in Galatians 2 : 11," *ITQ*, 17 (1922), 324-334.

1642. J. M. S. Baljon, "Gal. 2 : 11 b," *TS*, 5 (1887), 251-255.

1643. P. Gaechter, "Petrus in Antiochia," *ZKT*, 72 (1950), 177-212 [Gal. 2 : 11-14].

1644. M. W. Jacobus, "Paul and his Teaching in Galatians 2 : 11-21," *BW*, 24 (1904), 351-358.

1645. J. M. Bover, "Pauli oratio ad Petrum (Gal. 2, 11-21)," *VD*, 4 (1924), 48-55.

1646. Anonymous, "Hieronymus und Augustinus im Streit über Gal. 2, 14," *TQ*, 6 (1824), 195-219.

1647. C. H. Roberts, "A Note on Galatians 2 : 14," *JTS*, 40 (1939), 55-56.

1648. R. Schmidt, "Über Gal. 2, 14-21," *TSK*, 50 (1877), 638-705.

1649. L. Wetzel, "Versuch einer Erklärung der Stelle Gal. 2, 14-21," *TSK*, 53 (1880), 432-464.

1650. F. Zimmer, "Paulus gegen Petrus; Gal. 2, 14-21 erläutert," *ZWT*, 25 (1882), 129-188.

1651. A. Klöpper, "Zur Erläuterung von Gal. II, 14-21," *ZWT*, 37 (1894), 373-395.

1652. G. G. Warren, "A Study in Galatians 2 : 15-21," *BR*, 11 (1926), 356-367.

1653. D. R. Goodwin, "'Εὰν μή, Gal. ii. 16," *JBL* (June, 1886), 122-127.

1654. D. Lipsius, "Über Gal. 2, 17 f.," *ZWT*, 4 (1861), 72-82.

1655. W. Mundle, "Zur Auslegung von Gal. 2, 17-18," *ZNW*, 23 (1924), 152-153.

1656. C. F. D. Moule, "A Note on Galatians 2 : 17, 18," *ET*, 56 (1944-1945), 223.

1657. W. F. Arndt, "Brief Studies: On Gal. 2 : 17-19," *CTM*, 27 (1956), 128-132.

1658. J. Leal, " 'Christo confixus sum cruci' (Gal. 2, 19)," *VD*, 19 (1939), 76-80, 98-105.

1659. Carpus, "Heaven," *Exp*, 1st series, 3 (1876), 62-73 [Gal. 2 : 20].

1660. H. C. G. Moule, "A Study in the Connexion of Doctrines," *Exp*, 3rd series, 2 (1885), 447-455 [Gal 2 : 20].

1661. M. J. v. d. Hoogt, "Het ware leven," *GTT*, 6 (1905), 10-12, 48-53 [Gal. 2 : 20].

1662. Laurentius di Fonzo, "De semine Abrahae, promissionum herede, iuxta S. Paulum in Gal. 3," *VD*, 21 (1941), 49-58.

1663. H. M. Rettig, "Exegetische Analekten, I," *TSK*, 3 (1830), 96-100 [Gal. 3 : 1].

1664. Vacher Burch, "To Placard the Crucified (Gal. 3 : 1)," *ET*, 30 (1918-1919), 232-233.

1665. J. M. Bover, " 'Quis vos fascinavit?' (Gal. 3, 1)," *VD*, 2 (1922), 240-242.

1666. P. Jung, "Das paulinische Vocabular in Gal. 3 : 6-14," *ZKT*, 74 (1952), 439-449.

1667. Ragnar Bring, "Till frågen om Pauli syn på lagens förhållande till tron. En studie över Gal. 3 : 10-12 och Rom. 10 : 2-8," *STK*, 21 (1945), 26-54.

1668. H. Hanse, "Δῆλον: zu Gal. 3, 11," *ZNW*, 34 (1935), 299-303.

1669. F. Ruffenach, " 'Iustus ex fide vivit' (Gal. 3, 11)," *VD*, 3 (1923), 337-340.

1670. D. Bähr, "Exegetische Erörterungen: II. Gal. 3, 13," *TSK*, 22 (1849), 917-935.

1671. U. Holzmeister, "De Christi crucifixione quid e Deut. 21,22 et Gal. 3, 13 consequatur," *B*, 27 (1946), 18-29.

1672. E. DeW. Burton, "Redemption from the Curse of the Law (Exposition of Gal. 3 : 13-14)," *AJT*, 11 (1907), 624-646.

1673. A. H. Blom, "Handhaving mijner verklaring van Gal. III : 13, 16, 20. Antwoord aan Dr. J. J. Prins," *TT*, 12 (1878), 614-625.

1674. W. Hauck, "Exegetischer Versuch über Galat. 3, 15-22," *TSK*, 35 (1862), 512-548.

1675. H. Findeisen, "Zu Galater 3 : 15-29," *NKZ*, 9 (1898), 241-250.

1676. M. Conrat, "Das Erbrecht im Galaterbrief (3, 15-4, 7)," *ZNW*, 5 (1904), 204-227.

1677. Frederic Gardiner, "Note on Galatians 3 : 16," *BS*, 36 (1879), 23-27.

1678. B. W. Bacon, "Notes on New Testament Passages," *JBL*, 16 (1897), 136-142 [Gal. 3 : 16].

1679. C. P. Coffin, "Seeds, or Seed, in Gal. 3 : 16," *BW*, 32 (1908), 267-268.

1680. J. M. Bover, " 'Et semini tuo qui est Christus' (Gal. 3, 16)," *VD*, 3 (1923), 365-366.

1681. P. X. M. a Vallisoleto, " 'Et semini tuo qui est Christus' (Gal. 3, 16)," *VD*, 12 (1932), 327-332.

1682. H. Liese, "Promissiones Abrahae factae complentur per fidem, non per legem (Gal. 3, 16-22)," *VD*, 13 (1933), 257-263.

1683. G. B. Winer, "Über die Stelle Galater 3, 19-20, vorzüglich gegen Steudel, Kern und Sack," *ZWTh*, 2 (1827), 31-46.

1684. A. Hilgenfeld, "Die Stelle Gal. 3, 19.20 und ihre neueste Auslegung," *ZWT*, 8 (1865), 452-457.

1685. W. L. Davidson, "The Mediator-Argument of Galatians iii. 19, 20," *Exp*, 3rd series, 7 (1888), 377-386.

1686. [Fr.] Lücke, "Noch ein Versuch über Galat. 3 : 20," *TSK*, 1 (1828), 83-109.

1687. [M.] Schneckenberger, "Noch etwas über Galater 3, 20," *TSK*, 6 (1833), 121-143.

1688. W. F. Rinck, "Über Gal. 3, 20," *TSK*, 7 (1834), 309-312.

1689. Mack, "Über Galat. 3, 20," *TQ*, 17 (1835), 453-492.

1690. W. von Schütz, "Über Galat. 3, 20," *TQ*, 17 (1835), 623-645.

1691. T. F. K. Gurlitt, "Noch ein Wort über Gal. 3, 20," *TSK*, 10 (1837), 805-829.

1692. E. H. K. Reinhardt, "Noch ein Wort über Gal. 3, 20," *TSK*, 15 (1842), 990-1011.

1693. J. F. K. Gurlitt, "Über Gal. 3, 20," *TSK*, 16 (1843), 715-721.

1694. A. Vogel, "Zur Auslegung der Stelle Gal. 3, 20," *TSK*, 38 (1865), 524-538.

1695. [W.] Hauck, "Ein Wort zur Auslegung der Stelle Gal. 3, 20 v. Prof. D. Vogel in Wien,'" *TSK*, 39 (1866), 699-701.

1696. Anonymous, "Die crux interpretum Gal. 3, 20," *TSK*, 40 (1867), 331-349.

1697. A. H. Blom, "Verklaring van Gal. III : 20," *TT*, 12 (1878), 216-227.

1698. J. J. Prins, "Nog iets over Gal. III : 20 en, in verband daarmede, over vs. 13 en 16. Open brief aan Dr. A. H. Blom," *TT*, 12 (1878), 410-420.

1699. John Forbes, "Brevia — Galatians 3 : 20," *Exp*, 3rd series, 4 (1886), 150-156.

1700. Walther Bleibtreu, "Das Wort vom Mittler im Galaterbriefe, Kap. 3, 20," *NKZ*, 6 (1895), 534-560.

1701. Wilh. Siebert, "Exegetisch-theologische Studie über Galater 3 : 20 und 4 : 4," *NKZ*, 15 (1904), 699-733.

1702. Fr. Walther, "Miszellen. Gal. 3, 20," *NKZ*, 32 (1921), 706-709.

1703. W. H. Isaacs, "Galatians 3 : 20," *ET*, 35 (1923-1924), 565-567.

1704. W. K. L. Clarke, "Studies in Texts: Gal. 3 : 20," *Th*, 9 (1924), 215.

1705. G. H. Tremenheere, "Studies in Texts — Gal. 3 : 20," *Th*, 22 (1931), 35.

1706. Adolf Stegmann, "ὁ δὲ μεσίτης ἑνὸς οὐκ ἔστιν, Gal. 3, 20," *BibZ*, 22 (1934), 30-42.

1707. J. Danieli, "Mediator autem unius non est," *VD*, 33 (1955), 9-17 [Gal. 3 : 20].

1708. L. T. Wohlfeil, "Gal. 3, 24," *CTM*, 6 (1935), 192-196.

1709. J. M. Bover, " 'In Christo Iesu' filii Dei omnes unus, semen Abrahae (Gal. 3, 26-29)," *VD*, 4 (1924), 14-21.

1710. Augustin Grail, "Le baptême dans l'épître aux Galates (3.26-4.7)," *RB*, 58 (1951), 503-520.

1711. P. X. M. a Vallisoleto, " 'In Christo Iesu' ('Omnes vos unu(s) estis in Christo Iesu,' Gal. 3, 28)," *VD*, 12 (1932), 16-24.

1712. Georg Kurze, "Die στοιχεῖα τοῦ κόσμου, Gal 4 und Kol 2," *BibZ*, 15 (1918-1921), 335-337.

1713. E. Y. Hincks, "The Meaning of the Phrase τὰ στοιχεῖα τοῦ κόσμου in Gal. iv. 3 and Col. ii. 8," *JBL*, 15 (1896), 183-192.

1714. W. H. P. Hatch, "Τὰ στοιχεῖα in Paul and Bardaiṣān," *JTS*, 28 (1926-1927), 181-182 [Gal. 4 : 3, 9].

1715. A. W. Mitchell, " 'The Fulness of Time' (Gal. 4 : 4)," *ET*, 19 (1907-1908), 237.

1716. J. M. Bover, "Un texto de San Pablo (Gal. 4, 4-5) interpretado por San Ireneo," *EE*, 17 (1943), 145-181.

1717. J. M. Bover, "Heres 'per Deum' (Gal. 4, 7)," *B*, 5 (1924), 373-375.

1718. G. A. Barton, "The Exegesis of ἐνιαυτούς in Galatians 4 : 10 and its Bearing on the Date of the Epistle," *JBL*, 33 (1914), 118-126.

1719. H. M. Rettig, "Exegetische Analekten," *TSK*, 3 (1830), 108-114 [Gal. 4 : 11-15].

1720. Rudolf Hermann, "Über den Sinn des μορφοῦσθαι Χριστὸν ἐν ὑμῖν in Gal. 4, 19," *TLZ*, 80 (1955), 713-726.

1721. P. E. Kretzmann, "Miscellanea," *CTM*, 3 (1932), 457 [Gal. 4 : 25].

1722. K. H. Rengstorf, "Zu Gal. 5, 1," *TLZ*, 76 (1951), 659-662.

1723. E. DeW. Burton, "Religion and Ethics in the Thought of the Apostle Paul: Gal. 5 : 6," *BW*, 36 (1910), 307-315.

1724. Clement Bird, "Notes on Galatians 5 : 8," *Exp*, 4th series, 7 (1893), 471-472.

1725. Florentinus Ogara, " 'Spiritu ambulate', Gal. 5, 16-24," *VD*, 18 (1938), 257-261, 289-293.

1726. John Massie, "Professor Alexander Roberts on Galatians 5 : 17," *ET*, 3 (1891-1892), 219-220.

1727. Paul Althaus, " '. . . Dass ihr nicht tut, was ihr wollt,' (Zur Auslegung von Gal. 5, 17)," *TLZ*, 76 (1951), 15-18.

1728. E. Bäumlein, "Über Galat. 5, 23," *TSK*, 35 (1862), 551-553.

1729. J. D. Robb, "Galatians 5 : 23. An Explanation," *ET*, 56 (1944-1945), 279-280.

1730. E. Hirsch, "Zwei Fragen zu Gal. 6," *ZNW*, 29 (1930), 192-197.

1731. O. Holtzmann, "Zu E. Hirsch, Zwei Fragen zu Gal. 6," *ZNW*, 30 (1931), 76-83.

1732. J. D. Robb, "Galatians 6 : 1," *ET*, 57 (1945-1946), 222.

1733. George Matheson, "The Paradox of Christian Ethics," *Exp*, 1st series, 10 (1879), 81-98 [Gal. 6 : 1-5].

1734. H. P. Berlage, "De juiste verklaring van Gal. 6 : 2," *TT*, 25 (1891), 47-61.

1735. B. G. Hall, "Φορτίον and βάρη (Gal. 6 : 2, 5)," *ET*, 34 (1922-1923), 563.

1736. Arthur Jones, "Βάρος and φορτίον," *ET*, 34 (1922-1923), 333 [Gal. 6 : 2, 5].

1737. P. A. van Stempvoort, "Gal. 6 : 2," *NTT*, 7 (1952-1953), 362-363.

1738. Harry Smith, "Galatians 6 : 9," *ET*, 13 (1901-1902), 139.

1739. J. S. Clemens, "St. Paul's Handwriting," *ET*, 24 (1911-1912), 380 [Gal. 6 : 11].

1740. W. K. L. Clarke, "St. Paul's 'Large Letters,' " *ET* 24 (1912-1913), 285 [Gal. 6 : 11].

1741. H. A. A. Kennedy, "Galatians 6 : 12, 13," *ET*, 22 (1910-1911), 419-420.

1742. A. H. McNeile, "Studies in Texts," *Th*, 19 (1929), 108-109 [Gal. 6 : 14].

1743. J. H. Moulton, " 'The Marks of Jesus,' " *ET*, 21 (1909-1910), 283-284 [Gal. 6 : 17].

1744. H. J. Kouwenhoven, "Paulus' beroep op de litteekenen van den Heere Jezus in zijn lichaam," *GTT*, 13 (1912), 105-115 [Gal. 6 : 17].
On Gal. 1 : 11-17, see number 2831 ; 2 : 10, number 657 ; 2 : 20, numbers 817 and 2752 ; chap. 3, number 2764 ; 3 : 11, number 763 ; 3 : 13-14, number 2533 ; 4 : 22-31, number 1583.

6. The Epistle to the Ephesians

a. *Textual Criticism*

1745. J. M. S. Baljon, "Opmerkingen op het gebied van de Conjecturaalcritiek: de Brief aan de Epheziërs," *TS*, 3 (1885), 146-156.

1746. Alexander Souter, "The Epistle to the 'Ephesians' not a Secondary Production," *Exp*, 8th series, 2 (1911), 136-141.

1747. Alexander Souter, "The Non-Secondary Character of 'Ephesians,' " *Exp*, 8th series, 2 (1911), 321-328.

1748. Salvatore Garofalo, "Rettifica su Eph. 1, 1," *B*, 16 (1935), 342-343.

1749. J. P. Wilson, "Note on the Textual Problem of Ephesians 1 : 1," *ET*, 60 (1948-1949), 225-226.

1750. Alexander Souter, "An Interpretation of Ephesians 1 : 15," *ET*, 19 (1907-1908), 44.

1751. V. F. B[üchner], "A Marcionite Reading in Ephrem's Commentary on the Pauline Epistles," *BBC*, 5 (1927), 37-38 [Eph. 2 : 14].

b. *Historical and Literary Criticism*

1752. W. Fr. Rinck, "Kann der Epheserbrief an die Gemeinde zu Ephesus gerichtet sein?" *TSK*, 22 (1849), 948-958.

1753. A. Kiene, "Der Epheserbrief ein Sendschreiben des Paulus an die Heidenchristen der sieben (?) kleinasiatischen Gemeinden, welche mit Ephesus eine engere Verbindung bildeten," *TSK*, 42 (1869), 285-328.

1754. W. Seufert, "Das Verwandtschaftsverhältniss des ersten Petrusbriefs und Epheserbriefs," *ZWT*, 24 (1881), 178-197, 332-379.

1755. C. H. van Rhijn, "De jongste literatuur over de Schriften des Nieuwen Verbonds: De Brief aan de Efeziërs," *TS*, 3 (1885), 265-312.

1756. F. Godet, "The Epistle to the Gentile Churches," *Exp*, 3rd series, 5 (1887), 376-391.

1757. J. A. Beet, "The Epistle to the Ephesians: Hints for Study," *ET*, 2 (1890-1891), 85-86.

1758. W. C. Shearer, "To Whom was the so-called Epistle to the Ephesians actually addressed?" *ET*, 4 (1892-1893), 129.

1759. P. Ladeuze, "Les déstinataires de l'épître aux Éphésiens," *RB*, 11 (1902), 573-580.

1760. S. J. Case, "To Whom was 'Ephesians' Written?" *BW*, 38 (1911), 315-320.

1761. James Moffatt, "The Problem of Ephesians," *Exp*, 8th series, 2 (1911), 193-200.

1762. H. Coppieters, "Les récentes attaques contre l'authenticité de l'épître aux Éphésiens," *RB*, N.S. 9 (1912), 361-390.

1763. E. C. Caldwell, "Unity in Christ — Outline Study of the Epistle to the Ephesians," *USR*, 35 (1923-1924), 121-143.

1764. J. de Zwaan, "Le 'Rythme logique' dans l'épître aux Éphésiens," *RHPR*, 7 (1927), 554-565.

1765. E. J. Goodspeed, "The Place of Ephesians in the First Pauline Collection," *ATR*, 12 (1929-1930), 189-212.

1766. Manuel de los Ríos, "Los destinatarios de la carta a los Efesios," *EB*, 3 (1931), 298-316; 4 (1932), 22-26.

1767. C. R. Bowen, "The Place of Ephesians Among the Letters of Paul," *ATR*, 15 (1933), 279-299.

1768. Paul Joüon, "Notes philologiques sur quelques versets de l'épître aux Éphésiens," *RSR*, 26 (1936), 454-464.

1769. J. de Zwaan, "Ephesen niet 'deuteropaulinisch,'" *NTS*, 20 (1937), 172-174.

1770. C. L. Mitton, "Unsolved New Testament Problems: Goodspeed's Theory Regarding the Origin of Ephesians," *ET*, 59 (1947-1948), 323-327.

1771. C. L. Mitton, "E. J. Goodspeed's Theory Regarding the Origin of Ephesians," *ET*, 60 (1948-1949), 320-321.

1772. C. F. D. Moule, "E. J. Goodspeed's Theory Regarding the Origin of Ephesians," *ET*, 60 (1948-1949), 224-225.

1773. E. J. Goodspeed, "Ephesians and the First Edition of Paul," *JBL*, 70 (1951), 285-291.

1774. A. C. King, "Ephesians in the Light of Form Criticism," *ET*, 63 (1951-1952), 273-276.

1775. Friedrich Cornelius, "Die geschichtliche Stellung des Epheser-Briefes," *ZRGG*, 7 (1955), 74-76.

1776. C. L. Mitton, "Important Hypotheses Reconsidered; VII. The Authorship of the Epistle to the Ephesians," *ET*, 67 (1955-1956), 195-198.

1777. G. Schille, "Der Autor des Epheserbriefes," *TLZ*, 82 (1957), 325-334.

See also numbers 390, 415, 418, and 456.

(1). Relation to the Epistle to the Colossians

1778. J. Wiggers, "Beiträge zur Einleitung in die Briefe des Paulus an die Epheser, an die Kolosser und an den Philemon," *TSK*, 14 (1841), 413-456.

1779. S. Hoekstra, "Vergelijking van de brieven aan de Efeziërs en de Colossers," *TT*, 2 (1868), 599-652.

1780. W. Hönig, "Über das Verhältniss des Epheserbriefes zum Briefe an die Kolosser," *ZWT*, 15 (1872), 63-87.

1781. Th. Innitzer, "Zur Frage der Priorität des Epheser- oder des Kolosserbriefes," *ZKT*, 29 (1905), 579-588.

1782. E. Percy, "Zur den Problemen des Kolosser- und Epheser-briefes," *ZNW*, 43 (1950-1951), 178-194.

1783. Eduard Schweizer, "Zur Frage der Echtheit des Kolosser- und das Epheserbriefes," *ZNW*, 47 (1956), 287.

c. *Theological Studies*

1784. J. Méritan, "L'ecclésiologie de l'épître aux Éphésiens," *RB*, 7 (1898), 343-369.

1785. Arthur Carr, "Truth in Jesus: The Revelation of Christ and the Example of Christ; A Study in the Epistle to the Ephesians," *Exp*, 6th series, 3 (1901), 118-127.

1786. G. W. H. Thomas, "The Doctrine of the Church in the Epistle to the Ephesians," *Exp*, 7th series, 2 (1906), 318-339.

1787. James Moffatt, "Four Notes on Ephesians," *Exp*, 8th series, 10 (1915), 89-96.

1788. James Moffatt, "Three Notes on Ephesians," *Exp*, 8th series, 15 (1918), 306-317.

1789. A. M. Pope, "The All Embracing Faith," *CJRT*, 3 (1926), 401-410.

1790. G. H. Whitaker, "Studies in Texts — The Building and the Body," *Th*, 13 (1926), 335-336.

1791. C. H. Dodd, "The Message of the Epistles; Ephesians," *ET*, 45 (1933-1934), 60-66.

1792. L. H. Hough, "The Message of the Epistles; Ephesians," *ET*, 45 (1933-1934), 103-108.

1793. P. Benoît, "L'horizon paulinien de l'épître aux Éphésiens," *RB*, 46 (1937), 342-361, 506-525.

1794. John McNicol, "The Spiritual Blessings of the Epistle to the Ephesians," *EQ*, 9 (1937), 64-73.

1795. N. A. Dahl, "Dopet i Efesierbrevet," *STK*, 21 (1945), 85-103.

1796. B. M. Metzger, "Paul's Vision of the Church; A Study of the Ephesian Letter," *TTod*, 6 (1949-1950), 49-63.

1797. Leonhard Fendt, "Die Kirche des Epheserbriefs," *TLZ*, 77 (1952), 147-150.

1798. M. H. Scharlemann, "Human Relations According to Ephesians," *CTM*, 24 (1953), 705-714.

1799. J. W. Bowman, "The Epistle to the Ephesians," *Interp*, 8 (1954), 188-205.

1800. Werner Bieder, "Das Geheimnis des Christus nach dem Epheserbrief," *TZ*, 11 (1955), 329-343.

1801. Ernst Käsemann, "Christus das All und die Kirche," *TLZ*, 81 (1956), 585-590.

1802. S. S. Smalley, "The Eschatology of Ephesians," *EQ*, 28 (1956), 152-157.
See also numbers 578 and 2624.

d. *Exegesis of Individual Passages*

1803. W. O. Carver, "An Outline Study of the First Chapter of Ephesians," *RE*, 1 (1904), 211-218.

1804. [M. V.] Aberle, "Über eine Äusserung des Origenes zu Eph. 1, 1," *TQ*, 34 (1852), 108-122.

1805. Paul Ewald, "Exegetische Miszellen. Zu Eph. 1, 1," *NKZ*, 15 (1904), 560-617.

1806. C. H. van Rhijn, "Oud en Nieuw over den Epheser-brief," *TS*, 29 (1911), 255-273.

1807. W. Bartlett, "The Saints at Ephesus," *Exp*, 8th series, 18 (1919), 327-341 [Eph. 1 : 1].

1808. M. Zerwick, " 'Benedictus Deus et Pater D. N. I. Ch., qui benedixit nos . . .' (Eph. 1, 3)," *VD*, 22 (1942), 3-7.

1809. H. J. Flowers, "Election in Jesus Christ — A Study of Ephesians 1 : 3-4," *RE*, 26 (1929), 55-67.

1810. Th. Innitzer, "Der 'hymnus' im Epheserbriefe (1, 3-14)," *ZKT*, 28 (1904), 612-621.

1811. H. Coppieters, "La doxologie de la lettre aux Éphésiens," *RB*, N.S. 6 (1909), 74-106 [Eph. 1 : 3-14].

1812. J. M. Bover, "Doxologiae Epistulae ad Ephesios logica partitio," *B*, 2 (1921), 458-460 [Eph. 1 : 3-14].

1813. J. R. Mackay, "Paul's Great Doxology," *EQ*, 2 (1930), 150-161 [Eph. 1 : 3-14].

1814. Manuel de los Ríos,, "División y breve comentario de Ef. 1, 3-14," *EB*, 5 (1933), 83-94; 6 (1934), 184-194.

1815. Eng. Driessen, "De auxilio Dei et salute hominis apud S. Paulum (Eph. 1, 3-14)," *VD*, 20 (1940), 201-209, 225-233.

1816. E. Driessen, "Aeternum Dei propositum de salute hominis et de redintegratione omnium rerum per Christum," *VD*, 24 (1944), 120-124, 151-157, 184-191 [Eph. 1 : 3-14; Col. 1 : 19 f.].

1817. J. T. Trinidad, "The Mystery Hidden in God," *B*, 31 (1950), 1-26 [Eph. 1 : 3-14].

1818. J. Coutts, "Ephesians i. 3-14 and I Peter i. 3-12," *NTSt*, 3 (1957), 115-127.

1819. H. J. Flowers, "Adoption and Redemption in the Beloved; a Study of Ephesians 1 : 5-7," *ET*, 39 (1927-1928), 16-21.

1820. F. V. Pratt, "Ephesians 1 : 6," *ET*, 23 (1910-1911), 331.

1821. W. H. G. Thomas, "Ephesians 1 :6," *ET*, 29 (1917-1918), 561.

1822. Andreas ab Alpe, " 'Instaurare omnia in Christo' (Eph. 1, 10)," *VD*, 23 (1943), 97-103.

1823. D. A. Conchas, "Redemptio acquisitionis," *VD*, 30 (1952), 14-29, 81-91, 154-169 [Eph. 1 : 14].

1824. J. M. Holladay, "One of Paul's Prayers — Eph. 1 : 15-23," *USR*, 22 (1910-1911), 181-187.

1825. H. J. Flowers, "Paul's Prayer for the Ephesians; a Study of Ephesians 1 : 15-23," *ET*, 38 (1926-1927), 227-233.

1826. C. F. D. Moule, "A Note on Ephesians 1 : 22, 23," *ET*, 60 (1948-1949), 53.

1827. J. A. Robinson, "The Church as the Fulfilment of the Christ: a Note on Ephesians 1 : 23," *Exp*, 5th series, 7 (1898), 241-259.

1828. A. E. N. Hitchcock, "Ephesians 1 : 23," *ET*, 22 (1910-1911), 91.

1829. R. H. Riensch, "Exegesis of Eph. 2 : 1-7," *LQ*, 2 (1950), 70-74.

1830. H. Sahlin, " 'Omskärelsen i Kristus'. En interpretation av Ef. 2 : 11-22," *STK*, 23 (1947), 11-24.

1831. Alfred Gill, "Note upon Ephesians 2 : 14," *ET*, 2 (1890-1891), 93.

1832. R. Scott, "Ephesians 2 : 14," *ET*, 2 (1890-1891), 106.

1833. Peter Fraenkel, "A Note on Ephesians 2 : 14: αὐτὸς γάρ ἐστιν ἡ εἰρήνη ἡμῶν," *ET*, 53 (1941-1942), 242.

1834. Norman Snaith, "Further Note on Ephesians 2 : 14," *ET*, 53 (1941-1942), 325-326.

1835. P. Feine, "Eph. 2, 14-16," *TSK*, 72 (1899), 540-574.

1836. R. E. Bartlett, "St. Paul on the Trinity — Ephesians 2 : 18," *Exp*, 2nd series, 4 (1882), 321-331.

1837. A. Kolbe, "Auslegung der Stelle Eph. 2, 19-22," *TSK*, 51 (1878), 135-150.

1838. L. Spreer, "Über Ephes. 2, 19-22," *TSK*, 52 (1879), 128-130.
1839. G. H. Whitaker, "The Chief Corner-Stone," *Exp*, 8th series, 22 (1921), 470-472 [Eph. 2 : 20].
1840. S. Lyonnet, "De Christo summo angulari lapide secundum Eph. 2, 20," *VD*, 27 (1949), 74-83.
1841. F. H. Chase, "Note on the Word ναός in Ephesians 2 : 21," *Exp*, 3rd series, 6 (1887), 318-319.
1842. B. Borucki, "Paulus vinctus Iesu Christi," *VD*, 6 (1926), 342-348; 7 (1927), 20-23 [Eph. 3 : 1].
1843. H. J. Flowers, "The Grace of God Given to Paul — A Study of Ephesians 3 : 1-13," *RE*, 25 (1928), 155-172.
1844. Llynfi Davies, " 'I wrote afore in few words' (Eph. 3 : 3)," *ET*, 46 (1934-1935), 568.
1845. J. S. Purton, "Note on Ephesians III, 3-4," *Exp*, 2nd series, 7 (1884), 237-238.
1846. E. Preuschen, "Σύνσωμος," *ZNW*, 1 (1900), 85-86 [Eph. 3 : 6].
1847. R. E. Thomas, "Ephesians 3 : 8," *ET*, 39 (1927-1928), 288.
1848. H. Liese, "De interiore homine (Eph. 3, 13-21)," *VD*, 12 (1932), 257-263.
1849. Florentinus Ogara, " 'Scire . . . supereminentem scientiae caritatem Christi': Notae in Eph. 3, 13-21," *VD*, 15 (1935), 260-270.
1850. G. H. Whitaker, "Studies in Texts — The Address of the Prayer in Eph. 3 : 14 ff.," *Th*, 13 (1926), 220-223.
1851. F. M'Kenzie, "Exposition of Ephesians 3 : 15," *ET*, 2 (1890-1891), 93-94.
1852. Edward Spurrier, "Note on Ephesians 3 : 18," *ET*, 2 (1890-1891), 164.
1853. George Thompson, "The Fulness of God," *ET*, 3 (1891-1892), 225-226 [Eph. 3 : 19].
1854. H. Liese, " 'In vinculo pacis' (Eph. 4, 1-6)," *VD*, 13 (1933), 289-294.
1855. Florentinus Ogara, " 'Solliciti servare unitatem spiritus in vinculo pacis': Notae in Eph. 4, 1-6 et Eph. 4, 23-28," *VD*, 15 (1935), 292-301.
1856. W. N. Hall, "Fatherhood and Sonship," *ET*, 6 (1894-1895), 190 [Eph. 4 : 6].
1857. S. Hoekstra, "Wie is het subject van de verba in de pericope Efes. 4 : 7 vgg., God of Christus?" *TT*, 1 (1867), 73-78.

1858. E. Engelhardt, "Der Gedankengang des Abschnittes Eph. 4, 7-16," *TSK*, 44 (1871), 107-145.

1859. E. Nestle, "Zum Zitat in Eph. 4, 8," *ZNW*, 4 (1903), 344-345.

1860. J. Dalmer, "Bemerkungen zu 1 Kor. 10, 3-4 und Eph. 4, 8-10," *TSK*, 63 (1890), 569-592.

1861. E. Bröse, "Der descensus ad infernos, Eph. 4, 8-10," *NKZ*, 9 (1898), 447-455.

1862. F. W. Grosheide, "Ef. 4 : 9, κατέβη εἰς τὰ κατώτερα (μέρη) τῆς γῆς," *TS*, 28 (1910), 201-202.

1863. J. H. Smith, "Exegetical Note. Ephesians xiv [i.e. iv], 11-12," *USR*, 1 (1889-1890), 181-183.

1864. H. J. Flowers, "The Old Life and the New — A Study of Ephesians 4 : 17-24," *RE*, 26 (1929), 272-285.

1865. F. J. Briggs, "Ephesians 4 : 20, 21," *ET*, 39 (1927-1928), 526.

1866. C. A. Scott, "Ephesians 4 : 21: As the Truth is in Jesus," *Exp*, 8th series, 3 (1912), 178-185.

1867. M. B. Lang, "A Comparison: Isaiah 1 : 18 and Ephesians 4 : 25-29," *ET*, 8 (1896-1897), 405-406.

1868. [F. Fr] Zyro, "Ephes. 4, 26, ὀργίζεσθε, καὶ μὴ ἁμαρτάνετε," *TSK*, 14 (1841), 681-690.

1869. Hubert Foston, "Wrath's Quiet Curfew: An Expository Note on Eph. 4 : 26," *ET*, 18 (1906-1907), 480.

1870. W. D. Morris, "Ephesians 4 : 28," *ET*, 41 (1929-1930), 237.

1871. J. A. Findlay, "Ephesians 4 : 29," *ET*, 46 (1934-1935), 429.

1872. W. E. Wilson, "Ephesians 4 : 32," *ET*, 33 (1921-1922), 279.

1873. H. Liese, "Filii lucis, non iam tenebrarum (Eph. 5, 1-9)," *VD*, 12 (1932), 33-38.

1874. Florentinus Ogara, " 'Imitatores Dei . . . lux in Domino' (Eph. 5, 1-9)," *VD*, 17 (1937), 33-38, 70-74.

1875. J. N. Lindeboom, "De vrucht des Geestes. Ef. 5 : 9 en 10," *GTT*, 4 (1903), 4-8.

1876. Bent Noack, "Das Zitat in Ephes. 5, 14," *ST*, 5 (1951 [1952]), 52-64.

1877. Alfred Gill, "Ephesians 5 : 19: Psalms and Hymns of Spiritual Praise," *ET*, 2 (1890-1891), 165.

1878. A. B. Grosart, "Psalms and Hymns of Spiritual Praise," *ET*, 2 (1890-1891), 180 [Eph. 5 : 19].

1879. Manuel de los Ríos, "La prueba del sacramento del matrimonio en Ef. 5, 22-23," *EB*, 7 (1935), 189-200.

1880. John Dougherty, "The Confraternity Version of Eph. 5 : 32," *CBQ*, 8 (1946), 97.

1881. J. N. Lindeboom, "De H. Schrift over dienstknechten en heeren, Ef. 6 : 5-9," *GTT*, 4 (1903), 119-124, 150-156.

1882. J. N. Lindeboom, "De geestelijke Wapenrusting, Ef. 6 : 10-17," *GTT*, 7 (1906), 75-76, 84-88, 97-101, 134-139, 173-178.

1883. A. Vitti, "Militum Christi Regis arma iuxta S. Paulum (Eph. 6, 11-18)," *VD*, 7 (1927), 310-318.

1884. W. Röther, "Kritische Bemerkungen über die Stelle Ephes. 6, 12," *TSK*, 8 (1835), 970-975.

1885. John Rutherford, "Our Wrestling: Ephesians 6 : 12," *ET*, 2 (1890-1891), 181-182.

1886. D. E. H. Whiteley, "Expository Problems, Ephesians 6 : 12 — Evil Powers," *ET*, 68 (1956-1957), 100-103.

1887. L. L. Barclay, "Ephesians 6 : 14," *ET*, 2 (1890-1891), 117-118.

1888. A. J. Th. Jonker, "Ἡ ἑτοιμασία τοῦ εὐαγγελίου τῆς εἰρήνης (Ef. 6 : 15)," *TS*, 11 (1893), 443-451.

1889. A. F. Buscarlet, "The 'Preparation' of the Gospel of Peace," *ET*, 9 (1897-1898), 38-40 [Eph. 6 : 15].

1890. J. A. F. Gregg, "Ἐτοιμασία in Ephesians 6 : 15," *ET*, 56 (1944-1945), 54.
On Eph. 4 : 8-10, see number 1224 f.

7. The Epistle to the Philippians

a. *Textual Criticism*

1891. J. M. S. Baljon, "Opmerkingen op het gebied van de Conjecturaalcritiek: De Brief aan de Filippiërs," *TS*, 3 (1885), 220-233.

1892. J. H. Michael, "Two Brief Marginal Notes in the Text of Philippians," *ET*, 35 (1923-1924), 139-140 [Phil. 1 : 22].

b. *Historical and Literary Criticism*

1893. A. Hilgenfeld, "Der Brief an die Philipper, nach Inhalt und Ursprung untersucht," *ZWT*, 14 (1871), 309-335.

1894. E. Hinsch, "Untersuchungen zum Philipperbrief," *ZWT*, 16 (1873), 59-85.

1895. A. Hilgenfeld, "Hoekstra und der Philipperbrief," *ZWT*, 18 (1875), 566-576.

1896. S. Hoekstra, "Over de echtheid van den brief aan de Philippensen," *TT*, 9 (1875), 416-479.

1897. A. Hilgenfeld, "Der Brief des Paulus an die Philipper
und C. Holsten's Kritik desselben," *ZWT*, 20 (1877),
145-186.

1898. C. H. van Rhijn, "De jongste literatuur over de Schriften des
Nieuwen Verbonds: De Brief aan de Filippiërs," *TS*, 3
(1885), 291-300.

1899. D. Völter, "Zwei Briefe an die Philipper," *TT*, 26 (1892),
10-44, 117-146.

1900. [F. A.] Henle, "Philippi und die Philippergemeinde," *TQ*,
75 (1893), 67-104.

1901. H. A. A. Kennedy, "The Historical Background of the
Philippians," *ET*, 10 (1898-1899), 22-24.

1902. E. C. Selwyn, "The Christian Prophets at Philippi," *Exp*,
6th series, 4 (1901), 29-38.

1903. M. Albertz, "Über die Abfassung des Philipperbriefs des
Paulus zu Ephesus," *TSK*, 83 (1910), 551-594.

1904. A. van Veldhuizen, "Een vertaling van Paulus' Brief aan de
Filippenzen," *TS*, 31 (1913), 335-344.

1905. Gerard Ball, "The Epistle to the Philippians: a Reply," *Exp*,
8th series, 8 (1914), 143-154.

1906. Maurice Jones, "The Integrity of the Epistle to the Philippians," *Exp*, 8th series, 8 (1914), 457-473.

1907. Kirsopp Lake, "The Critical Problem of the Epistle to the
Philippians," *Exp*, 8th series, 7 (1914), 481-493.

1908. James Moffatt, "Literary Illustrations of Philippians,"
Exp, 8th series, 8 (1914), 473-480.

1909. J. H. Michael, "The Philippian Interpolation: Where does
it End?" *Exp*, 8th series, 19 (1920), 49-63.

1910. G. S. Duncan, "A New Setting for Paul's Epistle to the
Philippians," *ET*, 43 (1931-1932), 7-11.

1911. Paul Joüon, "Notes philologiques sur quelques versets de
l'épître aux Philippiens," *RSR*, 28 (1938), 223-233, 299-310.

c. *Theological Studies*

1912. F. Godet, "The Thanks of an Apostle," *Exp*, 3rd series,
6 (1887), 113-129.

1913. M. R. Vincent, "Some Aspects of Paul's Theology in the
Philippian Epistle," *AJT*, 3 (1899), 107-116, 570-577.

1914. Eugene Caldwell, "The Ideal Christian; a Book Study of Philippians," *USR*, 27 (1915-1916), 18-26.

1915. James Moffatt, "Expository Notes on the Epistle to the Philippians," *Exp*, 8th series, 12 (1916), 339-353.

1916. Lyder Brun, "Zur Formel 'in Christus Jesus' im Brief des Paulus an die Philipper," *SO*, 1 (1922), 19-38.

1917. W. H. Stuart, "The Heavenly Citizenship — A Study in the Book of Philippians," *USR*, 37 (1925-1926), 48-55.

1918. J. M. Shaw, "The Message of the Epistles; Philippians," *ET*, 45 (1933-1934), 203-209.

1919. George Johnston, "The Life of Christians in the World: An Exposition of Phil. 1 : 1 — 2 : 4," *CJT*, 3 (1957), 248-254.

d. *Exegesis of Individual Passages*

1920. James Moffatt, "A New Commentary upon Philippians," *Exp*, 8th series, 16 (1918), 215-221.

1921. Florentinus Ogara, " 'Socios gaudii mei omnes vos esse': Notae in Phil. 1, 6-11," *VD*, 15 (1935) 324-330.

1922. J. L. Davies, "St. Paul's Χάρις," *Exp*, 4th series, 5 (1892), 343-346 [Phil. 1 : 7].

1923. U. Holzmeister, " 'Viscera Christi,' " *VD*, 16 (1936), 161-165 [Phil. 1 : 8].

1924. T. Hawthorn, "Philippians 1 : 12-19, with special reference to vv. 15, 16, 17," *ET*, 62 (1950-1951), 316-317.

1925. R. F. Weymouth, "Notes on Philippians 1 : 22," *Exp*, 2nd series, 5 (1883), 396-398.

1926. Vernon Bartlet, "Philippians 1 : 22," *ET*, 4 (1892-1893), 177.

1927. Richard Roberts, "Old Texts in Modern Translation, Philippians 1 : 27 (Goodspeed)," *ET*, 49 (1937-1938), 325-328.

1928. Ch. Guignebert, "Exégèse sur Philippiens II," *RHPR*, 3 (1923), 512-533.

1929. Q. Hain, "Ein Versuch zur endgültigen Erklärung der Ellipse in Phil. 2, 5," *TSK*, 66 (1893), 169-172.

1930. U. Holzmeister, " 'Hoc enim sentite in vobis, quod et in Christo Iesu' (Phil. 2, 5)," *VD*, 22 (1942), 225-227.

1931. E. E., "The Mind That Was in Christ," *Exp*, 2nd series, 1 (1881), 319-320 [Phil. 2 : 5-8].

1932. J. H. Bindley, "Fresh Light upon Philippians 2 : 5-8," *Exp*, 8th series, 26 (1923), 442-446.

1933. A. J. McClain, "The Doctrine of the Kenosis in Philippians 2 : 5-8," *BR*, 13 (1928), 506-527.

1934. J. E. Swallow, "Philippians 2 : 5-8," *Th*, 30 (1935), 298-300.

1935. E. H. Gifford, "The Incarnation: A Study of Philippians 2 : 5-11," *Exp*, 5th series, 4 (1896), 161-177, 241-263.

1936. William Hull, "Epistle for Palm Sunday," *LQ*, 26 (1896), 533-539 [Phil. 2 : 5-11].

1937. J. B. Nisius, S. J., "Zur Erklärung von Phil. II, 5-11," *ZKT*, 21 (1897), 276-306; 23 (1899), 75-113.

1938. J. Labourt, "Notes d'exégèse sur Philip. II, 5-11," *RB*, 7 (1898), 402-415, 553-563.

1939. Buchanan Blake, "The True Kenosis (Phil. 2 : 5-11)," *ET*, 19 (1907-1908), 565-566.

1940. Jb. van Gilse, "Verklaring van Philippensen II, vers 5-11," *TT*, 51 (1917), 321-325.

1941. F. Loofs, "Das altkirchliche Zeugnis gegen die herrschende Auffassung der Kenosisstelle (Phil. 2, 5-11)," *TSK*, 100 (1927-1928), 1-102.

1942. Nathan Söderblom, "Concluding Meditation upon Phil. 2 : 5-11," *Th*, 17 (1928), 257-260.

1943. Dr. Bornhäuser, "Zum Verständnis von Philipper 2 : 5-11," *NKZ*, 44 (1933), 428-444, 453-462.

1944. Florentinus Ogara, " 'Hoc sentite in vobis, quod et in Christi Iesu': Notae in Phil. 2, 5-11," *VD*, 15 (1935), 99-109.

1945. A. A. Stephenson, "Christ's Self-Abasement; Phil. 2 : 5-11, the Epistle for Palm Sunday," *CBQ*, 1 (1939), 296-313.

1946. Josef Gewiess, "Zum altkirchlichen Verständnis der Kenosisstelle (Phil. 2, 5-11)," *TQ*, 128 (1948), 463-487.

1947. Thorleif Boman, "Fil. 2, 5-11," *NTT*, 53 (1952), 193-212.

1948. C. N. Kähler, "Bemerkungen zu Philipper 2, 5-14, besonders in Betreff des οὐχ ἁρπαγμὸν ἡγήσατο τὸ εἶναι ἴσα θεῷ," *TSK*, 30 (1857), 99-112.

1949. M. Stein, "Über Philipper 2, 6," *TSK*, 10 (1837), 165-180.

1950. H. Fr. Th. L. Ernesti, "Noch ein Wort über Philipper 2, 6," *TSK*, 24 (1851), 595-630.

1951. J. A. Beet, "Thought it not Robbery to be Equal with God," *Exp*, 3rd series, 5 (1887), 115-125 [Phil. 2 : 6].

1952. L. Wetzel "Über ἁρπαγμός in der Stelle Phil. 2, 6," *TSK*, 60 (1887), 535-552.

1953. J. A. Beet, "Some Difficult Passages in St. Paul's Epsitles; I, Phil. 2 : 6," *ET*, 3 (1891-1892), 307-308.

1954. J. S. Ff. Chamberlain, "The Kenosis," *ET*, 4 (1892-1893), 189-190. [Phil. 2 : 6].

1955. E. Nestle, "'Εν μορφῇ Θεοῦ ὑπάρχων, Phil. 2, 6," *TSK*, 66 (1893), 173-174.

1956. J. A. Beet, "Harpagmos, Philippians 2 : 6: A Reply," *ET*, 6 (1894-1895), 526-528.

1957. F. G. Chomondeley, "Harpagmos, Philippians 2 : 6," *ET*, 7 (1895-1896), 47-48.

1958. J. Massie, "Harpagmos, Philippians 2 : 6," *ET*, 7 (1895-1896), 141.

1959. E. P. Badham, "Phillipians [sic] 2 : 6; ἁρπαγμόν," *ET*, 19 (1907-1908), 331-333.

1960. Adhémar d'Alès, "Philip. II, 6, οὐκ ἁρπαγμὸν ἡγήσατο," *RSR*, 1 (1910), 260-269.

1961. Martin Dibelius, "ἁρπαγμός, Phil. 2, 6," *TLZ*, 40 (1915), 557-558.

1962. A. Jülicher, "Ein philologisches Gutachten über Phil. 2, 6," *ZNW*, 16 (1915), 1-17.

1963. P. E. Kretzmann, " 'Hielt er's nicht für einen Raub,' Phil. 2 : 6," *CTM*, 2 (1931), 244-258.

1964. F. Kattenbusch, "'Αρπαγμόν? Ἄπραγμον! Phil. 2, 6. Ein Beitrag zur paulinischen Christologie," *TSK*, 104 (1932), 373-420.

1965. Sigmund Mowinckel, "Et gammeltestamentlig analogen til ἁρπαγμός Fil. 2, 6," *NTT*, 40 (1939), 208-211.

1966. Anton Fridrichsen, " 'Nicht für Raub achten' Phil. 2 : 6," *TZ*, 2 (1946), 395.

1967. Hans Bruppacher, "Zur Redewendung 'nicht für Raub achten' Phil. 2, 6," *TZ*, 3 (1947), 234.

1968. H. Kruse, "Harpagmos (Ph. 2, 6)," *VD*, 27 (1949), 355-360.

1969. H. Kruse, "Iterum 'Harpagmos' (Phil. 2, 6)," *VD*, 29 (1951), 206-214.

1970. Tomas Arvedson, "Phil. 2, 6 und Mt. 10, 39," *ST*, 5 (1951 [1952]), 49-51.

1971. Louis Baugher, "Interpretation of Philippians 2 : 6, 7," *LQ*, 8 (1878), 119-124.

1972. A. J. Th. Jonker, "Is er verwantschap tusschen de doopliturgie van Severus en Filipp. 2 : 6 en 7 ?" *TS*, 10 (1892), 9-29.

1973. M. J. Gruenthaner, "The Confraternity Version of Phil. 2 : 6, 7a," *CBQ*, 7 (1945), 231-235.

1974. H. Fr. Th. L. Ernesti, "Philipp. II, 6 ff., aus einer Anspielung auf Genes. II. III. erläutert," *TSK*, 21 (1848), 858-924.

1975. B. W. Horan, "The Apostolic Kerygma in Philippians 2 : 6-9," *ET*, 62 (1950-1951), 60-61.

1976. Wilibald Grimm, "Über die Stelle Philipp. 2, 6-11," *ZWT*, 16 (1873), 33-59.

1977. Jacques Dupont, "Jésus-Christ dans son abaissement et son exaltation, d'après Phil. II, 6-11," *RSR*, 37 (1950), 500-514.

1978. Karl Petersen, "'Εαυτὸν ἐκένωσεν, Phil. 2, 7" *SO*, 12 (1933), 96-101.

1979. W. E. Wilson, "Philippians 2 : 7," *ET*, 56 (1944-1945), 280.

1980. Harald Riesenfeld, "Μέχρι θανάτου. Zu Phil. 2,8," *Nunt*, 5 (1951), cols. 35-36.

1981. P., "On Philippians ii. 12," *JCSP*, 2 (1855), 92.

1982. J. H. Burn, "Philippians 2 : 12," *ET*, 34 (1922-1923), 562.

1983. P. Thomson, "Philippians 2 : 12," *ET*, 24 (1922-1923), 429.

1984. G. S. Baker, "Note on St. Paul, Philippians ii. 12," *Herm*, 56 (1940), 146-147.

1985. J. Warren, "Work Out Your Own Salvation," *EQ*, 16 (1944), 125-137 [Phil. 2 : 12].

1986. J. J. Murray, "St. Paul on Predestination," *Exp*, 2nd series, 7 (1884), 145-160 [Phil. 2 : 12-13].

1987. [E.] Kühl, "Über Philipper 2, 12.13," *TSK*, 71 (1898), 557-581.

1988. R. Schmidt, "Über Philipper 2, 12 und 13," *TSK*, 80 (1907), 344-363.

1989. J. R. Linden, "Über Philipp. 2, 12.13.14., Hebr. 5, 7.8.9., und 2 Petri 1, 19.20.21.," *TSK*, 33 (1860), 750-762.

1990. A.-M. Denis, "Versé en libation (Phil. II, 17) = Versé son sang?" *RSR*, 45 (1957), 567-570.

1991. James Moffatt, "The Responsibility of Self-Assertion," *ET*, 10 (1898-1899), 445-449 [Phil. 3-4].

1992. M. Zerwick, "Gaudium et pax custodia cordium (Phil. 3, 1; 4, 7)," *VD*, 31 (1953), 101-104.

1993. W. J. Ferrar, "A Study of St. Paul," *Exp*, 8th series, 23 (1922), 353-359 [Phil. 3 : 5-18].

1994. J. T. Forestell, "Christian Perfection and Gnosis in Philippians 3, 7-16," *CBQ*, 18 (1956), 123-136.

1995. Sally N. Roach, "The Power of His Resurrection," *RE*, 24 (1927), 45-55, 297-304; 25 (1928), 29-38, 176-194 [Phil. 3 : 10].

1996. H. T. Kuist, "Does Philippians 3 : 10-14 Suggest a Method in Prayer?" *Exp*, 9th series, 3 (1925), 382-384.

1997. J. J. Owen, "Examination of Philip. 3 : 11 and Rev. 20 : 4," *BS*, 21 (1864), 362-383.

1998. A. Vitti, " 'Comprehensus sum a Christo Iesu' (Phil. 3, 12)," *VD*, 9 (1929), 353-359.

1999. E. Bröse, "Paulus durch Virgil kommentiert, zu Phil. 3, 12-14," *TSK*, 93 (1920-1921), 78-82.

2000. W. F. M'Micheal, " 'Be ye Followers together of Me,' " *ET*, 5 (1893-1894), 287 [Phil. 3 : 17].

2001. Florentinus Ogara, " 'Nostra conversatio in caelis est' Phil. 3, 17-4, 3," *VD*, 18 (1938), 321-328.

2002. Samuel Cox, "The Heavenly Citizenship," *Exp*, 2nd series, 3 (1882), 303-313 [Phil. 3 : 20].

2003. J. de Zwaan, "Philippenzen 3 : 20 en de κοινή," *TS*, 31 (1913), 298-300.

2004. Neal Flanagan, "A Note on Philippians 3, 20-21," *CBQ*. 18 (1956), 8-9.

2005. Erik Peterson, "Zu Philipper 4, 1," *Nunt*, 4 (1950), cols, 27-28.

2006. J. A. Beet, "Did Euodia and Syntyche Quarrel?" *ET*, 5 (1893-1894), 179-180 [Phil. 4 : 2].

2007. C. H. van Rhijn, "Euodia en Syntyche," *TS*, 21 (1903), 300-309 [Phil. 4 : 2].

2008. J. C. Watts, "The Alleged Quarrel of Euodia and Syntyche," *ET*, 5 (1893-1894), 286-287 [Phil. 4 : 2].

2009. Rendel Harris, "St. Paul and Aeschylus," *ET*, 35 (1923-1924), 151-153 [Phil. 4 : 4].

2010. James Moffatt, "The History of Joy; a Brief Exposition of Phil. 4 : 4-7 (R.V.)," *ET*, 9 (1897-1898), 334-336.

2011. Florentinus Ogara, " 'Dominus prope est' (Phil. 4, 4-7)," *VD*, 17 (1937), 353-359.

2012. U. Holzmeister, " 'Gaudete in Domino semper' (Phil. 4, 4-9)," *VD*, 4 (1924), 358-362.

2013. T. W. Chambers, "'Ο κύριος ἐγγύς, Philip. iv. 5.," *JBL* (December, 1886), 108-110.

2014. W. H. Weeda, "Filippenzen 4 vs 6 en 7. Over Bezorgdheid," *TS*, 34 (1916), 326-335.

2015. J. S. Stewart, "Old Texts in Modern Translation, Philippians 4 : 6, 7 (Moffatt)," *ET*, 49 (1937-1938), 269-271.
2016. J. A. Beet, "The Christian Secret," *Exp*, 3rd series, 10 (1889), 174-189 [Phil. 4 : 10].
2017. R. J. Drummond, "Note on Philippians 4 : 10-19," *ET*, 11 (1899-1900), 284.
2018. R. J. Drummond, "A Note on Philippians 4 : 10-19," *ET*, 11 (1899-1900), 381.
2019. J. C. Lambert, "Note on Philippians 4 : 10-19," *ET*, 11 (1899-1900), 333-334.
2020. H. A. A. Kennedy, "The Financial Colouring of Philippians 4 : 15-18," *ET*, 12 (1900-1901), 43-44.
2021. Leon Morris, "Καὶ ἅπαξ καὶ δίς," *NT*, 1 (1956), 205-208 [Phil. 4 : 16; I Thess. 2 : 18].
2022. J. A. Beet, "Epaphroditus and the Gift from Philippi," *Exp*, 3rd series, 9 (1889), 64-75 [Phil. 4 : 18].
On Phil. 1 : 27, see number 581; 2 : 5, number 657; 2 : 6, numbers 530 and 531; 2 : 20, numbers 555 and 556; 3 : 1, number 801; 4 : 16, number 643.

8. The Epistle to the Colossians
a. *Textual Criticism*

2023. J. M. S. Baljon, "Opmerkingen op het gebied van de Conjecturaalcritiek: De Brief aan de Kolossers," *TS*, 3 (1885), 313-343.
2024. Frank Alexander, "A Peculiar Reading of Colossians 2 : 5," *ET*, 51 (1939-1940), 394-395.
2025. Ernest Clapton, "A Suggested New Reading in Col. 2 : 23," *ET*, 36 (1924-1925), 382.
2026. George Farmer, "Colossians 3 : 14," *ET*, 332 (1920-1921), 427.

b. *Historical and Literary Criticism*

2027. [M.] Schneckenburger, "Bemerkungen über die Irrlehre zu Colossä," *TSK*, 5 (1832), 840-850.
2028. F. Wiggers, "Das Verhältniss des Apostels Paulus zu der christlichen Gemeinde in Kolossä," *TSK*, 11 (1838), 165-188.
2029. A. H. Blom, "De polemiek in den Brief aan de Kolossers," *TT*, 16 (1882), 393-427.

2030. H. Holtzmann, "Der Kolosserbrief und seine neueste Auslegung," *ZWT*, 26 (1883), 460-480.

2031. C. H. van Rhijn, "De jongste literatuur over de Schriften des
des Nieuwen Verbonds: De Brief aan de Kolossers," *TS*, 3
(1885), 301-312.

2032. F. Godet, "The First Indication of Gnosticism in Asia Minor,"
Exp, 3rd series, 4 (1886), 161-184.

2033. W. Soltau, "Die ursprüngliche Gestalt des Kolosserbriefs,"
TSK, 78 (1905), 521-562.

2034. A. van Veldhuizen, "Kolossenzen," *TS*, 35 (1917), 271-278.

2035. C. R. Bowen, "The Original Form of Paul's Letter to the
Colossians," *JBL*, 43 (1924), 177-206.

2036. John Knox, "Philemon and the Authenticity of Colossians,"
JR, 18 (1938), 144-160.

2037. Günther Bornkamm, "Die Häresie des Kolosserbriefes," *TLZ*,
73 (1948), 11-20.

2038. J. M. Robinson, "A Formal Analysis of Colossians 1 : 15-20,"
JBL, 76 (1957), 270-287.
See also number 309.

(1) Relation to the Epistle to the Ephesians
See numbers 1778-1783.

c. *Theological Studies*

2039. James Iverach, "The Epistle to the Colossians and its
Christology," *ET*, 25 (1913-1914), 150-153, 205-209.

2040. E. W. Work, "The Message of the Epistle to the Colossians,"
BR, 2 (1917), 100-129.

2041. E. Driessen, "De auxilio Dei et salute hominis apud S.
Paulum (Col. 1, 19-20; Eph. 1, 9-10)," *VD*, 21 (1941), 129-140.

2042. Edwin Lewis, "Paul and the Perverters of Christianity;
Revelation through the Epistle to the Colossians," *Interp*, 2
(1948), 143-157.

2043. Alexander Ross, "The Epistle to the Colossians and its
Message for To-day," *EQ*, 23 (1951), 19-29.
See also numbers 578 and 2624.

d. *Exegesis of Individual Passages*

2044. Alexander Maclaren, "The Epistle to the Colossians," *Exp*,
3rd series, 1 (1885), 12-28, 127-141, 187-200, 254-267, 321-334,

418-431; 2 (1885), 44-57, 106-119, 187-203, 263-276, 356-369;
3 (1886), 46-58, 98-109, 217-228, 302-315, 378-390, 434-445; 4
(1886), 44-60, 95-107, 204-216, 293-305, 346-361, 465-478; 5
(1887), 60-73, 125-138, 215-225.

2045. James Moffatt, "Expository Notes upon Colossians," *Exp*,
8th series, 14 (1917), 128-144.

2046. G. G. Findlay, "A Biblical Note, *Exp*, 1st series, 10 (1879),
74-80 [Col. 1 : 3-5].

2047. O. A. Piper, "The Saviour's Eternal Work; an Exegesis of
Colossians 1 : 9-29," *Interp*, 3 (1949), 286-298.

2048. Florentinus Ogara, "Qui nos transtulit in regnum Filii
dilectionis suae (Col. 1, 13)," *VD*, 17 (1937), 296-302.

2049. E. Preuschen, "Εἰκὼν τοῦ θεοῦ τοῦ ἀοράτου, Kol. 1, 15,"
ZNW, 18 (1917-1918), 243.

2050. A. W. Argyle, "πρωτότοκος πάσης κτίσεως (Colossians 1 : 15),"
ET, 66 (1954-1955), 61-62.

2051. F. Schleiermacher, "Über Koloss. 1, 15-20," *TSK*, 5 (1832),
497-537.

2052. L. E. Barton, "The Cosmic Christ," *RE*, 29 (1932), 459-469
[Col. 1 : 18].

2053. L. T. Wohlfeil, "What is Meant by 'All Fulness,' Col. 1 : 19?"
CTM, 4 (1933), 339-345.

2054. A. C. Oke, "A Hebraistic Construction in Colossians 1 : 19-
22," *ET*, 63 (1951-1952), 155-156.

2055. Johann Michl, "Die 'Versöhnung' (Kol. 1, 20)," *TQ*, 128
(1948), 442-462.

2056. B. N. Wambacq, "Per eum reconciliare . . . quae in caelis
sunt," *RB*, 55 (1948), 35-42 [Col. 1 : 20].

2057. J. E. Huther, "Versuch einer Erklärung von Kol. Kap. 1. V.
24," *TSK*, 11 (1838), 189-204.

2058. P. J. Gloag, "The Complement of Christ's Afflictions,"
Exp, 1st series, 7 (1878), 224-236 [Col. 1 : 24].

2059. J. S. Purton, "Biblical Notes," *Exp*, 1st series, 7 (1878),
474-476 [Col. 1 : 24].

2060. W. R. G. Moir, "Colossians 1 : 24," *ET*, 42 (1930-1931),
479-480.

2061. Josef Schmid, "Kol 1, 24," *BibZ*, 21 (1933), 330-344.

2062. G. Kittel, "Kol. 1, 24," *ZST*, 18 (1941), 186-191.

2063. B. N. Wambacq, " 'Adimpleo ea quae desunt passionum
Christi,' " *VD*, 27 (1949), 17-22 [Col. 1 : 24].

2064. J. B. Weatherspoon, "The Preacher of Reconciliation," *RE*, 31 (1934), 91-97 [Col. 1 : 24-2 : 5].

2065. George Matheson, "The Pauline Argument for a Future State," *Exp*, 1st series, 9 (1879), 264-284 [Col. 1 : 27].

2066. J. Leal, "Ut exhibeamus omnem hominem perfectum in Christo," *VD*, 18 (1938), 178-186 [Col. 1 : 28].

2067. A. H. Blom, "Verklaring van τὰ στοιχεῖα τοῦ κόσμου," *TT*, 17 (1883), 1-13 [Col. 2 : 8, 20; Gal. 4 : 3].

2068. J. van Wageningen, "Τὰ στοιχεῖα τοῦ κόσμου," *TS*, 35 (1917), 1-6 [Col. 2 : 8, 20].

2069. H. A. A. Kennedy, "Two Exegetical Notes on St. Paul: II, Colossians 2 : 10-15," *ET*, 28 (1916-1917), 363-366.

2070. G. Megas, "Das χειρόγραφον Adams. Ein Beitrag zu Col. 2, 13-15," *ZNW*, 27 (1928), 305-320.

2071. W. P. Workman, " 'Nailing it to His Cross,' " *ET*, 5 (1893-1894), 526 [Col. 2 : 14].

2072. P. X. M. a Vallisoleto, " 'Delens . . . chirographum' (Col. 2, 14)," *VD*, 12 (1932), 181-185.

2073. John Rutherford, "Note on Colossians 2 : 15," *ET*, 18 (1906-1907), 565-566.

2074. P. X. M. a Vallisoleto, " 'Et spolians principatus et potestates . . .' (Col. 2, 15)," *VD*, 13 (1933), 187-192.

2075. I. Heikel, "Kol. 2, 16-18," *TSK*, 107 (1936), 464-465.

2076. G. G. Findlay, "The Reading and Rendering of Colossians 2 : 18," *Exp*, 1st series, 11 (1880), 385-398.

2077. J. B. McClellan, "Colossians 2 : 18: A Criticism of the Revised Version," *Exp*, 7th series, 9 (1910), 385-398.

2078. A. Fridrichsen, "Θέλων, Col 2, 18," *ZNW*, 21 (1922), 135-137.

2079. S. Eitrem, "Ἐμβατεύω, Note sur Col. 2, 18," *ST*, 2 (1948 [1949]), 90-94.

2080. L. T. Wohlfeil, "A Few Remarks on Col. 2 : 18, 19a," *CTM*, 8 (1937), 424-433.

2081. Rendel Harris, "St. Paul and Aristophanes," *ET*, 34 (1922-1923), 151-156 [Col. 2 : 18, 23].

2082. B. G. Hall, "The Second Chapter of Colossians," *ET* 35 (1923-1924), 44 [Col. 2 : 18, 23; Eph. 4 : 14].

2083. G. H. Whitaker, "Studies in Texts — The Building and the Body," *Th*, 13 (1926), 335-336 [Col. 2 : 19].

2084. H. S. Bettenson, "Studies in Texts — Col. 2 : 20-23," *Th*, 26 (1933), 154-156.

2085. P. L. Hedley, "Ad Colossenes 2, 20-3, 4," *ZNW*, 27 (1928), 211-216.

2086. Robert Leaney, "Colossians 2 : 21-23 (The Use of πρός)," *ET*, 64 (1952-1953), 92.

2087. G. G. Findlay, "On Colossians 2 : 22-23," *Exp*, 1st series, 12 (1880), 289-303.

2088. B. G. Hall, "Colossians 2 : 23," *ET*, 36 (1924-1925), 285.

2089. Bo Reicke, "Zum sprachlichen Verständnis von Kol. 2, 23," *ST*, 6 (1952 [1953]), 39-53.

2090. F. W. Grosheide, "Kol. 3 : 1-4; I Petr. 1 : 3-5; I Joh. 3 : 1-2," *GTT*, 54 (1954), 139-147.

2091. C. M. Draper, " 'Your Life is hid with Christ in God' (Colossians 3 : 3)," *ET*, 27 (1915-1916), 427.

2092. Paul Joüon, "Notes sur Colossiens III, 5-11," *RSR*, 26 (1936), 186-189.

2093. Theodor Hermann, "Barbar und Skythe. Ein Erklärungsversuch zu Kol. 3, 11," *TB*, 9 (1930), 106-107.

2094. A. Vitti, "Animadversiones in Col. 3, 12-17," *VD*, 7 (1927), 35-41.

2095. Florentinus Ogara, " 'Caritatem habete, quod est vinculum perfectionis' (Col. 3, 12-17)," *VD*, 17 (1937), 335-343.

2096. J. M. Bover, "Caritas, perfectionis vinculum et virtus," *VD*, 1 (1921), 52-54 [Col. 3 : 14].

2097. Anton Fridrichsen, "Charité et perfection. Observation sur Col. 3, 14," *SO*, 19 (1939), 41-45.

2098. R. M. Pope, "Studies in Pauline Vocabulary; Redeeming the Time," *ET*, 22 (1910-1911), 552-554 [Col. 4 : 5].

2099. John Rutherford, "St. Paul's Epistle to the Laodiceans," *ET*, 19 (1907-1908), 311-314 [Col. 4 : 16].
On Col. 1 : 15, see number 963; 2 : 9, number 550.

9. The Two Epistles to the Thessalonians

a. *Textual, Historical, and Literary Criticism*

2100. W. Grimm, "Die Echtheit der Briefe an die Thessalonicher, gegen D. Baur's Angriff vertheidigt," *TSK*, 23 (1850), 753-816.

2101. A. Hilgenfeld, "Die beiden Briefe an die Thessalonicher, nach Inhalt und Ursprung," *ZWT*, 5 (1862), 225-264.

2102. C. H. van Rhijn, "De jongste literatuur over de Schriften des Nieuwen Verbonds: De Brieven aan de Thessalonikers," *TS*, 4 (1886), 282-309.

2103. Carl Clemen, "Paulus und die Gemeinde zu Thessalonike," *NKZ*, 7 (1896), 139-164.
2104. G. G. Findlay, "Recent Criticism of the Epistles to the Thessalonians," *Exp*, 6th series, 2 (1900), 252-261.
2105. G. R. Wynne, "The Problem of the Epistles to the Thessalonians," *Exp*, 7th series, 4 (1907), 364-372.
2106. E. J. Goodspeed, "The Epistles to the Thessalonians," *BW*, 34 (1909), 48-56.
2107. W. M. Ramsay, "Dr. Milligan's Edition of the Epistles to the Thessalonians," *Exp*, 7th series, 7 (1909), 1-17.
2108. E. H. Askwith, " 'I' and 'We' in the Thessalonian Epistles," *Exp*, 8th series, 1 (1911), 149-159.
2109. F. W. Grosheide, "De methode om de volgorde der Paulinische Brieven to bepalen, in het bijzonder in verband met de Brieven aan de Thessalonicensen onderzocht," *GTT*, 20 (1919-1920), 262-270, 305-319.
2110. W. Hadorn, "Die Abfassung der Thessalonicherbriefe auf der dritten Missionsreise und der Kanon des Marcion," *ZNW*, 19 (1919-1920), 67-72.
2111. T. H. Weir, "Notes on 1 and 2 Thessalonians," *ET*, 35 (1923-1924), 140.
2112. C. J. Costello, "Problems in Bible Revision, Saint Paul's Epistles to the Thessalonians," *CBQ*, 1 (1939), 256-263.
2113. L. O. Bristol, "Paul's Thessalonian Correspondence," *ET*, 55 (1943-1944), 223.
2114. Edward Thompson, "The Sequence of the Two Epistles to the Thessalonians," *ET*, 56 (1944-1945), 306-307.
2115. T. W. Manson, "St. Paul in Greece: the Letters to the Thessalonians," *BJRL*, 35 (1953), 428-447.
2116. F. Spadafora, "I e II lettera ai Tessalonicesi," *RivB*, 1 (1953), 5-24.
See also numbers 456 and 2811.

b. Theological Studies

2117. J. C. W. Laurent, "Der Pluralis maiestaticus in den Thessalonicherbriefen," *TSK*, 41 (1868), 159-166.
2118. F. Godet, "The First Love and Hope in Thessalonica," *Exp*, 3rd series, 1 (1885), 81-101.
2119. Buchanan Blake, "The Apocalyptic Setting of the Thessalonian Epistles," *Exp*, 9th series, 3 (1925), 126-139.

2120. J. B. Orchard, "Thessalonians and the Synoptic Gospels," *B*, 19 (1938), 19-42.
See also number 2662.

10. The First Epistle to the Thessalonians

a. *Textual, Historical, and Literary Criticism*

2121. R. A. Lipsius, "Über Zweck und Veranlassung des ersten Thessalonicherbriefs," *TSK*, 27 (1854), 903-934.

2122. J. J. Prins, "De eerste brief van Paulus aan de Thessalonikers," *TT*, 19 (1885), 552-559.

2123. [H.] von Soden, "Der erste Thessalonicherbrief," *TSK*, 58 (1885), 263-310.

2124. J. M. S. Baljon, "Opmerkingen op het gebied van de Conjecturaalcritiek: De 1e brief aan de Thessalonicensen," *TS*, 6 (1888), 188-195.

2125. James Moffatt, "Ethnic Parallels to I Thessalonians, etc.," *ET*, 14 (1902-1903), 568.

2126. Eberhard Nestle, "1 Thess. 3 : 3," *ET*, 18 (1906-1907), 479.

2127. C. E. Faw, "On the Writing of First Thessalonians," *JBL*, 71 (1952), 217-232.

b. *Theological Studies*

2128. E. Medley, "A Conception of Christ suggested by Paul's Earliest Extant Writing: a Study in 1 Thessalonians," *Exp*, 5th series, 4 (1896), 359-370.

2129. M. Mazien, "La résurrection des morts, d'après la première épître aux Thessaloniciens," *RB*, N.S. 4 (1907), 349-382.

2130. E. H. Askwith, "The Eschatological Section of 1 Thessalonians," *Exp*, 8th series, 1 (1911), 59-67.

2131. Edward Shillito, "Paul Upon Prayer," *Exp*, 8th series, 22 (1921), 438-444.

2132. W. F. Howard, "The Message of the Epistles; I Thessalonians," *ET*, 44 (1932-1933), 357-362.

2133. E. P. Blair, "The First Epistle to the Thessalonians," *Interp*, 2 (1948), 208-217.

2134. G. Bressan, "Dottrina ascetico-mistica della I ai Tessalonicesi," *RivB*, 1 (1953), 251-254.

c. *Exegesis of Individual Passages*

2135. L. Murillo, "In I Thess. 1, 1-10 annotationes homileticae," *VD*, 3 (1923), 328-332.

2136. T. H. Weir, "1 Thessalonians 1 : 3," *ET*, 34 (1922-1923), 525.

2137. H. J. Gibbins, "I Thessalonians 2 : 6," *ET*, 14 (1902-1903), 527.

2138. W. E. Wilson, "1 Thessalonians 2 : 6," *ET*, 35 (1923-1924), 43-44.

2139. R. Perdelwitz, "Zu σαίνεσθαι ἐν ταῖς θλίψεσιν ταύταις, 1 Thess. 3, 3," *TSK*, 86 (1913), 613-615.

2140. Florentinus Ogara, " 'Haec est . . . voluntas Dei, sanctificatio vestra,' " *VD*, 18 (1938), 65-72 [I Thess. 4 : 1-7].

2141. Willy Vogel, "Εἰδέναι τὸ ἑαυτοῦ σκεῦος κτᾶσθαι," *TB*, 13 (1934), 83-85 [I Thess. 4 : 3 ff.].

2142. J. R. Linder, "Exegetische Bemerkungen zu einigen Stellen des Neuen Testaments: I Thess. 4, 3-5," *TSK*, 40 (1867), 516-521.

2143. R. Beauvery, "Πλεονεκτεῖν in I Thess. 4, 6a," *VD*, 33 (1955), 78-85.

2144. T. I. Tambyah, "Θεοδίδακτοι, a Suggestion of an Implication of the Deity of Christ," *ET*, 44 (1932-1933), 527-528 [I Thess. 4 : 9].

2145. A. Wimmer, "Trostworte des Apostels Paulus an Hinterbliebene in Thessalonisch (I Th. 4, 13-17)," *B*, 36 (1955), 273-286.

2146. P. Rossano, "A che punto siamo con I Thess. 4, 13-17?" *RivB*, 4 (1956), 72-80.

2147, D. A. Hayes, "A Study of Pauline Apocalypse," *BW*, 37 (1911), 163-175 [I Thess, 4 : 13-18].

2148. Ernst Haack, "Eine exegetisch-dogmatische Studie zur Eschatologie über 1 Thessalonicher 4, 13-18," *ZST*, 15 (1938), 544-569.

2149. A. Romeo, " 'Nos qui vivimus qui residui sumus' (I Thess. 4, 13-18)," *VD*, 9 (1939), 307-312, 339-347, 360-364.

2150. A. van Veldhuizen, "1 Thessal. 4 : 15, 17," *TS*, 29 (1911), 101-106.

2151. F. Büttner, "Über die Entsuchung der Glaubigen (I Thess. 4, 17)," *NKZ*, 9 (1898), 707-721.

2152. G. Förster, "1 Thessalonicher 5, 1-10," *ZNW*, 17 (1916), 169-177.

2153. F. M. A. Hansel, "Über die richtige Auffassung der Worte Pauli 1 Thess. 5, 21 f.," *TSK*, 9 (1836), 170-184.
2154. Eduard Schweizer, "Zur Trichotomie von I Thess. 5, 23 und der Unterscheidung des πνευματικόν vom ψυχικόν in I Kor. 2, 14; 15, 44; Jak. 3, 15; Jud. 19," *TZ*, 9 (1953), 76-77.
2155. A. M. Festugière, "La trichotomie de I Thess. v, 28 et la philosophie grecque," *RSR*, 20 (1930), 385-415.
On I Thess. 2 : 18, see number 643.

11. The Second Epistle to the Thessalonians

a. *Textual, Historical, and Literary Criticism*

2156. J. M. S. Baljon, "Opmerkingen op het gebied van de Conjecturaalcritiek: De 2e brief aan de Thessalonicensen," *TS*, 6 (1888), 347-352.
2157. F. Zimmer, "Zur Textkritik des zweiten Thessalonicherbriefes," *ZWT*, 31 (1888), 322-342.
2158. Chr. Rauch, "Zum 2 Thessalonicherbrief," *ZWT*, 38 (1895), 451-464.
2159. H. Holtzmann, "Zum zweiten Thessalonicherbrief," *ZNW*, 2 (1901), 97-108.
2160. G. Hollmann, "Die Unechtheit des zweiten Thessalonicherbriefs," *ZNW*, 5 (1904), 28-38.
2161. George Milligan, "The Authenticity of the Second Epistle to the Thessalonians," *Exp*, 6th series, 9 (1904), 430-450.
2162. Wilhelm Michaelis, "Der zweite Thessalonicherbrief ein Philipperbrief?" *TZ*, 1 (1945), 282-286.
2163. Eduard Schweizer, "Der zweite Thessalonicherbrief ein Philipperbrief?" *TZ*, 1 (1945), 90-105.
2164. Eduard Schweizer, "Replik," *TZ*, 1 (1945), 286-289.
2165. Eduard Schweizer, "Zum Problem des zweiten Thessalonicherbriefes," *TZ*, 2 (1946), 74-75.
2166. H. Braun, "Zur nachpaulinischen Herkunft des zweiten Thessalonicherbriefes," *ZNW*, 44 (1952-1953), 152-156.

b. *Theological Studies*

2167. Robert Mackintosh, "The Antichrist of 2 Thessalonians," *Exp*, 7th series, 2 (1906), 427-432.

2168. J. A. Robertson, "The Message of the Epistles; 2 Thessalonians," *ET*, 44 (1932-1933), 407-408.
2169. E. Cothenet, "La IIe Épître aux Thessaloniciens et l'apocalypse synoptique," *RSR*, 42 (1954), 5-39.

c. *Exegesis of Individual Passages*

2170. J. R. Linder, "Exegetische Bemerkungen zu einigen Stellen des Neuen Testaments: 2 Thess. 1, 5-6," *TSK*, 40 (1867), 522-524.
2171. Peter Katz, "Ἐν πυρὶ φλογός," *ZNW*, 46 (1955), 133-138 [II Thess. 1 : 8].
2172. C. F. M. Deeleman, "2 Thess. 2 : 1-12," *TS*, 23 (1905), 252-276.
2173. J. Schmid, "Der Antichrist und die hemmende Macht," *TQ*, 129 (1949), 323-343 [II Thess. 2 : 1-12].
2174. H. Hamann, "Brief Exegesis of 2 Thess. 2 : 1-12 with Guideline for the Application of the Prophecy Contained Therein," *CTM*, 24 (1953), 418-433.
2175. M. Brunec, "De 'Homine peccati' in 2 Th 2, 1-12," *VD*, 35 (1957), 3-33.
2176. John Knox, "A Note on II Thessalonians 2 : 2," *ATR*, 18 (1936), 72-73.
2177. J. Th. Ubbink, "ὡς δι' ἡμῶν (2 Th. 2 : 2), een exegetisch-isogogische puzzle?" *NedTT*, 7 (1952-1953), 269-295.
2178. Eberhard Nestle, "2 Thess. 2 : 3," *ET*, 16 (1904-1905), 472-473.
2179. Henry Cowles, "On 'The Man of Sin' 2 Thess. 2 : 3-9," *BS*, 29 (1872), 623-640.
2180. J. G. Griffiths, "2 Thessalonians 2 : 4," *ET*, 52 (1940-1941), 38.
2181. J. C. Reimpell, "Das κατέχειν im 2 Thessalonicherbrief," *TSK*, 60 (1887), 713-736 [II Thess. 2 : 6].
2182. G. A. Alers, "τὸ κατέχον en ὁ κατέχων," *TS*, 6 (1888), 154-176 [II Thess. 2 : 6-7].
2183. F. Freese, "τὸ κατέχον und ὁ κατέχων (2 Thess. 2, 6 u. 7)," *TSK*, 93 (1920-1921), 73-77.
2184. O. Cullmann, "Le caractère eschatologique du devoir missionnaire et de la conscience apostolique de saint Paul. Etude sur le κατέχον (-ων) de 2 Thess. 2 : 6-7," *RHPR*, 16 (1936), 210-245.

2185. J. M. Gonzáles Ruiz, "La incredulidad de Israel y los impedimentos del Anticristo," *EB*, N.S. 10 (1951), 189-203 [II Thess. 2 : 6-7].

2186. E. E. Lofstrom, "Lawlessness and its Restrainer: A New Translation of 2 Thessalonians 2 : 6-8," *ET*, 28 (1916-1917), 379-380.

2187. H. W. Fulford, "ἕως ἐκ μέσου γένηται (2 Thess. 2 : 7)," *ET*, 23 (1910-1911), 40-41.

2188. V. Hartl, "ὁ κατέχων ἄρτι (2 Thess. 2, 7)," *ZKT*, 45 (1921), 455-475.

2189. P. H. Furfey, "The Mystery of Lawlessness," *CBQ*, 8 (1946), 179-191 [II Thess, 2 : 7].

2190. James Moffatt, "2 Thessalonians 3 : 14, 15," *ET*, 21 (1909-1910), 328.

12. The Pastoral Epistles

a. *Textual, Historical, and Literary Criticism*

2191. B. B. Edwards, "Introduction to the Pastoral Epistles," *BS*, 8 (1851), 318-346.

2192. W. H. Ward, "An Examination of the Various Readings of I Tim. 3 : 16," *BS*, 27 (1865), 1-50.

2193. H. R. Reynolds, "The Pastoral Epistles," *Exp*, 1st series, 1 (1875), 296-314, 380-392.

2194. O. Holtzmann, "Der zweite Timotheusbrief und der neueste mit ihm vorgenommene Rettungsversuch," *ZWT*, 26 (1883), 45-72.

2195. A. Hilgenfeld, "Die Gemeindeordnung der Hirtenbriefe des Paulus," *ZWT*, 29 (1886), 456-472.

2196. C. H. van Rhijn, "De jongste Literatuur over de schriften des Nieuwen Verbonds: De Pastorale Brieven," *TS*, 4 (1886), 309-322.

2197. M. J. Cramer, "Peculiarities of the Pastoral Epistles," *JBL* (December, 1887), 3-32.

2198. J. M. S. Baljon, "Opmerkingen op het gebied van de Conjecturaalcritiek: De 1e brief aan Timotheüs," *TS*, 6 (1888), 404-415.

2199. F. Godet, "The Pastoral Epistles, or the Closing Labours of the Apostle Paul," *Exp*, 3rd series, 7 (1888), 45-72.

2200. W. H. Simcox, "The Pauline Antilegomena," *Exp*, 3rd series, 8 (1888), 180-192.

2201. J. M. S. Baljon, "Opmerkingen op het gebied van de Con-jecturaalcritiek: De tweede brief aan Timotheüs," *TS*, 7 (1889), 261-268.

2202. J. M. S. Baljon, "Opmerkingen op het gebied van de Con-jecturaalcritiek: De brief aan Titus en de brief aan Phile-mon," *TS* 8 (1890), 118-124.

2203. W. M. Ramsay, "The Church and the Empire in the First Century: The Pastoral Epistles and Tacitus," *Exp*, 4th series, 8 (1893), 110-119.

2204. A. Hilgenfeld, "Die Hirtenbriefe des Paulus neu unter-sucht," *ZWT*, 40 (1897), 1-86.

2205. E. Y. Hincks, "The Authorship of the Pastoral Epistles," *JBL*, 16 (1897), 94-117.

2206. E. F. Krauss, "The Introductory Problems of the Pastorals," *LCR*, 29 (1910), 349-360.

2207. W. M. Ramsay, "Historical Commentary on the Epistles to Timothy," *Exp*, 8th series, 1 (1911), 262-273, 356-375.

2208. Vernon Bartlet, "The Historic Setting of the Pastoral Epistles," *Exp*, 8th series, 5 (1913), 28-36, 161-167, 256-263, 325-347.

2209. E. F. Brown, "Some Considerations of the Pastoral Epistles," *Exp*, 8th series, 13 (1917), 212-221.

2210. F. Torm, "Über die Sprache in den Pastoralbriefen," *ZNW*, 18 (1917), 225-243.

2211. W. B. Sedwick, "The Authorship of the Pastorals," *ET*, 30 (1918-1919), 230-231.

2212. G. Kittel, "Die γενεαλογίαι der Pastoralbriefe," *ZNW*, 20 (1921), 49-69 [I Tim. 1 : 4; Tit. 3 : 9].

2213. Dr. Kühn, "Das Problem der Pastoralbriefe," *NKZ*, 32 (1921), 163-181.

2214. A. H. Sayce, "Were the Pastoral Epistles written by St. Paul?" *BS*, 79 (1922), 487-491.

2215. F. R. M. Hitchcock, "The Latinity of the Pastorals," *ET*, 39 (1927-1928), 347-352.

2216. F. R. M. Hitchcock, "Classical Allusions in the Pastoral Epistles," *Th*, 17 (1928), 62-71.

2217. W. Michaelis, "Pastoralbriefe und Wortstatistik," *ZNW*, 28 (1929), 69-76.

2218. F. R. M. Hitchcock, "The Pastorals and a Second Trial of Paul," *ET*, 41 (1929-1930), 20-23.

2219. H. K. Moulton, "Scripture Quotations in the Pastoral Epistles," *ET*, 49 (1937-1938), 94.
2220. Philip Carrington, "The Problem of the Pastoral Epistles, Dr. Harrison's Theory Reviewed," *ATR*, 21 (1939), 32-39.
2221. F. R. M. Hitchcock, "Philo and the Pastorals," *Herm*, No. 56 (1940), 113-135.
2222. E. K. Simpson, "The Authenticity and Authorship of the Pastoral Epistles," *EQ*, 12 (1940), 289-311.
2223. Christian Maurer, "Eine Textvariante klärt die Entstehungsgeschichte der Pastoralbriefe auf," *TZ*, 3 (1947), 321-337.
2224. P. N. Harrison, "Important Hypotheses Reconsidered; III, The Authorship of the Pastoral Epistles," *ET*, 67 (1955-1956), 77-81. [cf. *ET*, 70, 91-94.]
2225. P. N. Harrison, "The Pastoral Epistles and Duncan's Ephesian Theory," *NTSt*, 2 (1956), 250-261.
2226. B. M. Metzger, "A hitherto neglected early Fragment of the Epistle to Titus," *NT*, 1 (1956), 149-150.
See also numbers 226, 229, 234, 456, and 2238.

b. *Theological Studies*

2227. H. Wettler, "Die Hauptgrundsätze der Pastoraltheologie, welche die Briefe an Timotheus und Titus auch noch für unsere Zeit enthalten," *TSK*, 37 (1864), 329-354.
2228. A. Hilgenfeld, "Die Irrleher der Hirtenbriefe des Paulus," *ZWT*, 23 (1880), 448-463.
2229. J. G. Duncan, "Πιστὸς ὁ λόγος," *ET*, 35 (1923-1924), 141.
2230. Joseph Johnston, "The Message of the Epistles; The Pastoral Epistles," *ET*, 45 (1933-1934), 270-274.
2231. H. Windisch, "Zur Christologie der Pastoralbriefe," *ZNW*, 34 (1935), 213-238.
2232. J. M. Bover, " 'Fidelis sermo,' " *B*, 19 (1938), 76-79.
2233. Raphael Mingioli, "The Idea of Christian Orthodoxy in the Pastoral Epistles," *ATR*, 21 (1939), 186-189.
2234. H. B. Blakely, "The Gospel of Paul, A Study in the Pastoral Epistles," *TTod*, 3 (1946-1947), 345-357.
2235. Paul Galtier, "La réconciliation des pécheurs dans la première Épître à Timothée," *RSR*, 39 (1951-1952), 317-320.
2236. J. W. Bowman, "The Pastoral Epistles," *Interp*, 9 (1955), 436-455.

c. *Exegesis of Individual Passages*

(1). First Timothy

2237. Alexander Souter, "The Pastoral Epistles; Timothy 1 and 2," *Exp*, 8th series, 6 (1913), 424-438.

2238. [M. V.] Aberle, "Exegetische Studien über die Abfassungszeit des ersten Timotheusbriefs," *TQ*, 45 (1863), 120-134.

2239. H. R. Reynolds, "The First Epistle to Timothy," *Exp*, 1st series, 2 (1875), 59-71, 131-146, 209-226, 317-323, 396-404, 465-471; 3 (1876), 74-80, 142-151, 224-235, 380-398; 4 (1876), 47-55, 191-212.

2240. H. E. Jacobs, "Notes in First Timothy," *LCR*, 6 (1887), 253-271.

2241. W. M. Ramsay, "Historical Commentary on the First Epistle to Timothy," *Exp*, 7th series, 7 (1909), 481-494; 8 (1909), 1-21, 167-185, 264-282, 339-357, 399-416, 557-568; 9 (1910), 172-187, 319-333, 433-440.

2242. E. H. Askwith, "On Two Points in I Timothy 1," *Exp*, 8th series, 7 (1914), 377-382.

2243. R. J. Drummond, "Grace, Mercy, and Peace," *EQ*, 20 (1948), 81-83 [I Tim. 1 : 2].

2244. O. E. Sohn, "Study on 1 Timothy 1 : 3-11," *CTM*, 21 (1950), 419-428.

2245. C. Lindeboom, "Wat hebben we te verstaan onder 'twistvragen en woordenstrijd'?" *GTT*, 2 (1901), 11-13 [I Tim. 1 : 4; 6 : 4; Tit. 3 : 9].

2246. W. Warren, "Note on I Timothy 1 : 11," *ET*, 12 (1900-1901), 431.

2247. F. Rendall, "Faithful is the Word," *Exp*, 3rd series, 5 (1887), 314-320 [I Tim. 1 : 15; 3:1; 4 : 9; II Tim. 2 : 11; Tit. 3 : 8].

2248. J. Turmel, "Histoire de l'interprétation de I Tim. II, 4," *RHLR*, 5 (1900), 385-415.

2249. [G. C. F.] Lücke, "Exegetische Miscellen über 1 Timotheus 2, 6.7," *TSK*, 9 (1836), 651-653.

2250. Robert Falconer, "I Timothy 2 : 14-15," *JBL*, 60 (1941), 375-379.

2251. U. Holzmeister, "Si quis episcopatum desiderat, bonum opus desiderat," *B*, 12 (1931), 41-69 [I Tim. 3 : 1].

2252. C. Spicq, "Si quis episcopatum desiderat...," *RSPT*, 29 (1940), 316-325 [I Tim. 3 : 1].

2253. C. W. Emmet, " 'The Husband of One Wife,' " *ET*, 19 (1907-1908), 39-40 [I Tim. 3 : 2, 12].

2254. J.-B. Frey, "La signification des termes μόνανδρος et univira," *RSR*, 20 (1930), 48-60 [I Tim. 3 : 2, 12].

2255. W. F. Slater, "I Timothy 3 : 15," *ET*, 5 (1893-1894), 64-66.

2256. R. W. Micou, "On ὤφθη ἀγγέλοις, I. Tim. iii 16," *JBL*, 11 (1892), 201-205.

2257. J. P. Jones, "Justified in the Spirit," *Exp*, 6th series, 4 (1901), 153-156 [I Tim. 3 : 16].

2258. C. Spicq, "Gymnastique et morale, d'après I Tim. 4, 7.8," *RB*, 54 (1947), 229-242.

2259. Ed. Riggenbach, "Zur Auslegung von I Tim. 5, 13," *NKZ*, 7 (1896), 586-591.

2260. M. J. v. d. Hoogt, "Wat zegt de Schrift van de verzorging der hulpbehoevenden?" *GTT*, 1 (1900), 138-141, 150-151, 170-185 [I Tim. 5 : 16; 5 : 4; I Cor. 14 : 40; Rom. 12 : 13].

2261. L. Lindeboom, "Een loon-quaestie?" *GTT*, 7 (1906), 17-19 [I Tim. 5 : 18].

2262. J. S. MacArthur, "On the Significance of ἡ γραφή in I Timothy 5 : 18," *ET*, 53 (1941-1942), 37.

2263. H. Rönsch, "Exegetisches zu I Tim. 6, 10," *ZWT*, 27 (1884), 140-146.

2264. S. T. Byington, "I Timothy 6 : 10," *ET*, 56 (1944-1945), 54.

2265. S. E. Rodhe, "Gudskunskap och gudstro," *STK*, 17 (1941), 34-43 [I Tim. 6 : 16].

2266. C. Spicq, "Saint Paul et la loi des dépôts," *RB*, 40 (1931), 481-501 [I Tim. 6 : 20; II Tim. 1 : 14].
On I Tim. 1 : 14, see number 595; 2 : 11, numbers 2884 ff.

(2). Second Timothy

2267. H. R. Reynolds, "The Second Epistle to Timothy — The Last Words of St. Paul," *Exp*, 1st series, 10 (1879), 116-134, 195-215, 291-313, 365-386.

2268. I. M. Bover, " 'Illuminavit vitam,' " *B*, 28 (1947), 136-146 [II Tim. 1 : 10].

2269. Andreas ab Alpe, "S. Paulus 'praedicator et apostolus et magister,' " *VD*, 23 (1943), 199-206, 238-244 [II Tim. 1 : 11].

2270. Rendel Harris, "Pindar and St. Paul," *ET*, 33 (1921-1922), 456-457 [II Tim. 2 : 7].

2271. U. Holzmeister, "Assumptionis Deiparae mysterium verbis S. Pauli 2 Tim. 2, 11 s. explicatur," *VD*, 18 (1938), 225-226.

2272. F. M. D., "Miscellanea — 2 Tim. 2 : 14-16," *Th*, 31 (1935), 229-230.

2273. W. Arndt, "ἔγνω, 2 Tim. 2 : 19," *CTM*, 21 (1950), 299-302.

2274. v. d. W. te G., "Onderscheidene vaten in 's Heeren huis; 2 Tim. 2 : 20, 21," *GTT*, 3 (1902), 171-173, 184-185.

2275. L. H. Bunn, "2 Timothy 2 : 23-26," *ET*, 41 (1929-1930), 235-237.

2276. F. R. M. Hitchcock, "Miscellanea — New Light on a Passage in the Pastorals," *Th*, 34 (1937), 108-112 [II Tim. 2 : 25-26].

2277. J. P. Wilson, "The Translation of 2 Timothy 2 : 26," *ET*, 49 (1937-1938), 45-46.

2278. G. H. Whitaker, "2 Timothy 3 : 10 f.," *Exp*, 8th series, 18 (1919), 342-344.

2279. R. M. Spence, "2 Timothy 3 : 15, 16," *ET*, 8 (1896-1897), 563-564.

2280. O. Olafsen, "Om oversaettelsen og fortstaaelsen af 2 Tim. 3, 16," *NTT*, 9 (1908), 321-333.

2281. F. W. Grosheide, "2 Tim. 3 : 16," *GTT*, 41 (1940), 225-227.

2282. J. H. Bennetch, "2 Timothy 3 : 16a, A Greek Study," *BS*, 106 (1949), 187-195.

2283. G. H. Whitaker, " 'In Season, out of Season,' " *ET*, 34 (1922-1923), 332-333 [II Tim. 4 : 2].

2284. John Torrance, "Ps. 22 — as used by Christ and St. Paul," *ET*, 44 (1932-1933), 382 [II Tim. 4 : 10-18].

2285. [Samuel Cox], "St. Paul's Cloak, and Books, and Parchments," *Exp*, 1st series, 1 (1875), 286-296 [II Tim. 4 : 13].

2286. J. S. Stevenson, "2 Timothy 4 : 13 and the Question of St. Paul's Second Captivity," *ET*, 34 (1922-1923), 524-525.

2287. Max Meinertz, "Worauf bezieht sich die πρώτη ἀπολογία 2 Tim. 4, 16?" *B*, 4 (1923), 390-394.

2288. Llynfi Davies, "Pauline Readjustments," *Exp*, 9th series, 1 (1924), 446-456 [II Tim. 6 : 9 ff.].
On II Tim. 2 : 8, see number 796; 4 : 9-21, number 1067.

(3). Titus

2289. J. O. Dykes, "The Epistle to Titus," *Exp*, 2nd series, 5 (1883), 177-185, 267-274; 6 (1883), 26-36, 108-119, 283-293, 391-398; 7 (1884), 205-214, 365-373.

2290. Alexander Souter, "The Pastoral Epistles; Titus," *Exp*, 8th series, 7 (1914), 73-76.

2291. George Edmundson, "The Enigma of Titus," *Exp*, 8th series, 11 (1916), 321-334.

2292. A. J. Dickinson, "The Genetic History of Titus," *RE*, 14 (1917), 479-488.

2293. E. Lyttelton, "Miscellanea — Another Paraphrase," *Th*, 31 (1935), 286-287 [Tit. 1 : 1].

2294. C. Lattey, "Unius uxoris vir (Tit 1, 6)," *VD*, 28 (1950), 288-290.

2295. G. G. Findlay, "The Reproach of the Cretans," *Exp*, 2nd series, 4 (1882), 401-410 [Tit. 1 : 12].

2296. L. Lemme, "Über Tit. 1, 12," *TSK*, 55 (1882), 133-144.

2297. Rendel Harris, "The Cretans Always Liars," *Exp*, 7th series, 2 (1906), 305-317 [Tit. 1 : 12].

2298. Rendel Harris, "A Further Note on the Cretans," *Exp*, 7th series, 3 (1907), 332-337 [Tit. 1 : 12].

2299. Rendel Harris, "St. Paul and Epimenedes," *Exp*, 8th series, 4 (1912), 348-353 [Tit. 1 : 12].

2300. Basilius Haensler, "Zu Tit. 1, 15," *BibZ*, 13 (1915), 121-129.

2301. Th. Vargha, "Apparuit gratia Dei (Tit. 2, 11 ss. — Ep. 1 Miss. Nat. et Circumcisionis)," *VD*, 14 (1934), 3-6.

2302. J. M. Bover, "In festo Circumcisionis D. N. I. C. (Tit. 2, 11-15)," *VD*, 2 (1922), 10-14.

2303. U. Holzmeister, " 'Apparuit gratia Dei Salvatoris nostri' (Tit. 2, 11-15)," *VD*, 11 (1931), 353-356.

2304. Florentinus Ogara, "Apparuit gratia Dei Salvatoris nostri," *VD*, 15 (1935), 363-372 [Tit. 2 : 11-15; 3 : 4-7].

2305. Anonymous, "Exegetical. Titus 2 : 13," *LQ*, 3 (1873), 285-288.

2306. Ezra Abbot, "On the Construction of Titus ii. 13," *JBL* (June and December, 1881), 3-19.
2307. J. N. Lindeboom, "Noemt de Schrift den Doop 'het bad der wedergeboorte'?" *GTT*, 1 (1900), 187-192 [Tit. 3 : 5].

13. The Epistle to Philemon

a. *Textual, Historical, and Literary Criticism*

2308. H. Holtzmann, "Der Brief an den Philemon, kritisch untersucht," *ZWT*, 16 (1873), 428-441.
2309. F. Godet, "The Epistle to Philemon — The Oldest Petition for the Abolition of Slavery," *Exp*, 3rd series, 5 (1887), 138-154.
2310. G. H. van Rhijn, "De jongste literatuur over de Schriften des Nieuwen Verbonds: De brief aan Philémon," *TS*, 5 (1887), 356-359.
2311. J. K. Demarest, "The Epistle to Philemon," *LQ*, 20 (1890), 514-523.
2312. J. Hulsebos, "De Brief van Paulus aan Filémon," *GTT*, 3 (1902), 5-7, 17-19, 35-39.
2313. E. Amling, "Eine Konjektur im Philemonbrief," *ZNW*, 10 (1909), 261-262 [Philemon 23-24].
2314. E. F. Knight, "The Reception of Onesimus by Philemon," *ET*, 28 (1916-1917), 92.
2315. W. Lock, "The Epistle to Philemon," *Th*, 15 (1927), 159-161.
2316. E. R. Goodenough, "Paul and Onesimus," *HTR*, 22 (1929), 181-183.
2317. P. N. Harrison, "Onesimus and Philemon," *ATR*, 32 (1950), 268-294.
2318. Heinrich Greeven, "Prüfung der Thesen von J. Knox zum Philemonbrief," *TLZ*, 79 (1954), 373-378.
See also number 2202.

b. *Theological and Exegetical Studies*

2319. S. E. C. T., "The Atonement — An Illustration," *Exp*, 1st series, 9 (1879), 221-233.
2320. Alexander Maclaren, "The Epistle to Philemon," *Exp*, 3rd series, 5 (1887), 270-282, 363-375, 443-453; 6 (1887), 150-159, 180-191, 297-306.
2321. C. A. Scott, "The Epistle of Philemon," *Exp*, 8th series, 2 (1911), 328-337.

2322. Eugene Caldwell, "The Ideal Brother: A Book Study of Philemon," *USR*, 27 (1915-1916), 139-143.

2323. A. T. Robertson, "Philemon and Onesimus: Master and Slave," *Exp*, 8th series, 19 (1920), 29-48.

2324. James Reid, "The Message of the Epistles; Philemon," *ET*, 45 (1933-1934), 164-168.

2325. J. E. Jones, "The Letter to Philemon — An Illustration of Koinonia," *RE*, 46 (1949), 454-466.

2326. O. E. Sohn, "The Forgotten Epistle," *CTM*, 20 (1949), 13-29.

SECTION IV

PAULINE APOCRYPHA

A. THE ACTS OF PAUL

2327. B. Pick, "The Acts of St. Paul and Thecla," *LQ*, 18 (1888), 585-601.

2328. Adolf Harnack, "Die Entdeckung bez. Identificirung der Πράξεις Παύλου," *TLZ*, 22 (1897), 625-629.

2329. Theo. Zahn, "Die wiedergefundenen Akten des Paulus," *NKZ*, 8 (1897), 933-940.

2330. C. Schmidt, "Notiz zu den *Acta Pauli*," *TLZ*, 23 (1898), 316-317.

2331. E. J. Goodspeed, "The Acts of Paul and Thecla," *BW*, 17 (1901), 185-190.

2332. D. De Bruyne, "Nouveaux fragments des Actes de Pierre, de Paul, de Jean, d'André et de l'Apocalypse d'Élie," *RBén*, 25 (1908), 149-160.

2333. C. F. M. Deeleman, "Acta Pauli," *TS*, 26 (1908), 1-44, 273-301.

2334. A. Wilmart, "Extraits d'*Acta Pauli*," *RBén*, 27 (1910), 402-412.

2335. H. A. Sanders, "A Fragment of the Acta Pauli in the Michigan Collection," *HTR*, 31 (1938), 73-90.

2336. W. D. McHardy, "A Papyrus Fragment of the *Acta Pauli*," *ET*, 58 (1946-1947), 279.

2337. E. Peterson, "Einige Bemerkungen zum Hamburger Papyrus-Fragment der Acta Pauli," *VC*, 3 (1949), 142-162.

2338. Hieronymus Engberding, "Bemerkungen zu den äthiopischen Acta Petri et Pauli," *OC*, 41 (1957), 65-66.

B. THE THIRD EPISTLE TO THE CORINTHIANS

2339. P. Better, "Der apokryphe dritte Korintherbrief," *TQ*, 72 (1890), 611-639.

2340. W. T. Smith, "The Third Epistle to the Corinthians," *ET*, 3 (1891-1892), 413.

2341. [P.] Better, "Eine rabbinische Quelle des apokryphen dritten Korintherbriefes," *TQ*, 77 (1895), 622-633.

2342. Eberhard Nestle, "Zwei syrische Zitate aus dem III Korintherbrief," *TLZ*, 30 (1905), 140-141, 220.

2343. D. De Bruyne, "Un nouveau manuscrit de la troisième lettre de saint Paul aux Corinthiens," *RBén*, 25 (1908), 431-434.

2344. C. F. M. Deeleman, "De apocriefe briefwisseling tusschen Paulus en de Corinthiërs," *TS*, 27 (1909), 37-56.

2345. Karl Pink, "Die pseudo-paulinischen Briefe," *B*, 6 (1925), 68-91, 179-200.

2346. D. De Bruyne, "Un quatrième manuscrit latin de la correspondance apocryphe de S. Paul avec les Corinthiens," *RBén*, 45 (1933), 189-195.

2347. H. Boese, "Über eine bisher unbekannte Handschrift des Briefwechsels zwischen Paulus und den Korinthern," *ZNW*, 44 (1952-1953), 66-76.

C. The Epistle to the Laodiceans

2348. E. J. Goodspeed, "The Madrid Manuscript of Laodiceans," *AJT*, 8 (1904), 536-588.

2349. B. W. Bacon, "St. Paul to the Laodiceans," *Exp*, 8th series, 17 (1919), 19-36.
See also number 2099.

D. Correspondence with Seneca, and Miscellaneous Apocrypha

2350. F. C. Baur, "Seneca und Paulus, das Verhältnis des Stoicismus zum Christentum nach den Schriften Seneca's," *ZWT*, 1 (1858), 161-246, 441-470.

2351. F. X. Kraus, "Der Briefwechsel Pauli mit Seneca, Ein Beitrag zur Apokryphen-Litteratur," *TQ*, 49 (1867), 603-624.

2352. Emil Schürer, "Notiz zur Apokalypse des Paulus," *TLZ*, 18 (1893), 267-268.

2353. F. Nau, "La version syriaque inédite des martyres de S. Pierre, S. Paul et S. Luc," *ROC*, 3 (1898), 39-57, 151-190.

2354. H. Böhlig, "Das Gewissen bei Seneca und Paulus: Religionsgeschichtliche Untersuchung," *TSK*, 87 (1914), 1-24.

2355. J. Th. Ubbink, "Seneca en Paulus," *NTS*, 1 (1918), 275-282.

2356. E. G. Sihler, "St. Paul and Seneca," *BR*, 12 (1927), 540-560.

2357. C. H. Kraeling, "The Apocalypse of Paul and the 'Iranische Erlösungsmysterium,' " *HTR*, 24 (1931), 209-244.
2358. R. P. Casey, "The Apocalypse of Paul," *JTS*, 34 (1933), 1-32.
2359. P. Benoit, "Sénèque et Saint Paul," *RB*, 53 (1946), 7-35.
2360. Alfons Kurfess, "Zum apokryphen Briefwechsel zwischen Seneca und Paulus," *ZRGG*, 2 (1949-1950), 67-70.

SECTION V

THEOLOGICAL STUDIES

A. GENERAL

2361. S. R. Asbury, "The Doctrine of the Apostles," *BS*, 27 (1870), 135-162.

2362. A. Hilgenfeld, "Zur Geschichte des Unions-Paulinismus," *ZWT*, 15 (1872), 469-509.

2363. W. Sanday, "Some Leading Ideas in the Theology of St. Paul," *Exp*, 1st series, 8 (1878), 40-58.

2364. A. H. Blom, "Paulinische Studien: Paulus' leer van de geloofsgerechtigheid van Abraham," *TT*, 14 (1880), 48-73.

2365. A. B. Grosart, "St. Paul and the Objective," *ET*, 3 (1891-1892), 250-255.

2366. A. B. Bruce, "Paul's Conception of Christianity," *Exp*, 4th series, 7(1893), 1-20, 118-136, 197-215, 267-282, 353-366, 416-430; 8 (1893), 21-37, 81-95, 192-207, 266-282, 348-361, 432-446; 9 (1894), 81-97, 189-203, 265-275, 342-355, 416-429; 10 (1894), 32-46, 112-126, 199-213, 300-313.

2367. A. S. Carman, "The New Testament Use of the Greek Mysteries," *BS*, 50 (1893), 613-639.

2368. G. B. Stevens, "The Theology of Paul and of John Compared," *BW*, 3 (1894), 166-175.

2369. Marcus Dods, "St. Paul's View of the Greek Gods," *Exp*, 5th series, 1 (1895), 237-240.

2370. [P.] Kölbing, "Studien zur paulinischen Theologie," *TSK*, 68 (1895), 7-51.

2371. G. F. Magoun, "Paul's Phraseology and Roman Law," *BS*, 52 (1895), 439-457.

2372. A. B. Bruce, "Four Types of Christian Thought; II, The Pauline Epistles," *BW*, 7 (1896), 6-19.

2373. J. S. Banks, "Back to St. Paul," *ET* 8 (1896-1897), 55-59.

2374. S. Baring-Gould, "St. Paul's Mind and Method," *Exp*, 5th series, 6 (1897), 200-207.

2375. E. I. Bosworth, "The Influence of the Damascus Vision Upon Paul's Theology," *BS*, 56 (1899), 278-300.

2376. Arthur Carr, "St. Paul's Attitude towards Greek Philosophy," *Exp*, 5th series, 9 (1899), 372-378.

2377. J. S. Banks, "A Note on Pauline and Johannine Doctrine," *ET*, 11 (1899-1900), 461-462.

2378. E. P. Boys-Smith, "St. Paul's Equivalent for the Kingdom of God," *ET*, 12 (1900-1901), 380-382.

2379. J. W. Diggle, "Suffering with Christ," *ET*, 12 (1900-1901), 521-524.

2380. A. S. Laidlaw, "Pauline Anthropology and Christian Doctrine," *ET*, 12 (1900-1901), 258-261, 505-507.

2381. C. Clemen, "Die Auffassung des Alten Testaments bei Paulus," *TSK*, 75 (1902), 173-187.

2382. V. Rose, "Études sur la théologie de saint Paul," *RB*, 11 (1902), 321-346; 12 (1903), 337-361.

2383. E. I. Bosworth, "Paul's Method of Evangelization," *BW*, 22 (1903), 416-423.

2384. Edward Caird, "St. Paul and the Idea of Evolution," *HJ*, 2 (1903), 1-19.

2385. W. H. H. Marsh, "Genesis of Paul's Theology," *BS*, 60 (1903), 60-83.

2386. J. H. Ropes, " 'Righteousness' and 'the Righteousness of God' in the Old Testament and in St. Paul," *JBL*, 22 (1903), 211-227.

2387. James Denney, "Adam and Christ in St. Paul," *Exp*, 6th series, 9 (1904), 147-160.

2388. L. A. Fox, "St. Paul as a Witness to the Supernatural," *LQ*, 35 (1905), 221-245.

2389. J. A. C. van Leeuwen, "Wedergeboorte," *TS*, 23 (1905), 459-488.

2390. H. W. Clark, "Paul's Doctrine of the Transformation of Experience," *Exp*, 7th series, 1 (1906), 171-178.

2391. O. P. Eashes, "Paul's Use of the Term 'Man,' " *RE*, 5 (1908), 522-529.

2392. A. E. Garvie, "The Experience of Paul," *Exp*, 7th series, 5 (1908), 193-207.

2393. A. E. Garvie, "Studies in Pauline Theology," *Exp*, 7th series, 7 (1909), 30-41, 126-138, 241-254, 333-346, 508-521; 8 (1909), 33-48, 130-143, 231-244, 325-338, 417-431, 542-556.

2394. G. H. Gilbert, "The Greek Element in Paul's Letters," *BW*, 33 (1909), 113-122.

2395. William Heathcote, "The Apologetic Value of St. Paul," *LQ*, 39 (1909), 63-74.

2396. H. A. A. Kennedy, "The Scope and Function of the Apostolate in the New Testament," *BW*, 33 (1909), 160-170.

2397. Superintendent Scholz, "Paulus als Seelsorger," *NKZ*, 20 (1909), 593-625.

2398. D. H. Rolston, "The Union of Christ with the Believer and the Inferences Therefrom," *USR*, 21 (1909-1910), 285-292.

2399. J. L. Davies, "St. Paul's Beliefs: Some Reconciliations," *Exp*, 7th series, 9 (1910), 254-263.

2400. D. C. Mackintosh, "The Pragmatic Element in the Teaching of Paul," *AJT*, 14 (1910), 361-381.

2401. Alexis Vanbeck, "La discipline pénitentielle dans les écrits de saint Paul," *RHLR*, N.S. 1 (1910), 241-251.

2402. E. Weber, "Die Genesis der paulinischen Theologie," *NKZ*, 21 (1910), 253-281.

2403. The Hon. Lady Welby, "The Message of Paul to the Present Age," *HJ*, 8 (1910), 603-611.

2404. G. A. J. Ross, "The Earlier Emphasis of St. Paul," *ET*, 22 (1910-1911), 327-329.

2405. A. E. Garvie, "The Gentile Influence on Paul," *Exp*, 8th series, 2 (1911), 470-474.

2406. W. M. Ramsay, "The Thought of Paul," *Exp*, 8th series, 2 (1911), 289-310, 434-455, 481-498.

2407. C. A. Scott, "The Dualistic Element in the Thinking of St. Paul," *ET*, 23 (1911-1912), 488-492, 560-564.

2408. J. Chapman, "St. Paul and the Revelation to St. Peter, Matt. xvi, 17," *RBén*, 29 (1912), 133-147.

2409. H. A. A. Kennedy, "St. Paul and the Mystery-Religions," *Exp*, 8th series, 3 (1912), 289-305, 420-441; 4 (1912), 60-88, 212-237, 306-327, 434-451, 539-554; 5 (1913), 62-75, 115-126.

2410. Ferdinand Prat, "Le triomphe du Christ sur les principautés et les puissances," *RSR*, 3 (1912), 201-229.

2411. W. M. Ramsay, "The Teaching of Paul in Terms of the Present Day," *Exp*, 8th series, 3 (1912), 52-69, 137-152, 276-288, 354-373, 442-468, 557-568; 4 (1912), 88-96, 171-192, 275-288, 370-384.

2412. J. W. Buckham, "Dualism or Duality?" *HTR*, 6 (1913), 156-171.

2413. M. Maas, "Die antiken Mysterien und ihre Beziehungen zum Apostel Paulus," *TLZ*, 38 (1913), 125.

2414. H. J. Toxopeüs, "Het karakter van het Paulinische christendom," *TT*, 47 (1913), 18-47.

2415. Johannes Weiss, "The Significance of Paul for Modern Christians," *AJT*, 17 (1913), 352-367.

2416. Jakob Wirz, "Keime des Paulinism," *STZ*, 30 (1913), 6-22, 49-66.

2417. H. E. Kirk, "The Oriental Mystery Religions and the Christianity of Paul," *USR*, 25 (1913-1914), 253-270.

2418. H. A. A. Kennedy, "St. Paul and the Conception of the 'Heavenly Man,' " *Exp*, 8th series, 7 (1914), 97-110.

2419. J. L. Rosser, "Paul's Valuation of his Ministry," *RE*, 11 (1914), 74-82.

2420. A. J. Rowland, "Paul the Interpreter," *RE*, 11 (1914), 407-416.

2421. P. W. H. Frederick, "The Kingdom of God according to St. Paul," *LCR*, 34 (1915), 59-67.

2422. F. C. Grant, "St. Paul and Stoicism," *BW*, 45 (1915), 268-281.

2423. G. H. Trever, "The Apostle Paul's Contribution to the Philosophy of Religion," *BS*, 72 (1915), 177-207.

2424. F. L. Anderson, "Paulinism," *BR*, 1 (1916), 262-277.

2425. H. A. A. Kennedy, "The Regulative Value for the Pauline Theology of the Conception of Christian Sonship," *Exp*, 8th series, 12 (1916), 26-37, 447-463.

2426. K. F. Proost, "Adam — Christus — Satan," *TT*, 50 (1916), 373-386.

2427. H. Windisch, "Christuskult und Paulinismus," *TT*, 50 (1916), 216-225.

2428. Vacher Burch, "The Exegetical Basis of Paul's Thought," *Exp*, 8th series, 14 (1917), 298-308.

2429. B. S. Easton, "The Pauline Theology and Hellenism," *AJT*, 21 (1917), 358-382.

2430. A. S. Peake, "The Quintessence of Paulinism," *BJRL*, 4 (1917), 285-311.

2431. W. S. Bishop, "Two Pauline Antitheses," *Exp*, 8th series, 15 (1918), 233-240.

2432. Maurice Jones, "St. Paul and the Angels," *Exp*, 8th series, 15 (1918), 356-370, 412-425.

2433. H. A. A. Kennedy, "St. Paul's Conception of the Knowledge of God," *Exp*, 8th series, 16 (1918), 241-269.

2434. E. J. Price, "Paul and Plato," *HJ*, 16 (1918), 263-282.

2435. T. B. Foster, "Credal Formulation in the New Testament," *ATR*, 1 (1918-1919), 164-183.

2436. J. Weiss, "Die Bedeutung des Paulus für den modernen Christen," *ZNW*, 19 (1919-1920), 127-142.

2437. J. M. Bover, "Perfectio spiritualis secundum mentem S. Pauli," *VD*, 1 (1921), 16-18.

2438. W. W. Everts, "Paul's Treatment of Knowledge," *RE*, 18 (1921), 416-427.

2439. J. H. Ropes, "Le radicalisme de Jésus et la *via media* de Paul," *RHPR*, 1 (1921), 507-517.

2440. George Henslow, "Paul's Religion — Whence was it?" *ET*, 33 (1921-1922), 330.

2441. B. R. Lacy, Jr., "The Spoken Messages of Paul," *USR*, 34 (1922-1923), 110-116, 233-239, 325-330.

2442. J. M. Bover, "Spiritualis B. Mariae V. maternitas 'in Christo Iesu' B. Pauli documentis comprobata," *VD*, 3 (1923), 307-310.

2443. L. Murillo, "Universalismus evangelii in aevo apostolico," *VD*, 3 (1923), 151-155.

2444. E. Rodhe, "Gottesglaube und Kyriosglaube bei Paulus," *ZNW*, 22 (1923), 43-57.

2445. W. E. Scofield, "Paul's Place in Christian Revelation," *BR*, 8 (1923), 510-521,

2446. J. M. Bover, "Los fundamentos de la Mariología en las Epístolas de San Pablo," *EE*, 2 (1923), 79-93, 134-151; 3 (1924), 38-50.

2447. H. Dieckmann, "De 'nationalismo' in re religiosa quid S. Paulus censeat," *VD*, 4 (1924), 119-127.

2448. A. Merk, " 'Traditionis' momentum apud S. Paulum," *VD*, 4 (1924), 332-336, 362-368.

2449. A. E. Garvie, "Paul's Personal Religion," *ET*, 36 (1924-1925), 248-254.

2450. J. M. Bover, "Christi Regnum in Epistulis Pauli," *VD*, 5 (1925), 225-229.

2451. Ch. Guignebert, "Contribution à l'étude de l'expérience religieuse chez Paul," *RHPR*, 7 (1927), 253-264.

2452. E. C. Hoskyns, "The Other-Wordly Kingdom of God in the New Testament," *Th*, 14 (1927), 249-255.

2453. E. Lohmeyer, "Probleme paulinischer Theologie," *ZNW*, 26 (1927), 158-173; 28 (1929), 177-207.

2454. A. E. J. Rawlinson, "The Kingdom of God in the Apostolic Age," *Th*, 14 (1927), 262-266.

2455. E. Buonaiuti, "Il pensiero di S. Paolo," *RR*, 4 (1928), 62-65.

2456. Vittorio Macchioro, "Orphism and Paulinism," *JR*, 8 (1928), 337-370.

2457. H. L. MacNeil, "Paul, the First Christian Protestant," *CJRT*, 5 (1928), 199-208.

2458. Ernst von Dobschütz, "Gedanken zur paulinischen Hermeneutik," *TB*, 8 (1929), 151-154.

2459. L. J. Koch, "Paulinsk teologi," *NTT*, 30 (1929), 126-141.

2460. E. de los Ríos, "S. Paulus de angelicis hierarchiis," *VD*, 9 (1929), 289-297.

2461. D. MacGillivray, "Paul's Sense of Beauty," *ET*, 41 (1929-1930), 566.

2462. M. Goguel, "Paulinisme et Johannisme," *RHPR*, 10 (1930), 504-526; 11 (1931), 1-19, 129-156.

2463. E. M. Martinson, "Spiritual Freedom as Paul's Thesis," *BR*, 15 (1930), 538-545.

2464. D. S. Traill, "St. Paul's Estimate of Paganism," *CJRT*, 7 (1930), 130-138, 239-249.

2465. W. Mackeown, "Paul at Athens," *ET*, 42 (1930-1931), 382-383.

2466. J. de Zwaan, "Paulinische Weltanschauung," *ZST*, 8 (1930-1931), 539-578.

2467. O. Michel, "Luthers 'deus absconditus' und der Gottesgedanke des Paulus," *TSK*, 103 (1931), 189-194.

2468. J. A. Robilliard, "Le symbolisme du mariage selon S. Paul," *RSPT*, 21 (1932), 242-247.

2469. J. Schneider, " 'Mysterion' im Neuen Testament," *TSK*, 104 (1932), 255-278.

2470. Hans Windisch, "Das johanneische Christentum und sein Verhältnis zum Judentum und zu Paulus," *TB*, 11 (1932), 340-341.

2471. C. H. Dodd, "The Mind of Paul: a Psychological Approach," *BJRL*, 17 (1933), 91-105.

2472. C. Król, "De sacrificiis iudaicis quid senserit S. Paulus," *VD*, 14 (1934), 296-305.

2473. W. T. Rivière, "The God of Mercy," *EQ*, 6 (1934), 82-88.

2474. M. E. Andrews, "Paul and Repentance," *JBL*, 54 (1935), 125.

2475. A. E. Garvie, "Paul as Christian Apostle and Jewish Rabbi, *RL*, 4 (1935), 243-252.

2476. P. P. Anspach, "The Race Problem in Paul's Epistles," *LCQ*, 9 (1936), 39-49.

2477. E. F. Harrison, "The Evidential Value of Paul's Conversion and Ministry," *BS*, 93 (1936), 187-192.

2478. W. H. P. Hatch, "Jesus' Summary of the Law and the Achievement of the Moral Ideal According to St. Paul," *ATR*, 18 (1936), 129-140.

2479. M. Goguel, "Les fondements de l'assurance du salut chez l'apôtre Paul," *RHPR*, 17 (1937), 105-144.

2480. Karl Karner, "Die Stellung des Apostels Paulus im Urchristentum," *ZST*, 14 (1937), 142-193.

2481. Eugeniusz Król, "Wpływ misteriów hellenistycznych na ideę Ofiary Krzyżowej w listach św Pawła," *PB*, 1 (1937), 57-78.

2482. G. B. King, "Paul's Use of the Figure of Abraham," *CQ*, 15 (1938), 283-285.

2483. A. Škrinjar, "Dicta Paulina de martyrio," *VD*, 19 (1939), 52-59, 91-96.

2484. H. Doergens, "Seneca im Gegensatz zu Paulus," *ZKT*, 64 (1940), 14-26.

2485. R. M. Grant, "The Anthropology of St. Paul," *ATR*, 22 (1940), 199-203.

2486. J. E. Bear, "Christian Liberty and the Christian Conscience," *USR*, 52 (1940-1941), 236-257.

2487. W. W. Gauld, "St. Paul and Nature," *ET*, 52 (1940-1941), 337-340, 392-394.

2488. Paul Althaus, "Das Bild Gottes bei Paulus," *TB*, 20 (1941), 81-92.

2489. A. R. Cripps, "A Layman Studies St. Paul," *HJ*, 40 (1941), 75-81.

2490. E. G. Gulin, "Die Freiheit in der Verkündigung des Paulus," *ZST*, 18 (1941), 458-481.

2491. Eric Montizambert, "St. Paul and the Vision of God," *ATR*, 23 (1941), 147-153.

2492. P. H. Furfey, "Social Action in the Early Church," *ThSt*, 3 (1942), 89-108.

2493. E. J. Goodspeed, "Paul and Slavery," *JBR*, 11 (1943), 169-170.

2494. Pierson Parker, "Paul Kept the Faith," *ATR*, 25 (1943), 399-402.

2495. Richard Hanson, "Moses in the Typology of St. Paul," *Th*, 48 (1945), 174-177.

2496. R. C. Klick, "St. Paul and the Problem of Suffering," *LCQ*, 19 (1946), 252-260.

2497. H. J. Schoeps, "The Sacrifice of Isaac in Paul's Theology," *JBL*, 65 (1946), 385-393.

2498. C. Spicq, "L'origine évangélique des vertus épiscopales selon saint Paul," *RB*, 53 (1946), 36-46.

2499. J. W. Bailey, "Paul and Matthew and the Primitive Jewish Christian Drama," *CQ*, 24 (1947), 326-333.

2500. Rudolf Bultmann, "Paulus und der Hellenismus," *TLZ*, 72 (1947), 77-80.

2501. Johs. Munck, "La vocation de l'Apôtre Paul," *ST*, 1 (1947 [1948]), 131-145.

2502. Werner Bieder, "Gebetswirklichkeit und Gebetsmöglichkeit bei Paulus," *TZ*, 4 (1948), 22-40.

2503. P. E. Davies, "Paul's Missionary Message," *JBR*, 16 (1948), 205-211.

2504. A. G. Hebert, "St. Paul's Defense of his Apostolate," *Th*, 51 (1948), 323-327.

2505. Ragnar Leivestad, "Dualism hos Paulus," *NTT*, 50 (1949), 209-225.

2506. M. Pohlenz, "Paulus und die Stoa," *ZNW*, 42 (1949), 69-103.

2507. O. Cullmann, "Paradosis et Kyrios. Le problème de la tradition dans le paulinisme," *RHPR*, 30 (1950), 12-30.

2508. A. H. Forster, "The Meaning of Power for St. Paul," *ATR*, 32 (1950), 177-185.

2509. R. P. C. Hanson, "St. Paul's Quotations of the Book of Job," *Th*, 53 (1950), 250-253.

2510. S. V. McCasland, "The Image of God According to Paul," *JBL*, 69 (1950), 85-100.

2511. H. Sahlin, "Frälsnivgens nya exodus hos Paulus," *STK*, 26 (1950), 24-34.

2512. Hans Wedell, "The Idea of Freedom in the Teaching of the Apostle Paul," *ATR*, 32 (1950), 204-216.

2513. Rudolf Bultmann, "Gnosis," *JTS*, 3 (1952), 10-26.

2514. D. M. Stanley, "Theologica promissionis apud S. Paulum," *VD*, 30 (1952), 129-142.

2515. H. Greeven, "Propheten, Lehrer, Vorsteher bei Paulus," *ZNW*, 44 (1952-1953), 1-43.

2516. P. H. Menoud, "Revelation and Tradition; the Influence of Paul's Conversion on his Theology," *Interp*, 7 (1953), 131-141.

2517. J. B. Bedenbough, "Paul's Use of 'Wrath of God,'" *LQ*, 6 (1954), 154-157.

2518. Matthew Black, "The Pauline Doctrine of the Second Man," *SJT*, 7 (1954), 170-179.

2519. G. H. C. Macgregor, "Principalities and Powers: the Cosmic Background of St. Paul's Thought," *NTSt*, 1 (1954), 17-28.

2520. C. E. Mason, "A Study of Pauline Motives," *BS*, 111 (1954), 213-228.

2521. S. G. McAllister, "The Supreme Business; Features of Paul's Service," *Interp*, 8 (1954), 155-162.

2522. D. M. Stanley, "The Theme of the Servant of Yahweh in Primitive Christian Soteriology, and its Transposition by Saint Paul," *CBQ*, 16 (1954), 385-425.

2523. Konrad Weiss, "Paulus — Priester der christlichen Kultgemeinde," *TLZ*, 79 (1954), 355-364.

2524. W. D. Stacey, "St. Paul and the 'Soul,'" *ET*, 66 (1954- 1955), 274-277.

2525. P. Rossano, "S. Paolo e l'ellenismo," *RivB*, 3 (1955), 332-347.

2526. O. A. Piper, "The Transforming Power of the Gospel," *TTod*, 12 (1955-1956), 438-450.

2527. H. H. Graham, "Continuity and Discontinuity in the Thought of St. Paul," *ATR*, 38 (1956), 137-146.

2528. Alfredo Vitti, "La dottrina di s. Paolo sul sacerdozio," *RivB*, 4 (1956), 1-16.

2529. Ioannis Hararis, "Τὸ κέντρον τῆς διδασκαλίας τοῦ 'Απ. Παύλου," II, 2 (1957), 311-314.

2530. B. Mariani, "San Paolo ed il 'Servo di Jahve,'" *RivB*, 5 (1957), 17-24.

2531. Donatien Mollat, "Théologie paulinienne," *RSR*, 45 (1957), 240-261.

2532. A. Penna, "Testi d'Isaia in San Paolo," *RivB*, 5 (1957), 163-179.
    See also numbers 2, 4, 7, 706, 712, 739, 2227, and the several sub-divisions within section III.

B. The Atonement (and/or Redemption)

2533. A. Schweizer, "Die Lehre des Apostels Paulus vom erlösenden

Tode Christi, von Galat. 3, 13 und 14 aus beleuchtet," *TSK*, 31 (1858), 425-473.

2534. F. C. Baur, "Die Lehre des Apostels Paulus vom erlösenden Tode Christi, mit Rücksicht auf Dr. A. Schweizer's Abhandlung in den Theol. Stud. u. Krit. 1858. S. 425 f.," *ZWT*, 2 (1859), 225-251.

2535. O. Pfleiderer, "Die paulinische Rechtfertigung. Eine exegetisch-dogmatische Studie," *ZWT*, 15 (1872), 161-199.

2536. J. A. Beet, "The Doctrine of the Atonement in the New Testament," *Exp*, 4th series, 5 (1892), 358-371, 432-443; 6 (1892), 27-34, 132-143.

2537. E. DeW. Burton, "The Biblical Doctrine of Atonement: IX, Atonement in the Teaching of Paul," *BW*, 32 (1908), 183-196, 252-261.

2538. Paul Galtier, "La réconciliation des pécheurs dans saint Paul," *RSR*, 3 (1912), 448-460.

2539. C. Lattey, "Theses Paulinae: IX. De Redemptione: Christus sacrificium propitiatorum Deo pro hominibus obtulit," *VD*, 5 (1925), 111-119.

2540. V. J. K. Brook, "St. Paul's Theory of Redemption," *Th*, 13 (1926), 302-311.

2541. J. E. Frame, "Paul's Idea of Deliverance," *JBL*, 49 (1930), 1-12.

2542. E. Stauffer, "Vom λόγος τοῦ σταυροῦ und seiner Logik," *TSK*, 103 (1931), 179-188.

2543. P. E. Kretzmann, "Der Schriftgrund für die Lehre von der 'satisfactio vicaria,'" *CTM*, 5 (1934), 863-866; 6 (1935), 121-124, 197-199, 430-432, 511-515, 592-594, 687-689, 746-749, 909-912; 7 (1936), 27-30, 123-126, 190-194, 445-446, 584-587, 752-754, 912-916.

2544. F. C. Lightbourn, "'Double Soteriology' in Paul," *ATR*, 18 (1936), 65-71.

2545. Eug. Driessen, "De auxilio Dei et salute hominis apud S. Paulum," *VD*, 20 (1940), 53-60.

2546. Eug. Driessen, "Promissio redemptoris apud S. Paulum (Rom. 3, 24-26; Hebr. 10, 5-7; I Cor. 2, 6-8)," *VD*, 21 (1941), 233-238, 264-271, 298-305.

2547. H. C. Thiessen, "The Place of Israel in the Scheme of Redemption," *BS*, 98 (1941), 78-91, 203-217.

2548. J. M. Bover, "El dogma de la redención en las Epístolas de San Pablo," *EB*, N.S. (1941-1942), 357-403, 517-541.

2549. J. R. Branton, "Paul and Salvation," *CQ*, 24 (1947), 228-240.

2550. Jacques Dupont, "La réconciliation dans la théologie de saint Paul," *EB*, 11 (1952), 255-302.

2551. J. W. Bailey, "Gospel for Mankind; the Death of Christ in the Thinking of Paul," *Interp*, 7 (1953), 163-174.

2552. D. E. H. Whiteley, "St. Paul's Thoughts on the Atonement," *JTS*, N.S. 8 (1957), 240-255.
See also numbers 1815 f., 1819, 1823, 2041, 2055 ff., 2319, 2670, 2749, and 2860.

C. Christology

2553. W. Beyschlag, "Zur paulinischen Christologie," *TSK*, 33 (1860), 431-479.

2554. [A.] Krawutzcky, "Über die Bedeutung des neutestamentlichen Ausdrucks Menschensohn und sein Verhältnis zur paulinischen Bezeichnung Christi als zweiten Menschen," *TQ*, 51 (1869), 600-657.

2555. A. Schweizer, "Die neueste Arbeit über die paulinische Christologie," *ZWT*, 13 (1870), 275-300.

2556. O. Pfleiderer, "Die paulinische Christologie," *ZWT*, 14 (1871), 502-534.

2557. E. Harmsen, "Versuch einer Beantwortung der Frage: Wird Christus als Mittler der Weltschöpfung Röm. 11, 36 und I Kor. 8, 6 gedacht und dargestellt?" *ZWT*, 19 (1876), 388-396.

2558. James Morison, "The Christology of St. Paul in the Superscription of his Epistle to the Romans," *Exp*, 1st series, 9 (1879), 105-122; 10 (1879), 149-162; 11 (1880), 309-320; 11 (1880), 458-475.

2559. H. Holtzmann, "Zur paulinischen Präexistenzlehre," *ZWT*, 27 (1884), 129-139.

2560. J. A. Beet, "Crucified and Risen with Christ," *Exp*, 3rd series, 6 (1887), 140-150.

2561. J. A. Beet, "Christ Crucified and Risen," *Exp*, 3rd series, 6 (1887), 372-380.

2562. H. Holtzmann, "Die paulinische Christologie in Verhältnis zu dem Gegensatze von σάρξ und πνεῦμα," *ZWT*, 31 (1888), 279-294.

2563. F. H. Stead, "The Chief Pauline Names for Christ," *Exp*‹ 3rd series, 7 (1888), 386-395.

2564. Emil Lingens, S.J., "Zur paulinischen Christologie," *ZKT*, 20 (1896), 449-470.

2565. S. Odland, "Nogle hovedpunkter af den paulinske kristologi," *NTT*, 4 (1903), 169-206.

2566. Vincent M'Nabb, "A Moot-Point of Pauline Christology," *ET*, 19 (1907-1908), 92-93.

2567. G. J. A. Jonker, "De paulinische formule 'door Christus,' " *TS*, 27 (1909), 173-208.

2568. C. M. Mead, "Paul on the Resurrection of Christ," *BS*, 67 (1910), 391-414.

2569. G. Kittel, "Jesus bei Paulus," *TSK*, 85 (1912), 366-402.

2570. A. T. Robertson, "Paul as an Interpreter of Christ," *RE*, 9 (1912), 3-23.

2571. H. Böhlig, "Zum Begriff Kyrios bei Paulus," *ZNW*, 14 (1913), 23-37.

2572. L. Coulange, "Le Christ de Paul." *RHLR*, N.S. 4 (1913), 20-44.

2573. G. M. Cummings, "Paul's Doctrine of the Logos," *BS*, 71 (1914), 381-392.

2574. H. H. Lindemann, "Apostolic Christology: A Comparison of Paul with his Predecessors," *BW*, 46 (1915), 14-25.

2575. William Houliston, "The Testimony of Paul the Apostle to the Resurrection of Jesus Christ," *BS*, 73 (1916), 546-569.

2576. B. B. Warfield, "The Christ that Paul Preached," *Exp*, 8th series, 15 (1918), 90-110.

2577. B. S. Easton, "The Development of Apostolic Christology," *ATR*, 1 (1918-1919), 148-163, 371-382.

2578. Hon. Lord Sands, "The Silence of Paul," *Exp*, 8th series, 19 (1920), 241-259.

2579. C. Lattey, "Theses Paulinae: II, S. Paulus clare docet Christum esse Deum," *VD*, 3 (1923), 198-206.

2580. H. A. A. Kennedy, "The Logos-Doctrine of St. Paul," *Exp*, 9th series, 1 (1924), 54-56.

2581. A. Medebielle, "Christus 'Dominus,' " *VD*, 4 (1924), 86-90, 117-119, 133-139.

2582. H. Offerman, "The Cross of Christ in the Epistles of Paul," *LCR*, 43 (1924), 228-237.

2583. Alonso Bárcena, "La resurrección de Cristo en el magisterio de San Pablo," *EE*, 5 (1926), 3-16.
5284. Alonso Bárcena, "El estado de Cristo glorioso según los escritos de San Pablo," *EE*, 5 (1926), 138-149, 373-389.
2585. A. Vitti, "Christus-Adam. De Paulino hoc conceptu interpretando eiusque ab extraneis fontibus independentia vindicanda," *B*, 7 (1926), 121-145, 270-285, 384-401.
2586. C. N. Bartlett, "Deity of Jesus Christ as set forth in the Epistles," *BS*, 86 (1929), 70-84.
2587. O. Michel, "Die Entstehung der paulinischen Christologie," *ZNW*, 28 (1929), 324-333.
2588. Emanuel Hirsch, "Zur paulinischen Christologie," *ZST*, 7 (1929-1930), 605-630.
2589. E. von Dobschütz, "Κύριος Ἰησοῦς," *ZNW*, 30 (1931), 97-123.
2590. Vincent McNabb, "Essai sur la christologie de saint Paul," *RB*, 42 (1933), 321-327.
2591. O. Michel, "Der Christus des Paulus," *ZNW*, 32 (1933), 6-31.
2592. Walter Dress, "Vom Problem paulinischer Christologie," *TB*, 13 (1934), 53-58.
2593. Ernst Lohmeyer, "Vom Problem paulinischer Christologie," *TB*, 13 (1934), 43-53.
2594. P. X. M. a Vallisoleto, "Christi 'Pleroma' iuxta Pauli conceptionem," *VD*, 14 (1934), 49-55.
2595. P. X. M. a Vallisoleto, " 'Christus-Adam,' " *VD*, 15 (1935), 87-93, 114-120.
2596. M. J. Lagrange, "Les origines du dogme paulinien de la divinité du Christ," *RB*, 45 (1936), 5-33.
2597. C. L. Feinberg, "Pauline Theology Relative to the Death and Resurrection of Christ," *BS*, 95 (1938), 290-308.
2598. G. J. Inglis, "St. Paul's Conception of Christ," *ET*, 50 (1938-1939), 456-460.
2599. S. L. Stealey, "Christ in You, the Hope of Glory," *RE*, 40 (1943), 55-59.
2600. H. W. Schmidt, "Das Kreuz Christi bei Paulus," *ZST*, 21 (1944), 145-159.
2601. A. C. Cotter, "The Divinity of Jesus Christ in Saint Paul," *CBQ*, 7 (1945), 259-289.
2602. R. G. Turnbull, "The Christology of Paul," *USR*, 57 (1945-1946), 121-138.

2603. R. G. Turnbull, "The Ascension in Paul's Christology," *USR*, 57 (1945-1946), 303-319.
2604. W. L. Conner, "Three Types of Teaching in the N.T. on the Meaning of the Death of Christ," *RE*, 43 (1946), 150-166.
2605. D. J. O'Herlihy, "Witnesses to Christ; 1, St. Paul," *Scr*, 3 (1948), 103-106.
2606. G. A. Daniel, "Did St. Paul Know the Tradition about the Virgin Birth?" *ST*, 4 (1950 [1951-1952]), 94-101.
2607. Trevor Ling, "Christ's Conquest of Satan in its Relation to the Individual," *Th*, 56 (1953), 327-332.
2608. J. M. Gonzáles Ruiz, "Teandrismo de la cristología de San Pablo," *EB*, 12 (1953), 257-272.
2609. G. H. Ranson, "The Primary Emphasis in Christology," *RE*, 52 (1955), 290-309.
2610. J. A. T. Robinson, "The Most Primitive Christology of All?" *JTS*, N.S. 7 (1956), 177-189.
2611. Neal Flanagan, "Messianic Fulfillment in St. Paul," *CBQ*, 19 (1957), 474-484.
    See also numbers 709, 1124, 1800 f., 1839 f., 1931 ff., 2039, 2049 ff., 2128, 2231, 2301 ff., 2387, 2410, and 2720.

D. THE CHURCH

2612. F. A. Christie, "One Body in Christ, Rom. xii, I Cor. xii," *JBL*, 16 (1897), 118-130.
2613. H. S. Nash, "St. Paul and the Church Ideal," *BW*, 32 (1908), 386-396.
2614. C. Lattey, "Theses Paulinae: X. De Ecclesiae unitate: Ecclesia est una, universalis, unica," *VD*, 5 (1925), 230-237.
2615. G. C. Pidgeon, "Members of Christ's Body," *CJRT*, 2 (1925), 393-401.
2616. C. Lattey, "Theses Paulinae: XI. De Ecclesiae potestate: Ecclesia habet potestatem regendi, docendi, sanctificandi," *VD*, 6 (1926), 43-48, 85-88.
2617. S. M. Gilmour, "Church Consciousness in the Letters of Paul," *JR*, 18 (1938), 289-302.
2618. J. M. Bover, "El cuerpo místico de Cristo en San Pablo," *EB*, 2 (1943), 249-277, 449-473.
2619. G. W. Forell, "A Neglected Aspect of St. Paul's Doctrine of the Church," *LCQ*, 17 (1944), 48-60.

2620. Léopold Malevez, "L'église, corps du Christ: sens et provenance de l'expression chez saint Paul," *SR* (= *RSR*, 32), (1944), 27-74.

2621. J. W. Dillistone, "How is the Church Christ's Body? A New Testament Study," *TTod*, 2 (1945-1946), 56-68.

2622. F. W. Grosheide, "Die zijn lichaam is," *GTT*, 47 (1947), 193-196.

2623. M. Goguel, "Ce que l'Église doit à l'apôtre Paul," *RHPR*, 31 (1951), 157-180.

2624. Otto Perels, "Kirche und Welt nach dem Epheser- und Kolosserbrief," *TLZ*, 76 (1951), 391-400.

2625. Albrecht Oepke, "Leib Christi oder Volk Gottes bei Paulus?" *TLZ*, 79 (1954), 363-368.

2626. Pierre Benoit, "Corps, tête, et plérôme dans les épîtres de la captivité," *RB* 63 (1956), 5-44.

2627. Thomas Krieder, "Ihr seid der Leib Christi, einzeln aber dessen Glieder (I Kor. 12, 27)," *FZPT*, 3 (1956), 407-417.

2628. Metropolitan Procopios of Corinth, "Οἱ χαρισματοῦχοι καὶ ὁ κλῆρος ἐν τῇ Ἐκκλησίᾳ κατὰ τὸν Ἀπόστολον Παῦλον," Π, 2 (1957), 280-284.

See also numbers 303, 1784, 1786, 1790, 1796, 1797, 1801, 1827, 2083, 2923, 2969, and 2984.

E. ESCHATOLOGY

2629. George Matheson, "Scriptural Studies of the Heavenly State," *Exp*, 2nd series, 5 (1883), 40-53, 185-198, 368-382.

2630. B. B. Warfield, "The Prophecies of St. Paul," *Exp*, 3rd series, 4 (1886), 30-44, 131-148, 439-464.

2631. J. A. Beet, "New Testament Teaching on the Future Punishment of Sin," *Exp*, 4th series, 1 (1890), 22-37, 130-142, 201-211.

2632. J. A. Beet, "New Testament Teaching on the Second Coming of Christ: The Teaching of St. Paul," *Exp*, 4th series, 10 (1894), 98-111.

2633. J. B. Henderson, "St. Paul and Death," *ET*, 7 (1895-1896), 431.

2634. E. H. Harding, "St. Paul's Certainty of a Future State, and Certainty that it would be Well with him in that State," *USR*, 8 (1896), 17-24.

2635. C. F. D'Arcy, "St. Paul on Life and Immortality," *Exp*, 6th series, 5 (1902), 428-434.

2636. Samuel MacComb, "The Eschatology of Paul," *BW*, 22 (1903), 36-41.

2637. T. G. Darling, "The Apostle Paul and the Second Advent," *PTR*, 2 (1904), 197-214.

2638. E. F. Scott, "The New Testament Idea of the Future Life: III, The Future Life in the Teaching of Paul," *BW*, 38 (1911), 185-193, 246-254.

2639. Geerhardus Vos, "The Pauline Eschatology and Chiliasm," *PTR*, 9 (1911), 26-60.

2640. I. F. Wood, "Paul's Eschatology," *BW*, 38 (1911), 79-91, 159-170.

2641. U. Holzmeister, "Zum Dekret der Bibelcommission über die Parusieerwartung in den paulinischen Briefen," *ZKT*, 40 (1916), 167-182.

2642. A. E. Whatham, "St. Paul's View of the Resurrection Body," *BW*, 49 (1917), 354-361; 50 (1917), 29-34.

2643. J. Th. Ubbink, "Paulus en de dood," *NTS*, 1 (1918), 3-10.

2644. T. J. Agius, "The Resurrection-Body in the Light of Present-Day Psychological Science," *ITQ*, 15 (1920), 1-23.

2645. F. C. Porter, "Paul's Belief in Life after Death," *RE*, 9 (1922), 280-309.

2646. W. S. Wood, "St. Paul and the Resurrection of the Body," *Exp*, 8th series, 23 (1922), 461-469.

2647. H. Meusel, "Zur paulinischen Eschatologie," *NKZ*, 34 (1923), 689-701.

2648. C. Lattey, "Theses Paulinae: XII, De Resurrectione carnis," *VD*, 6 (1926), 281-284, 309-317.

2649. A. Vitti, "De futura gloria adipiscenda iuxta S. Paulum," *VD*, 7 (1927), 225-233.

2650. J. M. Shaw, "The Resurrection of the Body," *ET*, 40 (1928-1929), 246-251.

2651. Geerhardus Vos, "The Pauline Doctrine of the Resurrection," *PTR*, 27 (1929), 1-35.

2652. Geerhardus Vos, "Alleged Development in Paul's Teaching on the Resurrection," *PTR*, 27 (1929), 193-226.

2653. Geerhardus Vos, "The Structure of the Pauline Eschatology," *PTR*, 27 (1929), 403-444.

2654. L. Kessler, "Die Eschatologie des Apostels Paulus und die religiös-bildliche Erkenntnis," *ZST*, 7 (1929-1930), 573-597.

2655. Lino Murillo, "La parusía en el apóstol san Pablo," *EB*, 3 (1930), 264-282.

2656. H. D. Wendland, "Ethik und Eschatologie in der Theologie des Paulus," *NKZ*, 41 (1930), 759-811.

2657. E. B. Allo, "Saint Paul et la double résurrection corporelle," *RB*, 41 (1932), 187-209.

2658. B. Brinkmann, "Die Lehre von der Parusie beim hl. Paulus in ihrem Verhältnis zu den Anschauungen des Buches Henoch," *B*, 13 (1932), 315-334, 445-461.

2659. J. Héring, "Saint Paul a-t-il enseigné deux résurrections?" *RHPR*, 12 (1932), 300-320.

2660. Jenö Kiss, "Zur eschatologischen Beurteilung der Theologie des Apostels Paulus," *ZST*, 15 (1938), 379-416.

2661. J. B. Orchard, "St Paul and the Book of Daniel," *B*, 20 (1939), 172-179.

2662. L. Fuerbringer, "Leading Thoughts on Eschatology in the Epistles to the Thessalonians," *CTM*, 13 (1942), 183-192, 265-273, 321-329, 401-414, 511-518, 591-603, 641-654.

2663. R. R. Hartford, "St. Paul, Plato and Immortality," *Herm*, No. 65 (1945), 74-79.

2664. Teófilo de Orbiso, "Los motivos de la esperanza cristiana, según S. Pablo," *EB*, 4 (1945), 61-85, 195-210.

2665. C. Lattey, "The Glorified Body in St. Paul's Epistles," *Scr*, 1 (1946), 55-56.

2666. Gerhard Delling, "Zur paulinischen Teleologie," *TLZ*, 75 (1950), 705-710.

2667. Maurice Carrez, "Souffrance et glorie dans les épîtres pauliniennes," *RHPR*, 31 (1951), 343-353.

2668. A. R. Ford, "The Second Advent in Relation to the Reign of Christ," *EQ*, 23 (1951), 30-39.

2669. J. W. Cobb, "The Nature of the Resurrection Body," *RE*, 49 (1952), 435-444.

2670. Bruce Vawter, "Resurrection and Redemption," *CBQ*, 15 (1953), 11-23.

2671. A. M. Hunter, "The Hope of Glory; the Relevance of the Pauline Eschatology," *Interp*, 8 (1954), 131-141.
See also numbers 41, 1123, 1343, 1802, 2065, 2129 f., 2167, 2169, 2172 ff., 2690, and 2947.

F. ETHICS

2672. Fr. Düsterdieck, "Ein feiner Zug paulinischer Ethik," *TSK*, 38 (1865), 517-524.

2673. Shailer Matthews, "The Social Teaching of Paul: I, The Social Content of Early Messianism," *BW*, 19 (1902), 34-46; "II, The Social Content of Messianism in New Testament Times," 113-120; "III, The Apocalyptic Messianism of the Pharisees," 178-189; "IV, The Messianism of Paul," 279-287, 370-376; "V, The Social Content of Apostolic Christianity in General," 433-442; "VI, The Christian Fraternity," 20 (1902), 31-47; "VII, The Family," 123-133; "VIII, Wealth and the State," 178-190.

2674. George Jackson, "The Ethical Teaching of St. Paul," *Exp*, 6th series, 11 (1905), "1. The Sources," 35-49; "2. Some General Characteristics," 139-151; "3. The Pagan Virtues," 194-208; "4. The Passive Virtues," 282-294; "5. The Intellectual Virtues," 358-372; "6. The Ethics of Controversy in the Teaching of St. Paul," 454-468; 12 (1905), "7. The Ethics of Speech," 61-73; "8. Asceticism True and False," 180-193; "9. Cases of Conscience," 269-280; "10. Anger and the Self-Assertive Virtues," 370-380.

2675. Arthur Carr, "St. Paul's Rule of Life," *Exp*, 7th series, 2 (1906), 111-120.

2676. A. W. Anthony, "The Ethics of Paul," *BW*, 34 (1909), 249-258.

2677. D. C. Mackintosh, "The Pragmatic Element in the Teaching of Paul," *AJT*, 14 (1910), 361-381.

2678. J. M. Hantz, "St. Paul's Sense of Duty," *LCR*, 30 (1911), 438-450.

2679. C. J. Cadoux, "St. Paul's Conception of the State," *Exp*, 8th series, 12 (1916), 135-147.

2680. H. B. Carré, "The Ethical Significance of Paul's Doctrine of the Spirit," *BW*, 48 (1916), 195-207.

2681. R. Bultmann, "Das Problem der Ethik bei Paulus," *ZNW*, 23 (1924), 123-141.

2682. F. O. Norton, "Legalism in the Churches of Paul's Day," *CQ*, 1 (1924), 52-65.

2683. Wilhelm Mundle, "Sammenhengen mellem religion og etik hos Paulus," *NTT*, 27 (1926), 1-20.

2684. Wilhelm Mundle, "Religion und Sittlichkeit bei Paulus in ihrem inneren Zusammenhang," *ZST*, 4 (1926-1927), 456-482.

2685. M. S. Enslin, "The Place of Morality in the Thought of Paul," *CQ*, 4 (1927), 159-170.

2686. Wilhelm Michaelis, "Ehe und Charisma bei Paulus," *ZST*, 5 (1927-1928), 426-452.

2687. Ch. Guignebert, "Quelques remarques sur la perfection (τελείωσις) et ses voies dans le mystère paulinien," *RHPR*, 8 (1928), 412-429.

2688. Herbert Preisker, "Ehe und Charisma bei Paulus," *ZST*, 6 (1928-1929), 91-95

2689. H. J. Cadbury, "The Ethics of Paul," *CQ*, 7 (1930), 423-428.

2690. H. D. Wendland, "Ethik und Eschatologie in der Theologie des Paulus," *NKZ*, 41 (1930), 757-811.

2691. E. de los Ríos, "Ad catalogos peccatorum apud S. Paulum animadversiones," *VD*, 12 (1932), 364-370.

2692. Mary E. Andrews, "The Problem of Motive in the Ethics of Paul," *JR*, 13 (1933), 200-213.

2693. O. Michel, "Wie spricht Paulus über Frau und Ehe?" *TSK*, 105 (1933), 215-225.

2694. Marian Morawski, "Pauliniści protestancey o naśladowaniu Chrystusa," *PB*, 2 (1938), 26-40.

2695. A. C. Piepkorn, "St Paul on Social Relationships," *CTM*, 11 (1940), 721-752.

2696. G. K. Wiencke, "Crucified with Christ: Paul's Ethical Interpretation of Christ's Death," *LCQ*, 14 (1941), 27-39.

2697. W. A. Smart, "Paul and his Persecution," *RL*, 12 (1943), 197-204.

2698. E. Mócsy, "Problema imperativi ethici in iustificatione paulina," *VD*, 25 (1947), 204-217, 264-269.

2699. Lucien Cerfaux, "L'antinomie paulinienne et la vie apostolique," *RSR*, 39 (1951-1952), 221-234.

2700. Walter Lowrie, " 'Glorify God in Your Body,' " *TTod*, 10 (1953-1954), 492-500.
See also numbers 709, 1798, 1919, 2258, 2260, 2309, 2390, 2478, 2486, 2492 f., 2656, and 2758.

G. Faith

2701. J. J. P. Valeton, "πίστις en ἱστορία," *TS*, 1 (1883), 339-369.

2702. P. W. Schmiedel, "Glaube und Dogma beim Apostel Paulus," *STZ*, 9 (1892), 211-230.

2703. Samuel MacComb, "Faith According to Paul," *BW*, 25 (1905), 292-299.

2704. G. Kittel, "Πίστις Ἰησοῦ Χριστοῦ bei Paulus," *TSK*, 79 (1906), 419-436.

2705. G. Schläger, "Bemerkungen zu πίστις Ἰησοῦ Χριστοῦ," *ZNW*, 7 (1906), 356-358.

2706. R. M. Pope, "Faith and Knowledge in Pauline and Johannine Thought," *ET*, 41 (1929-1930), 421-427.

2707. A Frövig, "Glaube und Geschichte bei Paulus," *ZST*, 13 (1936), 355-402.

2708. Rafael Gyllenberg, "Glaube bei Paulus," *ZST*, 13 (1936), 613-630.

2709. J. de Zwaan, "Persönlicher Glaube bei Paulus," *ZST*, 13 (1936), 114-149.

2710. A. M. Hunter, "Faith, Hope, Love — a Primitive Christian Triad," *ET*, 49 (1937-1938), 428-429.

2711. L. Baeck, "The Faith of Paul," *JJS*, 3 (1952), 93-110.

2712. J. E. Jones, "Now Faith is . . . Hope," *RE*, 52 (1955), 508-530.

2713. F. W. Danker, "Faith Without Works," *CTM*, 27 (1956), 513-535, 593-612.
See also numbers 709, 710, 712, and 2718.

H. The Holy Spirit

2714. O. Pfleiderer, "Das paulinische πνεῦμα," *ZWT*, 14 (1871), 161-181.

2715. G. Resch, "Was Versteht Paulus unter der Versiegelung mit dem Heiligen Geist ?" *NKZ*, 6 (1895), 991-1003.

2716. J. H. L. Roozemeyer, "Het wezen en de werking des H. Geestes," *TS*, 18 (1900), 341-356.

2717. H. A. A. Kennedy, "St. Paul's Conception of the Spirit as Pledge," *Exp*, 6th series, 4 (1901), 274-280.

2718. M. Steffer, "Das Verhältnis von Geist und Glauben bei Paulus," *ZNW*, 2 (1901), 115-139, 234-261.

2719. J. H. Hodson, "A Study in Christian Experience," *ET*, 26 (1914-1915), 398-402.

2720. J. W. Buckham, "Are Christ and the Spirit Identical in Paul's Teaching ?" *Exp*, 8th series, 22 (1921), 154-160.

2721. W. Moran, "Charismatic Ministry in the Primitive Church," *ITQ*, 17 (1922), 48-55, 101-111.

2722. R. B. Hoyle, "Spirit in St. Paul's Experience and Writings," *BR*, 11 (1926), 491-507.

2723. R. B. Hoyle, "Paul's Doctrine of the Spirit," *BR*, 13 (1928), 45-62.

2724. Fernando Quiroga, "Personalidad divina del Espíritu Santo en San Pablo," *EB*, 2 (1930), 113-121.

2725. P. E. Kretzmann, "Das 'Testimonium Spiritus Sancti,' " *CTM*, 6 (1935), 176-177.

2726. N. A. Waaning, "Enkele opmerkingen over de relatie πνεῦμα / γράμμα," *GTT*, 36 (1935), 161-169.

2727. F. W. A. Bosch, "The Freedom of the Spirit — II, The Teachings of Paul," *USR*, 54 (1942-1943), 213-230.

2728. D. W. Martin, " 'Spirit' in the Second Chapter of First Corinthians," *CBQ*, 5 (1943), 381-395.

2729. M. J. Shroyer, " 'The Lord is the Spirit,' " *RL*, 20 (1951), 21-35.

2730. H. D. Wendland, "Das Wirken des Heiligen Geistes in den Gläubigen nach Paulus," *TLZ*, 77 (1952), 457-470.

2731. Bernardin Schneider, "The Meaning of St. Paul's Antithesis, 'The Letter and the Spirit,' " *CBQ*, 15 (1953), 163-207.

2732. A. Penna, "Lo Spirito Santo nella vita di s. Paolo," *RivB*, 2 (1954), 325-328.

2733. B. Pelaia, "Lo Spirito Santo e la vida cristiana in s. Paolo," *RivB*, 3 (1955), 363-370.

2734. C. C. Oke, "Paul's Method not a Demonstration but an Exhibition of the Spirit," *ET*, 67 (1955-1956), 35-36.

2735. Armin Dietzel, "Beten im Geist; Eine religionsgeschichtliche Parallele aus den Hodajot zum paulinischen Beten im Geist," *TZ*, 13 (1957), 12-32.

See also numbers 712, 1128, 1144, 1409 ff., 2257, and 2680.

I. Justification

2736. K. Fromman, "Über den Widerspruch, welcher zwischen der Stelle Jak. 2, 14-26 und der paulinischen Lehre von der Rechtfertigung durch den Glauben statt finden soll," *TSK*, 6 (1833), 84-118.

2737. C. Schmitt, "Die Lehre der Apostel Paulus und Jacobus über die Rechtfertigung des Sünders," *TQ*, 56 (1874), 369-388.

2738. D. C. Thijm, "De verhouding van Jacobus tot Paulus, ten opzichte van de rechtvaardiging uit het geloof," *TS*, 1 (1883), 188-221, 479-547.

2739. Georg Schnedermann, "Der israelitische Hintergrund in der Lehre des Apostels Paulus von der Gottesgerechtigkeit aus Glauben," *NKZ*, 6 (1895), 649-658.

2740. F. E. Daubanton, "Paulus' leer der rechtvaardigmaking uit het geloof volgens den brief aan de Romeinen," *TS*, 17 (1899), 366-385.

2741. Josef Wieser, "Die Rechtfertigung durch Christus im Lehrsystem des Weltapostels," *ZKT*, 23 (1899), 649-685; 24 (1900), 267-281.

2742. Geerhardus Vos, "The Alleged Legalism in Paul's Doctrine of Justification," *PTR*, 1 (1903), 161-179.

2743. G. B. Stevens, "The Just Shall Live by Faith," *BW*, 23 (1904), 267-271.

2744. A. B. Curtiss, "Justification by Faithfulness: The True Doctrine of Jesus and Paul," *BS*, 65 (1908), 755-759.

2745. E. von Dobschütz, "Die Rechtfertigung bei Paulus, eine Rechtfertigung des Paulus," *TSK*, 85 (1912), 38-67.

2746. M.-J. Lagrange, "La justification d'après saint Paul," *RB*, N.S. 11 (1914), 321-343, 481-503.

2747. W. Macholz, "Zum Verständnis des paulinischen Rechtfertigungsgedankens," *TSK*, 88 (1915), 29-61.

2748. E. H. Wieringa, "De beteekenis van δικαιοσύνη Θεοῦ en de rechtvaardiging door 't geloof," *NTS*, 3 (1920), 219-226.

2749. A. M. Pope, "The Forensic Interpretation of the Cross," *ET*, 33 (1921-1922), 323-326.

2750. C. Lattey, "Theses Paulinae: V, De iustificatione per fidem: S. Paulus docet hominem per fidem dogmaticam et vivam iustificari, non autem per opera quae fide non informentur," *VD*, 4 (1924), 80-86.

2751. C. Lattey, "Theses Paulinae: VI, De iustitia impertita: Per iustificationem S. Paulus realem mutationem animae fieri intelligit," *VD*, 4 (1924), 149-153.

2752. C. Lattey, "Theses Paulinae: VII, De nova vita iusti: Secundum S. Paulum per iustificationem 'vivo iam non ego, vivit vero in me Christus' (Gal. 2, 20)," *VD*, 4 (1924), 196-200, 241-244.

2753. D. S. Sharp, "For Our Justification," *ET*, 39 (1927-1928), 87-90.

2754. T. C. Johnson, "Justification by Faith," *USR*, 41 (1929-1930), 178-190, 265-279.

2755. Th. Engelder, "Objective Justification," *CTM*, 4 (1933), 507-517, 564-577, 664-675.

2756. W. L. Conner, "Is Paul's Doctrine of Justification Forensic?" *RE*, 40 (1943), 48-54.

2757. J. M. Bover, "La justificación en San Pablo," *EB*, N.S. 4 (1945), 297-325.

2758. E. Mócsy, "Problema imperativa ethici in iustificatione paulina," *VD*, 25 (1947), 204-217, 264-269.
See also numbers 709, 734, 738, 2364, 2535, 2698, 2713, 2773, 2836, and 2986.

J. Law and Grace

2759. A. Klöpper, "Zwei merkwürdige Äusserungen des Apostels Paulus über die Genesis des Messaischen [i. e. Mosaischen] Gesetzes," *ZWT*, 13 (1870), 78-114.

2760. G. H. Gilbert, "The Scope of Paul's Doctrine of Grace," *AJT*, 1 (1897), 692-699.

2761. R. Zehnpfund, "Das Gesetz in den paulinischen Briefen," *NKZ*, 8 (1897), 384-419.

2762. James Wells, "Grace in Christ," *ET*, 9 (1897-1898), 25-26.

2763. M. Friedländer, "The 'Pauline' Emancipation from the Law a Product of the Pre-Christian Jewish Diaspora," *JQR*, 14 (1902), 265-301.

2764. O. Schulz, "Τί οὖν ὁ νόμος; Verhältnis von Gesetz, Sünde und Evangelium nach Gal. 3," *TSK*, 75 (1902), 5-56.

2765. S. J. Case, "The Legalistic Element in Paul's Religion," *BW*, 35 (1910), 151-158.

2766. F. O. Evers, "The Law with Jesus and Paul," *LCR*, 31 (1912), 438-450, 709-720.

2767. H. A. A. Kennedy, "St. Paul and the Law," *Exp*, 8th series, 13 (1917), 338-366.

2768. J. M. Bover, "Gratiae oeconomia per Christum independens a peccato secundum Pauli doctrinam," *VD*, 2 (1922), 79-87, 170-176.

2769. M. Müller, "Freiheit. Über Autonomie und Gnade von Paulus bis Clemens von Alexandrien," *ZNW*, 25 (1926), 177-236.

2770. Pierre Rousselot, "La grâce d'après saint Jean et d'après saint Paul," *RSR*, 18 (1928), 87-104.

2771. E. Lohmeyer, "Probleme paulinischer Theologie; II, 'Gesetzeswerke,' " *ZNW*, 28 (1929), 177-207.

2772. A. Pujol, "De salutatione apostolica 'gratia vobis et pax,' " *VD*, 12 (1932), 38-40, 76-82.

2773. W. Grundmann, "Gesetz, Rechtfertigung und Mystik bei Paulus," *ZNW*, 32 (1933), 52-65.

2774. P. Benoit, "La loi et la croix d'après saint Paul," *RB*, 47 (1938), 481-509.

2775. E. Mócsy, "De gratiarum actione in epistolis paulinis," *VD*, 21 (1941), 193-201, 225-232.

2776. E. G. Gulin, "Lagens positiva betydelse hos Paulus," *STK*, 18 (1942), 203-216.

2777. Gustave Bardy, "Saint Paul juriste," *SR* (= *RSR*, 31), (1943), 209-210.

2778. R. A. Bartels, "Law and Sin in Fourth Esdras and Saint Paul," *LQ*, 1 (1949), 319-329.

2779. Bo Reicke, "The Law and This World According to Paul," *JBL*, 70 (1951), 259-276.

2780. Gerard Bushell, "Law and Christian Spirituality According to St. Paul," *ABR*, 5 (1956), 99-117.

2781. Walter Grundmann, "Die Übermacht der Gnade; eine Studie zur Theologie des Paulus," *NT*, 2 (1957), 50-72.
See also numbers 709, 720, 722, and 726.

K. The Mysticism of Paul ("In Christ")

2782. E. Y. Hincks, "The Apostle Paul's Mysticism, *BW*, 2 (1893), 326-329.

2783. W. R. Inge, "The Mystical Element in St. Paul's Theology," *Exp*, 5th series, 4 (1896), 114-123.

2784. J. Weiss, "Paulinische Probleme, II: Die Formel ἐν Χριστῷ Ἰησοῦ," *TSK*, 69 (1896), 7-33.

2785. J. A. Rust, "Paulus Mysticus," *TS*, 28 (1910), 349-384.

2786. H. W. Clark, "Rational Mysticism and New Testament Christianity," *HTR*, 4 (1911), 311-329.

2787. J. W. Buckham, "The Mysticism of Jesus and of Paul," *BW*, 41 (1913), 309-313.

2788. J. de Zwaan, "Paulus Mysticus," *NTS*, 1 (1918), 171-174.

2789. J. M. Bover, "De mystica unione 'in Christo Iesu' secundum S. Paulum," *B*, 1 (1920), 309-326.

2790. H. Offerman, "St. Paul's Visions and Revelations of the Lord," *LCR*, 39 (1920), 185-194.

2791. Dr. Weber, "Die Formel 'in Christo Jesu' und die paulinische Christusmystik," *NKZ*, 31 (1920), 213-260.

2792. W. P. Hall, "A Biblical Study of Union with God in Christ," *BR*, 9 (1924), 181-198.

2793. W. E. Wilson, "The Development of Paul's Doctrine of Dying and Rising again with Christ," *ET*, 42 (1929-1930), 562-565.

2794. M. Goguel, "La mystique paulinienne," *RHPR*, 11 (1931), 185-210.

2795. P. X. M. a Vallisoleto, " 'In Christo Iesu,' " *VD*, 13 (1933), 311-319.

2796. Jules Lebreton, "La contemplation dans la vie de saint Paul," *RSR*, 30 (1940), 81-108.

2797. Eng. Driessen, "Notae de doctrina mystica S. Pauli," *VD*, 22 (1942), 240-245.

2798. B. N. Wambacq, "De relatione inter Corpus Christi mysticum et hierarchiam secundum S. Paulum," *VD*, 22 (1942), 193-203.

2799. E. Mócsy, "De unione mystica cum Christo," *VD*, 25 (1947), 270-279, 328-339.

2800. A. A. Fulton, "Schweitzer on the Mysticism of Paul: A Criticism," *EQ*, 20 (1948), 172-183.

2801. F. Büchsel, " 'In Christus' bei Paulus," *ZNW*, 42 (1949), 141-158.

2802. W. Bartling, "The New Creation in Christ: A Study of the Pauline ἐν Χριστῷ Formula," *CTM*, 21 (1950), 401-418.

2803. J. M. Bover, "Los carismas espirituales en San Pablo," *EB*, 9 (1950), 295-328.

2804. Pierre Bonnard, "Mourir et vivre avec Jésus-Christ selon saint Paul," *RHPR*, 36 (1956), 101-112.

2805. Theodoros Kastanas, "'Ο 'Απόστολος Παῦλος καὶ ἡ προσευχή," Π, 2 (1957), 303-305.
See also numbers 709, 1245, 1916, 2134, 2398, and 2773.

L. PAUL AND THE GOSPEL

2806. B. Spiegel, "Über εὐαγγέλιον und Χριστός bei Paulus," *ZWT*, 10 (1867), 330-331.

2807. A. H. Blom, "Beoordeling van Straatman's gevoelen over het ontstaan van het Evangelie van Paulus," *TT*, 9 (1875), 1-44.

2808. J. R. Lumby, "The Gospel in the Epistles," *Exp*, 1st series, 5 (1877), 1-11, 134-149, 289-304, 343-361, 451-470.

2809. A. H. Blom, "Paulinische Studiën: II, Paulus en de evangelische traditie," *TT*, 13 (1879), 343-357.

2810. A. H. Blom, "Paulinische Studiën: VII, Het ontstaan van het Evangelie van Paulus," *TT*, 15 (1881), 53-94.

2811. G. G. Findlay, "The Gospel of Paul at Thessalonica," *Exp*, 4th series, 2 (1890), 256-262.

2812. W. C. van Manen, "Het evangelie van Paulus verklaard? (naar aanleiding van Ch. C. Everett, *The Gospel of Paul*)," *TT*, 28 (1894), 358-373.

2813. F. H. Foster, "The Gospel of Paul," *BS*, 53 (1896), 89-99.

2814. [P.] Gennrich, "Studien zur Paulinischen Heilsordnung," *TSK*, 71 (1898), 377-431.

2815. C. Anderson, "The Gospel According to St. Paul, its Character and Source," *Exp*, 6th series, 2 (1900), 202-210.

2816. W. Sanday, "St. Paul's Gospel; an Eirenicon," *Exp*, 7th series, 3 (1907), 385-409.

2817. A. E. Garvie, "Did Paul Evolve his Gospel?" *Exp*, 8th series, 1 (1911), 180-192.

2818. A. E. Garvie, "Did Paul Borrow his Gospel?" *Exp*, 8th series, 1 (1911), 343-356.

2819. A. E. Garvie, "Did Paul Commend his Gospel?" *Exp*, 8th series, 1 (1911), 536-549.

2820. A. E. Garvie, "Is Paul's Gospel out of Date?" *Exp*, 8th series, 2 (1911), 367-379.

2821. J. H. Moulton, "The Gospel according to Paul," *Exp*, 8th series, 2 (1911), 16-28.

2822. Anton Fridrichsen, "τὸ εὐαγγέλιον hos Paulus," *NTT*, 13 (1912), 153-170, 209-256.

2823. Alfred Loisy, "L'évangile de Paul," *RHLR*, N.S. 5 (1914), 138-174.

2824. B. W. Bacon, "The Gospel Paul Received," *AJT*, 21 (1917), 15-42.

2825. J. B. Green, "The Gospel which Paul Preached," *USR*, 41 (1929-1930), 41-52.

2826. O. W. Heick, "The Fifth Gospel: The Gospel According to St. Paul," *LCQ*, 13 (1940), 223-243.

2827. B. Allo, "L'évolution' de l'évangile de Paul," *VP*, 1 (1941), 48-77, 165-193.

2828. T. E. Bleiben, "The Gospel of Luke and the Gospel of Paul," *JTS*, 45 (1944-1945), 134-140.

2829. G. F. Dowden, "The Abundance of the Gospel," *Th*, 58 (1955), 173-179.

2830. M. H. Franzmann, "The Inclusiveness and the Exclusiveness of the Gospel, as Seen in the Apostolate of Paul," *CTM*, 27 (1956), 337-351.

2831. William Baird, "What is the Kerygma? A Study of I Cor. 15 : 3-8 and Gal. 1 : 11-17," *JBL*, 76 (1957), 181-191.

See also numbers 68, 702, 712, 1094, 1975, 2120, 2234, 2385, 2402, 2440, 2845, and 2987.

M. PAUL AND JAMES

2832. E. P. Barrows, "The Alleged Disagreement Between Paul and James," *BS*, 9 (1852), 761-782.

2833. [P.] Schanz, "Jakobus und Paulus," *TQ*, 62 (1880), 3-46, 247-286.

2834. Otto Kuttner, "Einzelne Bemerkungen über das Verhältnis von Jac. ii und Röm. xii-xiv," *ZWT*, 31 (1888), 36-40.

2835. Theo. Zahn, "Are Paul and James in Contradiction?" *LCR*, 19 (1900), 107-112.

2836. F. W. Mozley, "Justification by Faith in St. James and St. Paul," *Exp*, 7th series, 10 (1910), 481-503.

2837. W. C. Cumming, "Do Paul and James Contradict Each Other?" *USR*, 31 (1919-1920), 46-48.

2838. A. Fernández, "Fides et opera apud S. Paulum et S. Iacobum," *VD*, 12 (1932), 177-180.

2839. Joachim Jeremias, "Paul and James," *ET*, 66 (1954-1955), 368-371.

See also numbers 2736 ff.

N. PAUL AND JESUS

2840. G. P. Fisher, "The Apostle Paul, A Witness for the Resurrection of Jesus," *BS*, 17 (1860), 620-634.

2841. J. H. McIlvaine, "Christ and Paul," *BS*, 35 (1878), 425-460.

2842. G. Matheson, "The Historical Christ of St. Paul," *Exp*, 2nd series, 1 (1881), 43-62, 125-138, 193-208, 264-275, 352-371, 431-443; 2 (1881), 27-47, 137-154, 287-301, 357-371.

2843. David Hill, "Paul as a Witness to Christ," *LQ*, 12 (1882), 405-414.

2844. H. U. Meyboom, "Jezus en Paulus in de Apokalypse," *TT*, 17 (1883), 58-80.

2845. J. S. Banks, "St. Paul and the Gospels," *ET*, 5 (1893-1894), 413-415.

2846. A. Hilgenfeld, "Jesus und Paulus," *ZWT*, 37 (1894), 481-541.

2847. O. Schmoller, "Die geschichtliche Person Jesu nach den paulinischen Schriften," *TSK*, 67 (1894), 656-705.

2848. P. Gloatz, "Zur Vergleichung der Lehre des Paulus mit der Jesu," *TSK*, 68 (1895), 777-800.

2849. Arthur Hoyle, "Paul and Jesus," *ET*, 8 (1896-1897), 487-492.

2850. R. R. Lloyd, "The Historic Christ in the Letters of Paul," *BS*, 58 (1901), 270-293.

2851. Eberhard Vischer, "Jesus und Paulus," *TR*, 8 (1905), 129-143, 173-188.

2852. M. Brückner, "Zum Thema Jesus und Paulus," *ZNW*, 7 (1906), 112-119.

2853. W. H. Johnson, "Was Paul the Founder of Christianity?" *PTR*, 5 (1907), 398-422.

2854. James Moffatt, "Paul and Jesus," *BW*, 32 (1908), 168-173.

2855. A. T. W. Steinhaeuser, "Paul and Jesus," *LCR*, 27 (1908), 217-225.

2856. W. Morgan, "The Jesus-Paul Controversy," *ET*, 20 (1908-1909), 9-12, 55-58.

2857. A. C. McGiffert, "Was Jesus or Paul the Founder of Christianity?" *AJT*, 13 (1909), 1-20.

2858. E. T. Horn, "Jesus and Paul," *LCR*, 30 (1911), 628-635.

2859. W. Heitmüller, "Zum Problem Paulus und Jesus," *ZNW*, 13 (1912), 320-337.

2860. B. B. Warfield, "The Essence of Christianity and the Cross of Christ," *HTR*, 7 (1914), 538-594.

2861. J. G. James, "The Theology of Paul and the Teaching of Jesus Christ," *ET*, 26 (1914-1915), 7-14.

2862. E. H. Wieringa, "Paulus en Jezus," *TS*, 33 (1915), 257-282.

2863. A. H. McNeile, "St. Paul in Relation to Our Lord," *Th*, 1 (1920), 9-18.

2864. Léonce de Grandmaison, "Le Christ de l'histoire dans l'oeuvre de saint Paul," *RSR*, 13 (1923), 481-490.

2865. A. M. Pope, "Paul's Reminiscences of Jesus," *Exp*, 9th series, 1 (1924), 283-296.

2866. Paul Feine, "Jesus und Paulus," *NKZ*, 36 (1925), 291-323.

2867. F. G. Bratton, "Continuity and Divergence in the Jesus-Paul Problem," *JBL*, 48 (1929), 149-161.
2868. R. Bultmann, "Die Bedeutung des geschichtlichen Jesus für die Theologie des Paulus," *TB*, 8 (1929), 137-151.
2869. H. Windisch, "Paulus und Jesus," *TSK*, 106 (1934-1935), 432-468.
2870. W. C. Robinson, "The Theology of Jesus and the Theology of Paul," *EQ*, 8 (1936), 373-397.
2871. J. H. Stelma, "Paulus Sotèr?" *NTS*, 22 (1939), 79-88.
2872. W. Kümmel, "Jesus und Paulus," *TB*, 19 (1940), 209-231.
2873. H. E. Guillebaud, "Paul's Gospel or Christ's?" *EQ*, 14 (1942), 281-290.
2874. Ray Knight, "Gospels and Epistles," *HJ*, 45 (1947), 304-308.
2875. Ray Knight, "Jesus or Paul? In Continuation of Gospels and Epistles," *HJ*, 47 (1948), 41-49.
2876. M. Goguel, "De Jésus à l'apôtre Paul," *RHPR*, 28-29 (1948-1949), 1-29.
2877. G. S. Duncan, "From Paul to Jesus," *SJT*, 2 (1949), 1-12.
2878. C. Lattey, "Quotations of Christ's Sayings in St. Paul's Epistles," *Scr*, 4 (1949), 22-24.
2879. W. G. Shepherd, "The Problem of Love," *ATR*, 31 (1949), 171-175.
2880. Anton Fridrichsen, "Jesus, John, Paul," *LQ*, 3 (1951), 243-254, 353-365.
2881. H. E. Turlington, "The Apostle Paul and the Gospel History," *RE*, 48 (1951), 35-66.
See also numbers 15, 292, 702, 1461-1466, 2439, 2569, 2744, 2766, 2787, and 2958.

O. PAUL ON THE PLACE OF WOMEN

2882. G. H. Gilbert, "Women in Public Worship in the Churches of Paul," *BW*, 2 (1893), 38-47.
2883. T. E. Schmauk, "St. Paul and Women," *LCR*, 18 (1899), 505-524.
2884. Margaret D. Gibson, " 'Let the Women Learn in Silence,' " *ET*, 15 (1903-1904), 374-380.
2885. G. Engel, " 'Let the Women Learn in Silence,' " *ET*, 16 (1904-1905), 189-190.
2886. H. W. Williams, " 'Let the Women Learn in Silence,' " *ET*, 16 (1904-1905), 188-189.

2887. R. Winterbotham, "St. Paul and Women," *Exp*, 8th series, 22 (1921), 445-454.
2888. W. S. Wood, "The Ministry of Women and St. Paul," *Exp*, 8th series, 21 (1921), 292-301.
2889. A. C. Kröger, "Die Stellung der Frau in der christlichen Kirche," *CTM*, 4 (1933), 85-95.
2890. Irene M. Robbins, "St. Paul and the Ministry of Women," *ET*, 46 (1934-1935), 185-188.
2891. J. T. Mueller, "St. Paul and Woman's Status," *CTM*, 9 (1938), 13-21.
2892. E. A. Leonard, "Saint Paul and the Status of Women," *CBQ*, 12 (1950), 311-320.
2893. John Foster, "St. Paul and Women," *ET*, 62 (1950-1951), 376-378.
See also numbers 1145, 1238 ff., and 2693.

P. THE RIGHTEOUSNESS OF GOD
2894. E. H. Blakeley, "The Righteousness of God," *ET*, 6 (1894-1895), 45-46.
2895. J. L. Davies, "The 'Righteousness of God' in St. Paul," *JTS*, 2 (1901), 198-206.
2896. James Drummond, "On the Meaning of 'Righteousness of God' in the Theology of St. Paul," *HJ*, 1 (1902), 83-95, 272-293.
2897. Karl Benz, "Δικαιοσύνη Θεοῦ beim Apostel Paulus," *TQ*, 94 (1912), 590-592.
2898. J. S. Simon, "The Righteousness of God," *LQ*, 43 (1913), 368-374.
2899. F. W. Stellhorn, "The Pauline Conception of the Righteousness of God," *LCR*, 34 (1915), 33-41.
2900. Otto Zänker, "Δικαιοσύνη Θεοῦ bei Paulus," *ZST*, 9 (1931-1932), 398-420.
2901. W. F. Lofthouse, "The Righteousness of God," *ET*, 50 (1938-1939), 441-445.
2902. Albrecht Oepke, "Δικαιοσύνη Θεοῦ bei Paulus in neuer Beleuchtung," *TLZ*, 78 (1953), 257-264.
2903. J. A. Bollier, "The Righteousness of God," *Interp*, 8 (1954), 404-413.
See also numbers 708, 712, 718, 761 f., 811, and 2386.

Q. The Sacraments

2904. Allan Menzies, "The Lord's Supper: St. Mark or St. Paul?" *Exp*, 5th series, 10 (1899), 241-262.

2905. R. Kern, "St. Paul's Conception of the Lord's Supper," *LCR*, 22 (1903), 239-246, 415-423.

2906. G. P. Wetter, "Die Auffassung des Apostels Paulus vom Abendmahl," *ZNW*, 14 (1913), 202-215.

2907. B. W. Bacon, "Reflections of Ritual in Paul," *HTR*, 8 (1915), 504-524.

2908. H. T. Andrews, " The Place of the Sacraments in the Teaching of St. Paul," *Exp*, 8th series, 12 (1916), 353-372.

2909. W. H. G. Thomas, "The Place of the Sacraments in the Teaching of St. Paul," *Exp*, 8th series, 13 (1917), 375-385.

2910. James Moffatt, "Discerning the Body," *ET*, 30 (1918-1919), 19-23.

2911. E. B. Allo, "La synthèse du dogme eucharistique chez saint Paul," *RB*, 18 (1921), 321-343.

2912. C. H. Dibble, "Primitive Symbolism in the Breaking of Bread," *ATR*, 5 (1922-1923), 187-210.

2913. C. Lattey, "Theses Paulinae: I, S. Paulus in SS. Eucharistia realem praesentiam et verum sacrificium agnovit," *VD*, 3 (1923), 108-112.

2914. F. Ruffenach, "Hoc est corpus meum, Hic est sanguis meus," *VD*, 4 (1924), 264-268, 296-298.

2915. J. Burnaby, "The Eucharist and St. Paul," *Th*, 27 (1933), 92-94.

2916. J. Jeremias, "Das paulinische Abendmahl — eine Opferdarbringung?" *TSK*, 108 (1937-1938), 124-141.

2917. Günther Bornkamm, "Taufe und neues Leben bei Paulus," *TB*, 18 (1939), 233-242.

2918. Teófilo de Orbiso, "La eucaristía en San Pablo," *EB*, N.S. 5 (1946), 171-213.

2919. J. J. Mueller, "St. Paul's Usus Practicus of Holy Baptism," *CTM*, 19 (1948), 417-439.

2920. E. H. Peters, "Saint Paul and the Eucharist," *CBQ*, 10 (1948), 247-253.

2921. Erich Fascher, "Zur Taufe des Paulus," *TLZ*, 80 (1955), 643-648.

2922. V. Iacono, "Il battesimo in s. Paolo," *RivB*, 3 (1955), 348-362.

2923. G. Bornkamm, "Herrenmahl und Kirche bei Paulus," *NTSt*, 2 (1956), 202-206.

See also numbers 381, 1125, 1185, 1189, 1221, 1258 ff., 1795, 1879, and 2307.

R. Sin

2924. Orello Cone, "The Pauline Doctrine of Sin," *AJT*, 2 (1898), 241-267.
2925. Paul Feine, "Der Ursprung der Sünde nach Paulus," *NKZ*, 10 (1899), 771-795.
2926. G. Wohlenberg, "Das Heidentum nach der Beurteilung des Apostels Paulus," *NKZ*, 23 (1912), 223-249.
2927. Robert Mackintosh, "The Roots of St. Paul's Doctrine of Sin," *Exp*, 8th series, 5 (1913), 441-458.
2928. C. Lattey, "Theses Paulinae; IV, De peccato originali: S. Paulus docet omnes homines per inobedientiam Adae formaliter constitui peccatores (Rom. 5, 12-21)," *VD*, 4 (1924), 21-26.
2929. E. Lohmeyer, "Probleme paulinischer Theologie; III, 'Sünde, Fleisch, und Tod,' " *ZNT*, 29 (1930), 1-59.
2930. G. Schnitzer, "Paolo e il peccato del Christiano," *RR*, 10 (1934), 539-545.
2931. Lyder Brun, "Seiren over synden i Paulus' frelsesforkynnelse og formaning," *NTT*, 37 (1936), 20-48.
2932. A. M. Dubarle, "Le péché originel dans saint Paul," *RSPT*, 40 (1956), 213-254.
2933. P. Rossano, "Il concetto di 'Hamartia' in Rom. 5-8," *RivB*, 4 (1956), 289-313.

See also numbers 712, 735, 1168, 2235, 2538, 2691, 2778, and 2986.

SECTION VI

THE HISTORY OF THE INTERPRETATION OF PAUL AND OF HIS WORK

2934. F. J. A. Hort, "On an Ancient Latin Version of Theodore of Mopsuestia's Lost Commentary on Ten of St. Paul's Epistles," *JCSP*, 4 (1859), 302-308.

2935. W. Böhmer, "Eine neue Ausgabe der melanthonischen Commentare zum Briefe des Paulus an die Römer," *ZWT*, 5 (1862), 335-336.

2936. A. Hilgenfeld, "Der Paulinismus und seine neueste Bearbeitung," *ZWT*, 17 (1874), 161-187.

2937. M. A. N. Rovers, "Een poging tot rehabilitatie van Petrus. Naar aanleiding van H. Rodrigues, St. Paul," *TT*, 11 (1877), 315-334.

2938. F. Klasen, "Pelagianistische Commentare zu 13 Briefen des h. Paulus," *TQ*, 67 (1885), 244-317, 531-577.

2939. S. M. Schiller-Szinessy, "St. Paul from a Jewish Point of View," *Exp*, 3rd series, 4 (1886), 321-335.

2940. G. H. Gilbert, "Dr. Lyman Abbott on Paul's Letter to the Romans," *BS*, 46 (1889), 229-244.

2941. C. G. Montefiore, "First Impressions of Paul," *JQR*, 6 (1894), 428-474.

2942. F. König, "Paulus und Schopenhauer," *STZ*, 12 (1895), 46-57.

2943. W. M. Ramsay, "A Study of S. Paul by Mr. Baring Gould," *Exp*, 5th series, 6 (1897), 49-65.

2944. T. E. Schmauk, "Canon Gore on the Latter Half of Romans," *LCR*, 19 (1900), 489-496.

2945. Alexander Souter, "The Commentary of Pelagius on the Epistles of St. Paul," *Exp*, 7th series, 3 (1907), 455-467.

2946. G. Morin, "Jean Diacre et le Pseudo-Jérôme sur les Épîtres de S. Paul," *RBén*, 27 (1910), 113-117.

2947. W. Montgomery, "Dr. Schweitzer on the Interpretation of St. Paul," *ET*, 23 (1911-1912), 209-211.

2948. E. F. Scott, "The Present Position of New Testament Theology," *HTR*, 6 (1913), 60-75.

2949. Alexander Brown, " 'Paul and His Interpreters,' " *ET*, 25 (1913-1914), 286.

2950. M.-J. Lagrange, "Le commentaire de Luther sur l'épître aux Romains," *RB*, N. S. 12 (1915), 456-484; 13 (1916), 90-120.

2951. Maurice Jones, "Pauline Criticism in the Present Day," *Exp*, 8th series, 14 (1917), 16-40.

2952. H. A. A. Kennedy, "A New Interpretation of Paulinism," *Exp*, 8th series, 14 (1917), 81-97, 175-194.

2953. A. Souter, "The Sources of Sedulius Scottus' *Collectaneum* on the Epistles of Paul," *JTS*, 18 (1917), 184-228.

2954. Maurice Jones, "St. Paul in the *Encyclopaedia of Religion and Ethics*," *Exp*, 8th series, 15 (1918), 39-55.

2955. Martin Dibelius, "Synthetische Methoden in der Paulus-Forschung," *TB*, 3 (1924), 60-65.

2956. Anton Fridrichsen, "Eduard Meyer om apostelhistorien og urkristendommen," *NTT*, 25 (1924), 54-64.

2957. D. De Bruyne, "Sommaires antipélagiens inédits des lettres de S. Paul," *RBén*, 39 (1927), 45-55.

2958. Luigi Salvatorelli, "From Locke to Reitzenstein: The Historical Investigation of the Origins of Christianity," *HTR*, 22 (1929), 263-369.

2959. Karl Staab, "Neue Fragmente aus dem Kommentar des Origenes zum Römerbrief," *BibZ*, 18 (1929), 72-82.

2960. J. W. van den Bosch, "Rondom den Romeinen-Commentaar van Martinus Bucer," *GTT*, 30 (1929-1930), 513-524.

2961. W. Völker, "Paulus bei Origenes," *TSK*, 102 (1930), 258-279.

2962. A. Landgraf, "Familienbildung bei Pauluskommentaren des 12. Jahrhunderts," *B*, 13 (1932), 61-71, 169-191.

2963. Martin Dibelius, "Zur Methode der Paulusforschung," *TB*, 12 (1933), 296-300.

2964. Johannes Hoh, "Zum Verständnis des Paulinismus. Eine psychanalytische Lösung?" *BibZ*, 21 (1933), 324-329.

2965. R. H. Walker, "Teaching the Pauline Epistles," *JBR*, 2 (1934), 12-15.

2966. H. Seesemann, "Das Paulusverständnis des Clemens Alexandrinus," *TSK*, 107 (1936), 312-346.

2967. Friedrich Büchsel, "Neue Wege der Paulusdeutung?" *TB*, 16 (1937), 272-275.

2968. R. Galdos, "Effigies divi Pauli biblicis ac patristicis citation-
ibus a P. Cornelio a Lapide composita," *VD*, 17 (1937), 166-
172, 212-218, 234-241.

2969. H. Koehnlein, "La notion de l'Église chez l'apôtre Paul. A
propos de publications récentes," *RHPR*, 17 (1937), 357-377.

2970. J. de Zwaan, "Photius over Galaten," *NTS*, 20 (1937),
34-40.

2971. A. Landgraf, "Der Paulinenkommentar des Hervaeus von
Bourg-Dieu," *B*, 21 (1940), 113-132.

2972. S. Zeitlin, "Erroneous Statements on Paul in Doctor Klaus-
ner's Book," *JQR*, 34 (1943-1944), 117-121.

2973. S. R. Harlow, "Teaching the Pauline Epistles," *JBR*, 12
(1944), 33-35.

2974. A. Landgraf, "Ein neuer Fund zur Kommentierung des
Paul.-Komm. des Petrus Lombardus," *B*, 25 (1944), 50-61.

2975. A. N. Wilder, "Paul through Jewish Eyes," *JBR*, 12 (1944),
181-187.

2976. Holmes Rolston, "A Theological Watershed, Barth's *Römerbrief*; a Digest with Notes," *TTod*, 1 (1944-1945), 103-120.

2977. Arthur Landgraf, "The Commentary on Saint Paul of the
Codex Paris Arsenal, Lat. 534, and Baldwin of Canterbury,"
CBQ, 10 (1948), 55-62.

2978. A. Landgraf, "Der Paulinenkommentar und der Psalmen-
kommentar des Petrus Cantor und die Glossa Magna des
Petrus Lombardus," *B*, 31 (1950), 379-389.

2979. A. S. Wood, "The Theology of Luther's Lectures on Romans," *SJT*, 3 (1950), 1-18, 113-126.

2980. [K. H.] Schelkle, "Erwählung und Freiheit im Römerbrief
nach der Auslegung der Väter," *TQ*, 131 (1951), 189-207.

2981. M. Zenwick, "Anders Nygren: Epistola ad Romanos," *VD*,
29 (1951), 355-361.

2982. Leonhard Fendt, "Anmerkungen zur Interpretation des
Römerbriefs," *TLZ*, 77 (1952), 75-80.

2983. Albrecht Oepke, "Irrwege in der neueren Paulusforschung,"
TLZ, 77 (1952), 449-458.

2984. [K. H.] Schelkle, "Kirche und Synagoge in der frühen Auslegung des Römerbriefs," *TQ*, 134 (1954), 290-318.

2985. J. M. Gonzáles Ruiz, "La antítesis paulina entre la letra y el
espíritu em la traducción y comentario de Juan Valdés," *EB*,
13 (1954), 167-183.

2986. Wilfried Joest, "Paulus und das Luthersche simul iustus et peccator," *KD*, 1 (1955), 269-320.

2987. Morton Smith, "Pauline Problems. Apropos of J. Munck's 'Paulus und die Heilsgeschichte,' " *HTR*, 50 (1957), 107-132.
See also numbers 35, 39, 292, 295, 297, 300, 862, 1155, 1415, 1421, 1646, 1804, and 2030.

INDEX OF AUTHORS